TACTICAL FLY FISHING

Lessons Learned from Competition for All Anglers

Devin Olsen

STACKPOLE
BOOKS

Guilford, Connecticut

STACKPOLE BOOKS

Published by Stackpole Books
An imprint of The Rowman & Littlefield Publishing Group, Inc.
4501 Forbes Blvd., Ste. 200
Lanham, MD 20706
www.rowman.com

Distributed by NATIONAL BOOK NETWORK
800-462-6420

British Library Cataloguing in Publication Information available

Library of Congress Cataloging-in-Publication Data available

ISBN 978-0-8117-1982-7 (hardcover)
ISBN 978-0-8117-6603-6 (e-book)

♾™ The paper used in this publication meets the minimum requirements of American National Standard for Information Sciences—Permanence of Paper for Printed Library Materials, ANSI/NISO Z39.48-1992.

Printed in the United States of America

CONTENTS

ACKNOWLEDGMENTS

feel incredibly fortunate to have led what I consider a charmed life. I consider it charmed because as a lower-middle-class kid in suburban Utah, my father Mark Olsen introduced me to fly fishing when I was young, and he did it in a way that let me enjoy discoveries on my own. With that ownership came a pride in learning, a hunger to know more, and a love of the places that trout call home. I thank him for giving me a start in the sport that has shaped my life in ways I never could have foreseen, from the moment that first cutthroat ate my dry fly on Slough Creek in Yellowstone National Park.

I am grateful that I had great friends during my middle and high school years who shared in the excitement of heading to the river as soon as we could race away from school. Thank you, Mike and Scott Peterson, Mark Hammond, and Jared Peterson for the days we spent on the water and the pivotal fly-fishing lessons I learned on those trips that kept me motivated to seek more.

When I started competing for Fly Fishing Team USA in 2006, I never could have imagined the path this pursuit would take me on. I owe a debt to my teammates, who teach me more at each competition than I could ever learn in months spent on my own. To the world championship teammates I've had—Lance Egan, Pat Weiss, Josh Graffam, Norman Maktima, Russell Miller, Bret Bishop, Pete Erickson, Mike Sexton, George Daniel, Anthony Naranja, and Loren Williams—I thank you for your shared expertise, much of which is distilled in this book without the direct credit it deserves. And to Jerry Arnold—without your support of Fly Fishing Team USA, and me individually, the dreams that I've been able to pursue, competitively and professionally, would not have been possible. Thank you so much for your generosity and faith in our team, and in me. I am truly indebted to you.

Thanks to Jay Nichols for taking a chance on me with an invitation to write this book. To be included with the other authors whose books you have helped to publish is an honor.

Last and most importantly, thank you to my loving and long-suffering wife, Julia. Our marriage has encompassed the entire time I've been competing. You have spent months each year alone or taking care of our kids while I've been training or traveling for competitions. You have supported me through it all, and I couldn't have done it without you. To say thank you is not nearly enough.

INTRODUCTION

The year 2005 was a momentous one for me. First, I married my wife Julia, who has been my anchor through thick and thin and has supported my piscine monomania. It was also the year that directed my path toward serious efforts at competitive fly fishing. The year prior I had competed against Lance Egan and Ryan Barnes at the Fly Fishing Masters tournament, which was a televised fly-fishing tournament put on by the Outdoor Life Network for several years.

The next fall, after finishing a summer guiding season, I was looking for work to get me through the winter and happened to apply at the Cabela's fly shop that was just opening in Lehi, Utah. To my surprise, when I showed up at employee orientation I found out that Lance and Ryan were going to be my colleagues in the new shop. While I was certainly excited to be working (and hopefully fishing) with anglers who were known to be the cream of the local crop, I could not fathom then how this good fortune would direct my future path.

Lance and Ryan were members of Fly Fishing Team USA at the time, and Lance still is 13 years later. Like most American anglers, I didn't even know that Fly Fishing Team USA existed, but I was instantly intrigued by the possibility of fishing for the Stars and Stripes. Over that winter I started learning the techniques that Lance and Ryan were using to adapt to the rules of Fédération Internationale de Peche Sportive Mouche (FIPS-Mouche)–regulated competitions. My early efforts were focused on learning the Polish nymphing methods that Lance and Ryan had picked up from former world champion Wladyslaw Trzebunia Niebies (Vladi), who had been coaching Team USA.

The next spring (2006), I entered my first Fly Fishing Team USA regional trial held in Heber City, Utah. I was so nervous the night before the competition that I didn't sleep more than half an hour. As I stepped into my first river session I was a shaky mess, until I caught my first few fish and settled down. Happily, I ended up winning my first two sessions of the tournament.

It was an honor to be a part of the first team from the United States to win a medal at the 2015 World Fly Fishing Championship in Bosnia. Here we pose with our silver medals in front of Pliva Lake. (L–R) Bret Bishop (team captain/coach), Russell Miller, the author, Pat Weiss, Norm Maktima, Josh Graffam, Jerry Arnold (team manager), John Knight (2016 world championship organizer), and Lance Egan.

Learning from great anglers will propel your fishing ability forward by leaps and bounds. Fishing with Lance Egan through the years has brought plenty of learning and laughs. Here he poses with trophies from his individual bronze medal and our team bronze medal at the 2016 World Fly Fishing Championship in Vail, Colorado.

Fly-fishing competitions are not for everyone, but they can be exhilarating, in addition to offering unparalleled learning experiences. Here I net a fish during my second session of the 2016 World Fly Fishing Championship on Colorado's Eagle River. (PHOTO BY TUCKER HORNE)

The stress turned into adrenaline. It was a transition I've repeated and come to love over the past 12 years, as the regional trials turned into world championships and the stakes got much higher. Following that first regional I fished in the first Fly Fishing Team USA national championship that June, which was held in Boulder, Colorado. I squeaked onto the last place on the team and was ecstatic to have gotten my foot in the door.

The ensuing years have brought a mountain of learning and changes to my fishing ability, the techniques I employ, and the way I approach water. When I started working with Lance and Ryan, I was a dyed-in-the-wool tailwater river junkie. Though I had grown up fishing lots of different waters, from lakes to tiny streams, as I entered my high school years I became enamored with difficult pressured fish in Western US tailwater rivers. In these waters blind-strike-indicator/suspension-nymphing and/or sight-nymph-fishing were, and still are, the dominant techniques employed by most fly anglers.

Before I began competing, my belief—and, consequently, my ability—concretely centered on my own dogma that there was no better way to catch numbers of fish from a river than a strike indicator and imitative nymphs. I couldn't be convinced otherwise. However, the rules of the competitions I began fishing in prohibited adding weight or floating devices to the leader. Split shot and strike indicators were out. Suddenly, if I wanted to compete, I had to adapt.

At first it was a difficult transition, and most of my early competitive success was basically achieved by fishing a yarn-laden dry fly to replace an indicator. In the right water type I still turn to this rig with a lot of success. However, as I continued to compete and fish with other competitors, especially regular trips with my teammates Lance Egan and Josh Graffam, I made great leaps forward, not only in my river nymphing ability, but in the all-around skill set that it takes to be a successful competitive angler.

In the past 12 years of competing with Fly Fishing Team USA, I've had the incredible good fortune to fish in nine world championships. I've fished an array of different types of rivers and lakes in Scotland, Poland, Italy, Slovenia, Norway, the Czech Republic, Bosnia, the USA, and Slovakia, and have qualified for the upcoming world championships in Italy (2018) and Tasmania, Australia (2019). During these years, I've been blessed with success in domestic competitions, and had the honor of being a part of the squad that won the first two USA team medals at a world championship (silver in Bosnia in 2015, and bronze in the USA in 2016). I was also fortunate enough to receive the individual bronze medal in Bosnia in 2015, and join Jeff Currier (bronze, 2003) and Lance Egan (bronze, 2016) as USA anglers who have medaled at a world fly-fishing championship.

Along this competitive path I've learned that good nymphing skills will certainly catch you a lot of trout, but world champions aren't crowned with nymphing ability alone. For example, during my medal run in Bosnia, 45 percent of the fish I caught during the river sessions were on dry flies. In addition to a mastery of nymphing, to be a world champion you must have a mastery of dry flies, streamers, and swung wet flies, and exhibit a similarly broad skill set on stillwaters. Furthermore, the way you approach water and tactically dissect it into fishable parts with specific techniques is what separates great anglers from good to mediocre ones.

You may be reading this and thinking to yourself, "I have no interest in competing, so why should I keep reading this book?" While competitions certainly don't appeal to all anglers, they have brought an array of technique and gear advancements to the sport. These include beadhead nymphs, a focus on long lightweight rods, unique fly patterns, European-nymphing, styles of nymphing without suspending strike indicator, and fly-line designs from casting competitions that focus on distance.

Competitions force successful anglers to refine every piece of gear they use and every approach they make on the water. As Mr. Keating said in *Dead Poets Society*, "For me, sport is actually a chance for us to have other human beings push us to excel."

My bronze individual medal and team silver medal from the 2015 World Fly Fishing Championship in Bosnia—the reason I keep chasing this crazy dream.

Above: Camaraderie is a great part of competitive fly fishing. In this photo from the 2016 World Fly Fishing Championship in Colorado, we are shaking hands with our good friends from the Spanish team after receiving our bronze medal. The Spaniards were receiving their second straight team gold medal.

Left: One of my proudest moments: hearing "The Star-Spangled Banner" while receiving my individual bronze medal at the 2015 World Fly Fishing Championship in Bosnia.

I have been fortunate to learn from some of the best in our sport as I've fished and competed with—and against—anglers from the USA and across the world. Without the lessons I've learned from these anglers, I would be a fraction of the fly angler that I am today. Most anglers have had a different experience in their angling career than mine, but they still want to improve their success on the water. While you may not be able to fish with a variety of world-class anglers regularly, I hope this book will impart some of what I've learned from top competitors to help your time on the water be more enjoyable.

During a world championship river competition session, each angler randomly draws a beat, which is simply a reach of the river marked by upstream and downstream flags. Most beats are between 100 and 200 yards long. Each angler fishes their beat for a period of three hours, and their score is compared against the other anglers in their group who are fishing the same venue, which is a continuous stretch of the same river. Their scores are determined by a formula that gives points for catching fish, as well as for the length of the fish. In general, the goal is to catch as many fish as possible within the beat during the three-hour session, and hope that you catch more and/or larger fish than the other competitors in your group.

Most everyday anglers cover a lot more than 100 to 200 yards in three hours of fishing. Typically, they fish their favorite runs or pools and skip the water in between. In fact, oftentimes anglers will skip a section of water in between honey holes, which is longer than a typical competition beat. While anglers who fish this way certainly still catch fish, I've come to realize that there are often more fish to be caught in the in-between water, considered inferior to the obvious pools and runs that receive the focus of most anglers. Moreover, because the fish in these in-between areas receive less pressure, they are often easier to catch than the fish in the prime lies, which repeatedly see artificial imitations passing their noses.

A comical example of the above situation occurred during a Fly Fishing Team USA regional in April 2016. My teammate Glade Gunther was fishing a river session when several anglers showed up who had driven

One exciting challenge of competing in the World Fly Fishing Championships is quickly adapting to new species and rivers. European grayling have become one of my favorite species as a result.

If you had three hours to fish 100 yards of this water, how would you spend your time? Here Joe Clark fishes the Little Juniata River during a Fly Fishing Team USA regional trial in April 2016.

all the way from Maryland—not just to fish the Little Juniata River in general, but to fish the specific pool that was in Glade's beat. Because of past success there, and a lack of it in other stretches of the river, they were convinced their best (or only) shot at catching fish was in that one pool alone. They ended up waiting to fish the pool until after Glade had caught half a dozen fish and moved on. Following his exit, they immediately started fishing the pool without letting the fish rest, and received a skunk for their drive from Maryland. While this situation was sadly funny, it illustrates a pattern I've seen time and again, and one that I used to exhibit myself.

Growing up in Utah, my favorite local river was the intensively fished Provo. As I learned to fish there in my middle school years, I saw anglers fishing essentially the same pieces of water each time I visited. I learned to fish that same water myself, with a few sneaky holding lies in between, but for the most part I fished the obvious holding water where other anglers fished, and where my strike-indicator nymphing rig was most effective. As I began guiding on the river, this pattern became further entrenched, and I would return to my confidence stretches of river time and again, whether by myself or with clients.

After competing for many years and expanding my technical skill set, as well as my ability to read in-between water, I've come to realize that during much of the year I used to pass by a large proportion of the places that hold fish. I am now able to fish a broader spectrum of the holding water available by letting the water type dictate the technique I fish, rather than letting my technique dictate the water I fish. By catering my approach to the water in front of me, I am able to fish a greater proportion of the river. I can cover fish that avoid much of the pressure in the popular locations, and have plenty of success even when surrounded by other anglers. I don't worry nearly as much about a crowded parking lot as I used to, because I know there will be lots of overlooked open water between the spots where most anglers concentrate their efforts.

Even if you have no competitive aspirations, I firmly believe you will increase your success on the water by adopting some strategies and approaches from competitive anglers. In the end, catching a trout is a competition of wits and ability between the angler and his/her

This photo shows some famous water on Utah's Provo River. The first decade I fished this river, I fished almost exclusively with split shot and nymphs under a strike indicator. I focused on the obvious water, such as where the angler is standing upstream. These days I fish a much higher proportion of the river with a range of tactics. I enjoy success in water I would have passed by before my days as a competitor.

quarry. By arming yourself with multiple techniques, you can cover much more of the holding water you encounter successfully and efficiently. As long as you present your flies effectively, covering more water = covering more fish = catching more fish.

Let's return to my example from the sojourning Maryland anglers above. Their unwillingness to fish more than one pool (that had already been fished immediately before they began) severely limited their prospects for success. If they had been prepared with a plan to fish other water, they would have had a much higher probability of being rewarded with a few or more brown trout for their long drive.

Do you make similar mistakes when you are on the water? Do you repeatedly fish the same water with the same techniques and flies, because that's what worked last time? Do you only fish obvious pools and runs and pass by the in-between water? If you do, I hope you will commit to expanding your quiver of techniques and the way you approach water, thereby expanding your catch.

In the rest of this book, I will guide you through what goes through my mind when I study a piece of river. You will learn the variables I assess to help me decide which rigs and methods to fish, and how to fish them. In addition to theory, I will provide real-world case studies where my friends and I implemented tactical approaches to cover specific water types. I am far more successful and versatile as an angler than I was before my competition years. If you study the methods found in the following pages, I am confident you will be as well.

A stout brown trout caught Euro-nymphing the skinny water on the left side of the previous photo. Fish like this can be found in abundance in water most anglers wade through to get to the next pool.

CHAPTER 1

European grayling have become one of my favorite fish to target during trips to the World Fly Fishing Championships. They can be maddeningly difficult at times, but they love to take dry flies. The grayling in Bosnia were no exception when we competed there in 2015.

Making and Adjusting a Plan Based on Observation

Before I began fly-fishing competitively, like most anglers I showed up on the river without a specific plan to approach the water. I usually rigged up my rod at the car and expected to be able to adjust on the river if I wasn't successful. Most of the time I just fished a nymphing rig with a strike indicator, and it worked well on rivers and water types I was familiar with. A lot changed for me in my first competition. I found myself restricted to a small section of river that I was to fish for three hours without water types I would have considered worth fishing in normal circumstances. I realized I would have to change the way I prepared in my regular outings if I wanted to be successful when it came time to compete.

In FIPS-Mouche–governed competitions, anglers rotate with their randomly drawn group of fellow competitors to fish three-hour sessions on each of the rivers or lakes chosen for a competition. As mentioned previously, each competitor randomly draws a 100- to 200-meter beat of water. The angler is restricted to fishing within the boundaries of this beat for their three-hour session at that venue. Once the angler arrives, he/she has 30 minutes to rig rods and scout the beat before the clock starts.

It took me several years of competition before I learned how critical the proper use of this time is to achieving success in each session. In my early years I spent a lot of time rigging rods, which left me little opportunity to survey my beat to devise an effective strategy. Now I prepare my rods ahead of time to the point where I just need to add flies and make appropriate adjustments in my rigging for the depth and water types in my beat. I try to spend as much time as possible surveying and studying my beat so I can fish it effectively and efficiently. I prepare a mental timeline for the session that includes where I plan to fish, with what progression of methods and flies, and how long I will fish each area with each method. There are plenty of times when my game plan has to be adjusted, but having a plan gives me a structure to fall back on that helps to support tough decisions throughout a session.

There is a lot to be gained for the recreational angler by following a similar pattern. I try to apply logical reasoning to each decision I make during preparation time and within each session. This gives me confidence in my plan, allows me to fish better, and provides a consistent framework I can rely on when confronted with similar decisions in the future. Even if my decisions do not end up being the best possible choice, they generally end up falling within the positive side of the decision spectrum. I believe this is because they are defensible based on significant prior experience and acquired knowledge of the behavior and physiology of trout under different environmental conditions, as well as their reactions to flies and presentations during different scenarios.

Given a similar basic understanding, every angler can form a defensible guide to their own fishing plans for the day. However, before any concrete plans are made, a survey must be made of variables that inform angling decisions. Based on these variables, many

After 12 amazing years of competing with Fly Fishing Team USA, I've learned the value of making a plan before each competition session. The individuals and teams that generate and execute the best plans, based on the conditions of the fisheries they face, are usually those who stand on the podium at the end of the World Fly Fishing Championships.

Whether I am competing or just fishing my local river for the day, I've come to learn the value of taking a few minutes by the side of the river to observe. Here I am studying the water before fishing a session in the 2017 Casting for Hope tournament in North Carolina. By taking the time to scout this location, I spotted several fish that I caught later during my session. (PHOTO BY TUCKER HORNE)

decisions become obvious. Whether I am in a competition, on a trip to a new river, or training on my local home rivers, I try to ask myself a series of questions with answers based on observation to guide my decisions regarding methods, flies, approach, and positioning. Common variables I observe are detailed in the rest of this chapter, but you may think of others that also apply to your own waters based on your experience.

Water Clarity

Water clarity, or turbidity, is a variable that changes a trout's view of the world around it. I often experience the best fishing when a river has that lovely aquamarine color that anglers in the Pacific Northwest often refer to as "steelhead green." In these conditions, the water is just turbid enough to hide my approach, but clear enough to allow trout to see my fly from a reasonable range. Each time I head to the river, I never quite know what it will look like when I arrive.

When fishing exceptionally clear water, the trout are often wary. They can detect predatory threats from a long distance, which predisposes them to spooking

When it comes to mixing the benefits of the fish being able to see your flies without being threatened by you, the most favorable water clarity is a nice medium gray-green with 2 to 4 feet of visibility. There is a reason many anglers refer to this type of clarity as "steelhead green," as evidenced by the Grande Ronde River steelhead trying to make a break for it in this photo. During these conditions, the clarity is good enough that fish can see your fly and track it down from a distance, but your presence is hidden enough to allow a close-proximity approach without spooking fish.

easily. They can also spot potential food items at long range and follow their behavior as they approach. This means that they may be able to see and track down your fly from afar, but it also means they will be able to spot inconsistencies in your presentation that raise a red flag, telling them your offering is not food.

On the opposite end of the spectrum, when the water is turbid, trout will be visually separated from much of the world around them. Try snorkeling in a dirty river and you will see firsthand how short the range of visibility can be. In these conditions, the approach of a predator will often go unnoticed, and you may be able to get within 10 feet or less of trout without worrying about spooking them. Shortening the distance between you and your quarry can help you minimize slack and eliminate the need to lay line or leader across different currents, which will hamper your drift. However, if you're not thorough in covering potential lies, your presentations may go unseen by trout. As such, I usually find it helpful to adapt my approach to the clarity of the river I am fishing.

Below are some approaches I take, depending on whether the water is clear or turbid.

Strategies for Clear Water

The first action I take when facing clear water is to try to spot fish. Learning to spot fish is an acquired skill in fly fishing that takes patience and practice, and may require training from someone skilled in the art. Sight-fishing is exciting, largely because if you can see a fish, you know you are making presentations to a fish instead of empty water, and can tailor your approach accordingly.

Let me share one of the most important examples I can recall where this strategy paid dividends. In 2015 I was fortunate enough to win an individual bronze medal and a silver medal with my team at the World Fly Fishing Championship in Bosnia. During my second session, I arrived at a beat on the gin-clear and technically challenging Pliva River. My beat was channelized and flowing at high velocity, with little structure. At first glance, it did not inspire confidence; I wasn't sure where to fish, since there was no obvious holding water. However, during my setup time before the session, I slowly walked a high bank above the river. To my pleasant surprise, as I scanned the water I spotted eight trout and grayling tucked up tight against the bank, out of the high velocity of the main flow. I made careful mental notes, marking each fish against a landmark. Slowly crawling my way up the bank and Euro-nymphing upstream to these landmarks was fruitful. I ended up winning the session by catching 15 fish in a river that was blanking some anglers.

Learning to spot fish takes focused effort. When the water is clear enough and the light angles allow it, each time I approach a new piece of water I stop and scan. If the water surface is broken and turbulent, I pause and wait for windows of reduced turbulence. Just like waves on the ocean, the turbulence and wave action on the surface of the river comes in pulses, and there will be periods when the surface flattens in normally rough water. You may need to watch a particular target piece

Dark fish over a light bottom are easy to spot and provide good practice for anglers learning to sight-fish. Look harder in this photo and you may notice fish over the darker substrate as well. If you can learn to spot fish over a variety of river bottom colors, the underwater world will be open to you.

My beat on the Pliva River during the 2015 World Fly Fishing Championship in Bosnia. Scouting and spotting fish on the left bank proved pivotal to my success during the session.

of water for 30 seconds to a minute or more before the surface conditions are right. However, your patience will often be paid back with a glimpse into the underwater world and the positions of fish in your target zone.

Spotting fish provides positive feedback on your abilities to read water when sighting conditions are poor. If you pay attention to the locations of fish you can see, you can match these water types to similar locations elsewhere in conditions where spotting fish is not possible. Conversely, if you understand how to

read water to identify likely holding lies when fish can't be spotted, you will learn to search the same types of water when trout-spotting conditions are good. The first step to spotting a trout is always believing that one is there to be seen.

Picking your viewing angle is a critical component of spotting fish. Obviously, polarized glasses are a crucial piece of gear to be able to cut the glare on the water's surface and increase your underwater visibility. However, your glasses cannot overcome shallow sun angles reflecting toward you with harsh sparkling glare.

In order to see fish, you may need to cross the river to a position where the sun is mostly behind you or at an angle to the side. In addition, dark riparian vegetation will absorb light and reduce incidental glare. Bright surfaces, such as snow, will reflect light and produce additional glare. I routinely take several steps up- or downstream to shift my viewing angle toward dark vegetation behind the location where I am trying to spot fish. Taking a position of elevation where you can look down on the river provides much greater visibility as well. Keep in mind that your shadow may cover the water, and the increased elevation will also help the fish see you. When moving to put yourself into a better viewing position, try to employ obstructions that obscure your body from the fish, or stand far enough from the river that you avoid posing a threat.

Separating fish from their surroundings is hard for most anglers. After all, a key component of a trout's survival is camouflaging itself to avoid predators. However, if you make spotting fish a goal, it is possible to identify the cues that separate trout from the substrate of the river. My core strategies for spotting fish are searching for abnormal color, bright versus dark light disparity, and movement. Rainbow trout are usually easiest to spot because their red/pink operculum and flank is easily differentiated from most underwater rocks and vegetation. Brown trout can be more difficult to spot, but they often sport a yellow/orange belly and dark-green back that distinguishes them from the surrounding rocks.

Shadows are another key identifying feature. They create hard light differentials that are easy to locate. Many times, a fish is so well camouflaged that I don't spot it initially, but I may pick up the hard dark/light line of a shadow, which will lead me back to the fish it belongs to. Lastly, looking for movement is the best way to confirm that what you are seeing is a trout. It is very common to stare at a color or shape that

Changing your position can drastically improve your underwater view and likelihood of spotting a trout. The rainbow trout in the center of this photo is still visible, but the vertical bands of white glare from snow on the opposite stream bank obscure the view through the water's surface. When I moved up- or downstream from where I took the photo, the reflection from the snow also shifted, and the trout became much more visible.

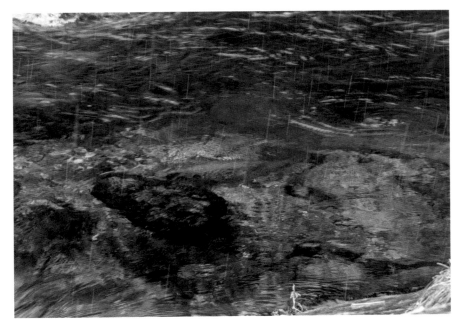

To consistently spot fish, it is important to train your eyes to see the typical colors of the trout species in the river. The rainbow trout in this photo is easy to spot because of its light coloration and the teal-over-red pattern, which is out of place in its surroundings. The brown trout holding next to it was much harder to see until it moved over the light-colored bottom in the photo. Prior to this photo, when it was over the darker bottom, its yellow pectoral fin gave away its presence.

appears fishy for an extended period. In this situation, the movement of a fin, or the lack thereof, will usually confirm whether or not the object is a fish.

Whether you have been able to spot fish or not, the next critical component of successful fishing in clear water is ensuring you don't alert fish to your presence. There is a complex interplay of light passing between aquatic and terrestrial environments. Whether a trout can see you or not is based on aspects of their anatomy and the physics of light refraction between water and air. I won't go into detail here on this relationship, because neither you nor I are likely to run the necessary calculations to ensure that you are below a trout's

cone of vision when we're on the water. If you would like to know more about the details of this topic, I suggest reading Jason Randall's excellent book, *Trout Sense*.

For everyday fishing applications I live by the simple rule that unless I'm downstream of a fish, if I can see a fish, it can likely see me. However, this rule does not apply solely to fish I can see. I apply it to any potential holding lie I plan to fish by remembering that if I can see the bottom clearly where I plan to fish, the trout that are there can likely see me as well. Even if a trout does not flee when it spots you, it is likely to alter its feeding pattern or to quit feeding altogether. I see this a lot in heavily pressured tailwaters where trout may stop feeding aggressively and sit hard on the bottom after they have recognized me as a threat. If you approach each piece of water carefully with the goal of avoiding spooking fish, especially when the water is clear, I can guarantee that you will catch more fish.

HOW TO PREVENT A FISH FROM SEEING YOU

So how do you avoid alerting fish to your presence? Here are five strategies I use to help prevent fish from seeing me and perceiving me as a threat:

1) **Fish a longer rod.** One way to avoid showing yourself to fish in clear water is to fish from a greater distance. A lot of the nymph fishing I do is based on Euro-nymphing methods. These techniques are inherently limited in their effective range. Many anglers start off Euro-nymphing with a 10-foot rod. However, one of the ways to increase your range is to fish a longer rod. My friend and former Fly Fishing Team USA mate Charlie Card spends much of his time fishing on his home water, Utah's Green River. This is a techy tailwater river often referred to as "The Aquarium" because its clarity is unsurpassed, and trout can be spotted everywhere, including at the bottom of pools more than 20 feet deep. A while back, I asked Charlie what strategies he uses to adapt to fishing the Green when Euro-nymphing. One of his simplest is that he only Euro-nymphs with rods 11 feet and longer at this river. With the longer rod, he is able to increase his successful radius of presentation; sometimes only a foot or two extra is needed to make the difference between spooking a fish and catching it.

2) **Use a fishing method tailored to distance presentations.** The other strategy for fishing farther away is choosing the proper technique and rig for the situation. In clear water, the distances required to avoid spooking fish can be significant if the water is smooth and the view between air and water is not obstructed by broken surface currents. In these situations, I often choose to forgo Euro-nymphing in favor of a longer-distance strategy.

Let me provide an example. In the 2013 World Fly Fishing Championship in Norway, we fished the large, low-gradient Vefsna River. The weather turned warm and dry for several weeks leading up to the championship, and the river dropped and

When Euro-nymphing, your rod loosely forms the hypotenuse of adjacent right triangles. With a little trigonometry it's possible to calculate the difference in reach between rods of different lengths. In short, an extra foot of rod leads to more than an extra foot of reach. When fishing large rivers or clear pressured rivers with spooky fish, a longer rod can mean the difference between catching fish and coming up short.

I find that large, low-gradient rivers—where fish are difficult to approach—are often the best waters to fish a typical suspension/strike-indicator nymphing rig or a dry-and-dropper substitute. This rig was critical to my success on the Vefsna River during the 2013 World Fly Fishing Championship in Norway.

became very clear. The densities of fish were low in the river, and most sessions were won with less than 10 fish. When I arrived at the river during the championship, I found that 90 percent of my beat was a smooth, medium-velocity glide between 2 and 5 feet deep. While I could not spot fish, I could see the bottom easily, and knew the fish would see me.

Most of the competitors from other countries chose to fish wet flies swung on floating and clear intermediate lines, which worked well. However, I chose to rely on my suspension/strike-indicator nymphing background, and rigged a rod with a dry and tungsten nymph dropper to use the same approach, while staying within the FIPS-Mouche rules, which don't allow floating devices on the leader other than flies. The dry fly was a large Chubby Chernobyl with extra yarn I added in the wing to increase the buoyancy and hold up heavy nymphs. I spent 90 percent of my session fishing this rig with a combination of dead drifts and twitches to move the dry fly. The grayling and brown trout fell hard for the duo, and I landed 16 fish for the session win, which was the highest

Anglers in New Zealand are known for wearing camouflage to hide their presence when stalking trout. Whether you sport full camo or not, avoid wearing bright colors, especially on your head and neck, and you will be able to approach more trout without spooking them. (PHOTO BY CONNOR MURPHY)

If there are not any rocks or trees to hide you from the trout, try using the currents of the river instead. The turbulent currents in the center of the river made an easy veil to hide behind to fish the eddy in this photo. (PHOTO BY MARK OLSEN)

number landed during any session of the championship. If I had stuck with the usual short-range Euro-nymphing approach, it's possible I would have landed a few fish, but I doubt I would have been nearly as successful.

3) **Use naturally occurring obstructions to shield you from the fish.** An often-overlooked way to minimize your chances of spooking fish is to use obstructions to block a trout's view of your body or to blend into your surroundings. One

The inside corner of bends in the river often feature high gravel or rock berms deposited during high flows, like the one upstream of me in this photo. Kneel on or step off these elevated locations to lower your profile. (PHOTO BY MARK OLSEN)

Keeping your shadow off the water you plan to fish is critical to avoid alerting trout to your presence. In this photo, Lance Egan gets into fishing position by crouching. The low afternoon sun angle on this December day cast long shadows; by keeping his shadow off the water, Lance avoided spooking the fish he was about to catch.

of my favorite examples of this strategy comes from Gary Lafontaine. In his book *Fly Fishing the Mountain Lakes,* Gary shared a story about how he caught a wise old brown trout from a friend's pond. In his first few encounters, Gary noticed that the fish would cruise its established path until swerving out into the pond after noticing Gary fishing from the bank. Gary placed an artificial tree on the bank near where the fish had established its territory and allowed the brown trout to become accustomed to it. On a subsequent trip, he used the tree to hide behind. As a result, he avoided signaling himself as a threat and easily caught the trout.

This story illustrates a strategy that few anglers use on the river. The fact is, there can be lots of types of obstructions to use while you're on the river. The obvious ones are physical objects like rocks and trees. When placed between yourself and the fish, these objects can break up your outline just like the artificial tree did for Gary Lafontaine. If I'm fishing pocketwater, I will kneel on, lean on, or crouch behind available boulders that will help to break my silhouette and allow me to

get closer to my target lie, or fish. I also look for dead trees hanging out over the river that I can use the same way.

The current itself is often the best and easiest veil to hide behind. When the surface of the river is broken enough to hide the riverbed, I place this current in between myself and my target lie, just like it was a tree or rock. If you force the fish to look through broken current, either they won't be able to see you, or their view will be broken enough that they won't consider you a threat. A common example of this strategy is fishing from a wading position in the river to the lies on the far bank. When there are waves and broken water running between you and your target lie, they will hide your outline and allow you to cut the distance between you and the trout you're after. When you can fish closer to your target, you can reduce the slack in your presentation, improve your strike detection and deadness of your drift, and quicken your hook-set reaction time.

If you can't find turbulent water or a physical object to put in between yourself and the fish, another strategy to try is blending into your

Though it may not look like good holding water, the area Antonio Rodrigues is fishing produced several fish in mid-winter. By kneeling, he kept his profile low and his head and shoulders below the cone of vision of the trout he was targeting. If you can get past the extra effort and the odd looks from fellow anglers, kneeling will produce extra opportunities to catch unsuspecting trout when the water is clear and the fish are spooky.

surroundings. If you have ever seen photos of anglers from New Zealand, or have taken a trip there, you will likely notice a lot of anglers wearing camouflage. While this may seem overzealous to some, they deal with the difficulties of spooky trout in clear water on a daily basis, and use any strategy they can to reduce the trout's perception of them as a threat. You may not need to dress fully like an archery hunter to avoid spooking fish on your local river, but I'm convinced it can pay dividends to dress in drab colors that don't stand out drastically from the vegetation in the riparian zone. This is particularly important when it comes to hats or shirts, since the parts of your body fish are most likely to see first are your head, shoulders, neck, and outstretched arms.

4) **Lower your elevation and profile.** Keep repeating the mantra, "If I can see the bottom or the fish, they can see me." As you wade into position to fish a lie, think about your position and your height. If where you plan to wade puts your head high above the water, fish are more likely to

If you find yourself kneeling very often in your local river, a pair of guards to protect your knees and shins can be a big help. I find they help take the edge off accidental falls and help save me from a cracked patella accompanied by a plethora of expletives. In addition, they are great at protecting waders from thorny plants and other sources of leaks.

see you. If you can wade into a depression between rocks or step off a gravel bar or shelf into deeper water, you will diminish your presence to the fish.

This is a common problem when fishing from an inside bend. These locations are deposition zones for the river, and flooding flows often deposit gravel or cobble that forms a steep slope. A single step toward the center of the river may lower your profile 6 to 12 inches in these types of locations. Even though stepping into the river will put you closer to your intended lie, the reduced height may decrease the angle between you and the water's surface sufficiently for you to get under the cone of vision of the trout you are pursuing. Be cognizant of your casts as well. Many of the best dry-fly anglers I know make sidearm casts to keep their line close to the water and out of view of the trout.

In addition, a lot of anglers overlook the position of their shadow as they approach the river. There is no better way to send trout scurrying for cover quickly than a shadow cast across their holding lie. If you have ever watched trout holding in a pool as a bird of prey flies over and casts a shadow on the water, you have likely seen the instant panic that ensues. As you approach the water, pay close attention to where your shadow extends, especially when the sun is at low angles during the day and your shadow is longer. Crouch to get into position if necessary and you will find more fish still willing to eat when you make your first cast.

If the water is less than knee-deep or if I'm fishing from the bank, I will often fish from my knees. During the session on the Pliva River in Bosnia I described earlier, the only way I could approach the fish I spotted was from dry land on the bank they were holding by. Heavy water in the middle of the channel prevented an across-the-river approach. I spent two and a half of my three hours in that session fishing from my knees on the bank. I firmly believe I would not have caught any fish had I been standing over them.

A similar strategy paid dividends during the 2011 National Fly Fishing Championship in North Carolina. I drew a beat on the Nantahala River in

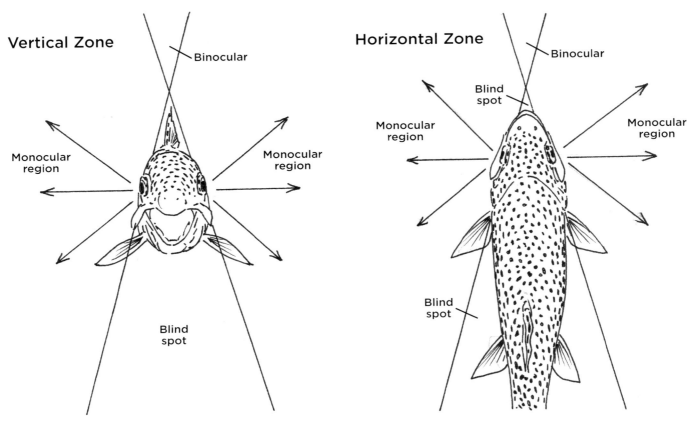

Vertical Zone

Binocular

Monocular region

Monocular region

Blind spot

Horizontal Zone

Binocular

Blind spot

Monocular region

Monocular region

Blind spot

The location of its eyes allows a trout to see much of the world around it in binocular or monocular vision. However, there is one blind spot behind its head where you can approach it and stay out of sight.

In smooth water an upstream fishing approach from a downstream position is often the best way to present your flies without spooking fish. My Fly Fishing Team USA mate Pat Weiss is a master of this approach, having honed his skills on the famous rivers surrounding State College, Pennsylvania. In this photo, Pat fights a fish he hooked fishing upstream on a flat glide of a Western tailwater, showing that the success of his approach is certainly not limited to his home rivers.

my final session that had produced poor results for other anglers in the previous four sessions. When I scouted the beat, there was a long section (80–100 yards) of shallow pocketwater at the bottom, which was difficult to approach in the low, clear flows. However, the temperatures were prime, and I thought there would be fish that hadn't been bothered by other competitors in this less-prime-looking water.

I spent the first two hours of my session on my knees slithering from rock to rock. Trout came easily in the turbulent yet shallow water. They were much harder to fool in the obvious pools and deep pockets above, which earlier competitors had likely targeted heavily. Though I did not win the session, I was able to get a third place on a tough beat, which was good enough to secure a silver individual medal for the championship. If I had taken the road heavily traveled in the deep pools and obvious pockets, my finish would have been much worse. Instead, a low-profile approach, to water that was prime for the river conditions, produced results.

5) **Approach fish from downstream to avoid being seen.** The anatomical position of a trout's eyes allows it a cone of monocular vision on the sides and binocular vision in the front, but it has a blind spot directly downstream. If you stay in that blind spot, the trout won't be able to see you until your proximity becomes too close.

My teammate Pat Weiss is a master of fishing upstream to trout. Reading back through my journals of the competitions we've fished together over the past few years, my comments from our practice sessions repeatedly refer to how well Pat fishes from a downstream position. It's become clear to me that there are many instances where I could incorporate this strategy more regularly into my own approach. Like George Daniel, Pat hails from State College, Pennsylvania, the capital of tuck casting and the upstream tight-line nymphing techniques made famous by Joe Humphreys and George Harvey. This region features a lot of lower-gradient trout rivers with flatter sections that make it difficult to avoid spooking fish when employing an across-the-river approach, except in higher flows.

Pat has adjusted his style to master lower-gradient rivers. He uses a Euro-nymphing leader specifically built with a thicker sighter so that it will float and suspend lightly weighted nymphs for an extended upstream drift. He prefers a fast 10-foot, 4-weight rod to assist in his complete command of the tuck cast, as opposed to the softer rods typically used by most Euro-nymphing anglers. I'll cover Pat's strategies in some specific fishing scenarios in later chapters.

Strategies for Turbid Water

One of the most disheartening sights for an angler is arriving to find the river looking more like coffee than an inviting azure color promising trout behind every rock. It can be intimidating to look at a river and think, "How is a trout going to see my fly in that muddy soup?" I'll be the first to admit that I'm not immune to this type of reaction.

When it comes to competitions, competitors learn to deal with whatever conditions they face, or else they would crumble. For instance, back in 2009 during my first session of the US National Fly Fishing Championships, I arrived at Penn's Creek when the river was flowing at under 250 cubic feet per second (cfs); by the time I left three hours later it had risen to over 3,000 cfs, on its way to 6,000 cfs. Picnic benches, construction barrels, and entire hardwood trees came down the river while I cast away, fruitlessly. This obviously was a dire circumstance. However, in less extreme cases, just because a river is turbid does not mean that all is lost.

Trout certainly feed in muddy water. I remember a trip I guided down the Rio Grande in Colorado back in August of 2007. The previous day had brought severe thunderstorm activity. I warned my clients before the trip that I did not expect much fishing success that day, but they wanted to enjoy the float whether the fish cooperated or not. Instead of fishing dry-and-dropper rigs like I had been doing previous to the storm, I pulled out dumbbell-eyed black articulated leeches. What ensued was one of the better days of fishing that I had all season, and all three of us ended the day with smiles and good memories.

Through the above experience and others, I have learned that trout do still feed in turbid water. In fact, whenever we have a heavy snow year in the Western United States, with a prolonged muddy snowmelt, the trout always come out of these conditions in prime shape, which is not what would be expected if they had been fasting for several months. You may find yourself on a vacation where persistent storms have roiled a normally placid river, or you may have a local river that seems to always be discolored when you have the chance to go fishing. The question then becomes, Do you head home when the river turns turbid, or do you make adjustments to have success?

Several of the changes I make when the water turns turbid have to do with fly selection. As with all fly-fishing situations, to catch a trout it must first see your fly and then be convinced that the fly is food. Because range of sight is greatly diminished in turbid water, it can be a challenge for fish to see your fly. Regardless of fly type (nymph, streamer, etc.), there are four characteristics that give me confidence in a fly during turbid conditions. They include a large size, a dark base color, flash and/or fluorescent hot spots, and contrast.

For most anglers, fishing a river below a Slovakian castle would be an exciting and surreal experience. However, arriving at the river with it running the color of a caffè latte might dampen the enthusiasm a bit. This was the scene that greeted me before my first session in the 2017 World Fly Fishing Championship on Slovakia's Orava River. Despite the color of the water, adjustments in strategy allowed me to find willing grayling.

When the water is turbid, it's time to put away the midge pupae and pull out the meat. Large flies might put trout off during clear conditions, but when it's turbid they are far more likely to be seen. I rarely fish nymphs smaller than 14 and streamers smaller than size 8 when a river is turbid. I also rarely fish dry flies unless fish are rising. Regarding color, unless I'm fishing a worm or mop pattern, which are consummate performers during muddy conditions, I opt for flies with black, peacock, dark brown, or dark olive for their base color in dirty water. Dark flies cast a harder-edged silhouette, which helps them to be seen from a greater distance. Adding flash or fluorescent beads, dubbing, thread, or tails to the dark base color can also increase the likelihood of having your fly be seen by trout. Lastly, a bit of contrast against the dark base can increase your fly's visibility even more. Combining these characteristics, I have tied successful large nymphs and streamers with black flashy bodies, pink, orange, or chartreuse collars or tails, and white or yellow legs to provide some contrast. These types of flies rarely make it out of my box in normal conditions, but they have saved the day for me when water clarity is a foot or less.

Once you have the proper fly design, you must also get your flies in front of fish and keep them there. Most of the time this means extra weight, unless you are fishing in shallows along the bank. Fish will be more forgiving of slight drag in dirty water. When Euro-nymphing in dirty water, I often choose to fish heavier flies than I normally would to get my flies to depth quickly. To keep them from constantly snagging the bottom, I will lead them downstream slightly with the rod tip or use a shorter section of tippet. Similar to fishing in cold water, I like to fish point flies such as eggs, mops, and stoneflies, which will roll along the bottom over rocks and snags as long as they are tied on jig hooks or with inverting tungsten beads. Stalling these flies intentionally on the bottom during the drift can increase the time

trout have to see them, and if you are fishing a second fly on a dropper tag, it will dangle seductively in the current, which provokes further takes. In addition, jigging your nymphs 3 to 5 inches once or twice during the drift can produce movements that will help trout find your flies and suggest they are alive.

When fishing streamers in dirty water, I also over-weight them to increase sink rate and get them to depth quickly. To avoid constant snagging, I move them more often or fish with more tension during the drift to halt their descent when necessary.

Another method that has worked in turbid water repeatedly is fishing a short dry-and-dropper on a Euro-nymphing leader in eddies. With a short tippet length between the dry and nymph and the sag-resistant properties of the long, thin leader, I can allow the rig to cycle repeatedly in the eddy, providing trout multiple chances to see and eat my nymph.

Heavily weighted flies also produce commotion when they enter the water. Trout are visual feeders more so than many fish. In clear water the visual image and behavior of your fly will determine their interest in it as potential food. However, in turbid water or during the night hours, trout rely on the vibrations they detect through their inner ear and their lateral line to identify sounds that are produced by potential prey. An audible splash may be a detriment in clear water, but it can help trout locate your fly in turbid water. When combined with a large bulbous body, extra weight can accentuate the entry splash and pique a trout's interest.

In turbid water, the difference between success and failure can simply be whether fish can see your fly or not. Choosing larger flies that feature flash, fluorescent materials, and/or contrasting colors can help fish to identify your fly in conditions with low light and short-range visibility.

Due to a lack of color changes and contrast, it can be difficult to identify which parts of a river offer good holding water. This photo shows the lower half of my beat during the first session of the 2017 World Fly Fishing Championship on the Orava River in Slovakia. The turbid water made finding fish in the nondescript flat water difficult. I found success upstream by focusing on the banks and faster water, where obvious current seams could be seen on the surface.

One of the harder aspects of fishing turbid water is reading the water to know where to focus your effort. Much of reading water is learning to look for structure and changes in depth that suggest where trout might hold. Turbid water hides rocks and logs from view and limits your ability to see underwater structure. Normally, looking for changes in water color is the best way to detect depth changes. When all you can see is brown, it's pretty hard to know whether the water you are fishing is inches or feet deep. Surface currents can still be read, however, and trout will still hold in feeding lies you would fish in clearer conditions. Keep in mind that they are more likely to frequent slower water where they have a longer time to see potential food items drifting past.

One grace of turbid conditions is that the fish pull to the banks. Here the depths are less variable and you're less likely to hook a snag that will hold your

fly like the jaws of a bear trap, where you can't wade to retrieve it. Light attenuates very quickly in turbid conditions, and the bottom of a deep pool or run can be a dark place where food is difficult to identify. If a muddy pulse of water is a short-lived event, then trout may ride out the swell in this type of refuge location. If it is prolonged, like a mountain snowmelt, then they are forced to seek out proper feeding locations. When the water is turbid, these locations are often in shallow water, where enough light still penetrates to allow trout to search for food.

This lesson was drilled into me a few years ago while fishing with my former Fly Fishing Team USA mate Kurt Finlayson during one of our frequent lunch dates on the river. We were fishing a local brown trout river experiencing an early snowmelt. This river is rarely clear during low flows, and visibility was only about 6 inches during the pulse. I was taking turns with Kurt

During turbid conditions, light attenuates quickly and deep water can be a dark place. Trout will usually seek shallow water near the banks where visibility is higher and finding food is easier. Bankside locations can also offer a refuge from moving objects that might be entrained in the current if the river is swollen and full of debris. If you find yourself fishing a turbid river, focus on the banks, and you will likely find willing trout. (PHOTO BY MARK OLSEN)

fishing water types that had produced fish in the weeks prior, catching the occasional fish, but far fewer than I was used to on this stream.

As we rounded a featureless run, Kurt started fishing water tight to the inside bend, which I was about to walk through on our way upstream. He quickly caught a fish in inches of water within a foot of the bank. I assumed it was a one-off, but we proceeded to take turns and land four more trout from the same area. The water offered no overhead cover, and there was no overt structure that suggested fish should be there. However, the turbid conditions provided the trout all the cover they needed to avoid being seen, and the shallow water allowed enough sun to penetrate for them to search for food. The fish would have been completely exposed and unlikely to reside there in clearer conditions. It's a lesson I haven't forgotten, and one I've applied many times since with similar pleasant surprises.

Let me share an experience that helps to combine the strategies for designing flies and fishing turbid water in the preceding paragraphs. Back in 2008 I had the chance to fish in the Teva Mountain Games in Vail, Colorado. During the fishing portion of the competition, we were scheduled to make two one-third-day floats down the upper Colorado River. The river was in full-blown snowmelt runoff, and the organizers had considered moving the fishing to another venue leading up to the competition. Ultimately, they chose to stay with the original plan. At that time, the competition rules allowed six flies total of the same pattern to

be fished during the tournament. During my preparation, I knew I needed to find a fly I was completely confident with, given the conditions.

My first thoughts on method were, "Fish a dark streamer with contrast as close to the bank as possible." To devise a suitable pattern, my teammate Lance Egan and I fished the Eagle River near where we were staying, which was experiencing the same runoff conditions. I tied a couple of streamers to test, which were more successful than I expected. Combining the fly characteristics covered above, I settled on a size 6, black-tailed, peacock-bodied Woolly Bugger. It featured flashabou in the tail, yellow rubber legs in the rear, white rubber legs in the front, a fluorescent chartreuse thread collar, and a very large 4.5 mm tungsten bead, in addition to a shank full of 0.030-inch lead wire.

After a good initial round, my mediocre results during the final casting round the day before put me in the back of the third out of four boats that floated competitors down the river. My boat partner had first shot at each of the potential lies we spotted, so I knew my presentations had to be more precise to be successful. Though I only had six flies to fish with, my goal was to place my fly within inches of the bank on every cast, unless I identified lies off the bank that were important to cover.

I caught fish consistently through the first float and the first half of our second float. I was able to put 17 fish in the net for first place in the tournament, and I landed a 20-inch rainbow for the "big fish" award. My boat partner netted only four fish during the two floats. What was the difference? My boat partner was also

In the 2008 Teva Mountain Games, high and muddy water greeted the anglers who made it through the casting portion of the tournament and into the fishing rounds. By designing a streamer specifically for the tough snowmelt runoff conditions and fishing it accurately and as tight to the bank as possible, the trout of the Colorado River cooperated, and I took home the gold medal and the "big fish" award.

fishing a Woolly Bugger, but it had much less weight and did not feature the same additions of flash, fluorescent colors, and intentional contrast. Furthermore, while he was casting toward the bank, his casts were usually feet off the bank instead of inches away, where the water was shallower and visibility for the trout was higher. The majority of my fish came from the time my fly hit the water to within my first or second strip. Several of them came from backwaters where I cast my streamer to stagnant water under willows, like I was fishing for bass.

The weight I had built into my fly not only got the fly to depth quickly, where the fish could see it, but I also believe the splash it created garnered attention from fish that provoked them to search for the source of the sound. The visual characteristics of the fly helped them to spot it in the sepia water and separate it as potential food. That day provided one of many examples that have shown me that success on the river is usually a matter of identifying small details, which will provide incremental advantages.

Water Temperature

There may not be a single environmental variable that affects trout more than water temperature. I can often predict how successful a day of fishing is likely to be and where I will find trout simply by taking the temperature. As such, one of the first things I like to do when I get to the river is pull out my thermometer. Because trout are *ectothermic* (cold-blooded), their

In addition to having clown colors during spawning time, arctic char require the coldest water out of any of the salmonids in order to thrive.

metabolism is ruled by the temperature of their surroundings. As the temperature rises and falls, enzymes that control the speed of metabolic reactions undergo conformational changes that result in corresponding accelerations and decelerations of a trout's metabolic rate. As their metabolic rate changes, their need for food responds accordingly.

This concept became very clear during my fisheries research in graduate school. As part of my thesis, I used a bioenergetics program to estimate the consumptive demand (i.e., metabolic rate) of the arctic char I was studying. The model was based on their growth and the temperature of the water in which they resided, in addition to other factors. From their basal metabolic rate to their peak rate, which occurs between 53 and 59 degrees F, their need for food nearly quadrupled.

As endothermic creatures, we simply cannot relate to this type of change. True, our metabolic rate changes some due to the extra energy required to maintain homeostasis when temperature or other variables change. But can you imagine if as the seasons changed, you needed to eat three or four times as many calories, or vice versa, to cope with the changes around you? This is a difficult scenario to visualize, and, if nothing else, I'm glad my grocery budget doesn't have to expand like it does for trout. If we humans did have to cope with similar changes to our energetic needs, our behaviors would change as a result, and it is likely we would focus more of our time directly on maintaining food when needed and more on energy conservation during times when we need less energy. It turns out this strategy is essentially the pattern that trout follow.

Most fly anglers do not find themselves fishing rivers that are inhabited by arctic char. The char species with a circumpolar native range (arctic char, Dolly Varden, bull trout, and lake trout) need the coldest water of all of the salmonids to thrive, which makes sense given the geography of where they evolved. However, the same metabolic relationship with temperature exists for other salmonid species as well. The temperatures just shift higher.

One of the most underutilized tools in an angler's tool kit is a thermometer. I take the water temperature when I arrive at the river in the morning and often several more times throughout the day. These readings help me to focus on techniques and water types that are most likely to be successful. I prefer infrared or digital thermometers over typical analog models, as the readings are quick and easy to read.

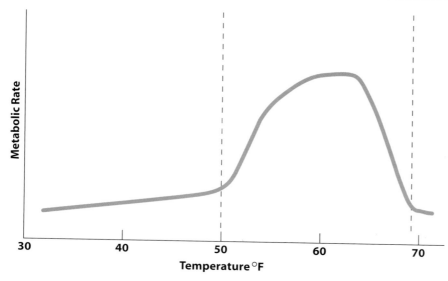

Temperature is one of the most critical variables affecting trout feeding behavior because it directly affects their metabolic rate. Trout metabolic rates follow a left-skewed bell curve. The shape of the curve is similar between different species, but the specific temperature where changes occur can differ by a few degrees. Their metabolic rate descends as stress increases once the water becomes too warm for their optimal function.

The typical metabolic curve for trout is a left-skewed bell curve. Their lowest metabolic rate will be at near-freezing temperatures. This rate will gradually increase until reaching an inflection point where their metabolic rate rises rapidly to an apex, and then rapidly descends as the temperatures reach stress and lethality. This inflection point is typically around 48 to 50 degrees. Depending upon the species and strain, most trout have maximum metabolic rates between 55 and 65 degrees. Once temperatures reach 68 to 70 degrees, most trout enter stress mode and their consumptive demand decreases drastically.

What does all this physiology mean for anglers? In my experience, three aspects of trout behavior change in relation to the temperature. First, trout are generally willing to move farther for food items when the water is near prime temperatures. Therefore, if the water is cold, I plan to fish each likely holding spot with more drifts from various angles. Additionally, I seek to ensure that my flies are very near the bottom if I'm nymphing so that trout have ample chances to take them in close proximity. On the other hand, if the temperatures are ideal, I am more confident that I can fish quickly through an area and show my flies to most of the willing fish without having to repeatedly drill a small pocket to get a fish to take.

Trout are more likely to come up through the column to take a suspended nymph or a dry fly during ideal temperatures. During these times I am more likely to fish a dry fly or dry-and-dropper to capitalize on the trout's willingness to move. Furthermore, I am also more likely to use an active presentation with a streamer, since the trout are more likely to chase.

Take readings at multiple times throughout the day, as the water temperature will change based on the conditions. Unless you are close to a dam on a tailwater or to the groundwater source(s) on a spring creek, you can expect the temperature to rise significantly on a sunny day. The amount of variation depends on a lot of factors, like stream shading, sun angle, volume of the water, and stream width-to-depth ratio, among others. Normally I expect to see a temperature change of 3 to 8 degrees from morning to late afternoon, when the river is at its warmest. However, I remember an April day on Montana's Beaverhead River where the water was 38 degrees when we started fishing and 54

With a little foresight, you can plan around predicted temperature fluctuations that will increase or decrease trout activity. For instance, in the winter it is best to focus your efforts during the warmest hours of the day, when the sun angle is at its highest, along with the water temperature. Conversely, during late summer it may be wise to fish only early or late in the day to capitalize on lower water temperatures and sun angles, and more-active trout. This trout fell to a Pliva Shuttlecock Emerger during a short afternoon *Baetis* hatch on a cold March day in Idaho.

Scientific studies have shown that riffles and pocketwater are the insect factories of a trout stream or large river, like this riffle on Utah's Green River. On average, not only are more insects produced in these habitats, but they tend to be larger than those in pools and glides as well. As such, these are prime feeding locations for trout when the temperatures are comfortable or there is a hatch in progress.

degrees during a blizzard caddis hatch that afternoon. To say the least, the morning fished a bit different than the afternoon.

You can use daily temperature fluctuation patterns to plan when to hit the water if you only have a few hours to fish for the day, or to focus on your favorite water when the conditions are best. For instance, in the winter I may not hit the river until ten or eleven a.m., after the sun has been up and the temperature is rising. Conversely, in late summer I may focus my efforts early in the day, before the water temperature reaches stressful levels for trout, or in the evening when the sun and water temperature are both dropping. If you are familiar with a stretch of river, one strategy is to pick what you deem to be the best water and plan your day to be in that water during the time and temperatures when fish will be at peak activity.

In my experience, the last and most important change to trout behavior in relation to temperature is the water types where fish hold. There is an ecological reasoning for the change. It has long been postulated that the riffles and fast-water areas of a river are the food-production zones within a stream, while the pools and slow-water areas are the food sinks.

A recent paper by Sean Naman et al. (2017) demonstrated this theory definitively. In their study they used a novel screening approach to separate streams into habitat types and isolate the sources of macroinvertebrate drift within the stream. They found that macroinvertebrate drift within riffles averaged three and a half

times higher than within pools. In addition, macroinvertebrate size was higher within riffles as well. So not only is food higher in quantity in riffle habitat, but the prey is higher in quality as well.

So why don't trout inhabit riffles all of the time? Remember from our discussion above that trout metabolic rates slow significantly in colder water. At these rates they may not be able to digest food quickly enough to make it energetically profitable to inhabit riffles and faster currents where they must expend more energy to hold station. During cold times, there is enough food in slow, deep currents to supply their energetic needs, and these areas also provide refuge from overhead predators while they are in energy-conservation mode. However, as the water warms, trout will spread out into faster water to take advantage of the increase in food availability.

I learned this lesson the hard way on a local river before my competitive angling days. During this period of my angling life, I spent an inordinate amount of time fishing a short stretch of a local tailwater. Interestingly, I found that my catch rates were often as good or better in the winter than in the summer, when water temperatures were cold and the fish were lethargic. At the time, I thought I had just dialed in the winter midge fishing. In reality, I was glued to my strike-indicator rig in the slower runs and pools in which it fished best.

While I realized that trout spread out during the summer, simply from seeing them in shallower water, I did not have a strategy that was well suited

Pools are important refuge locations for trout and provide depth, cover, and reduced energetic demands compared to faster water. This makes them prime locations for trout on winter days like the one in this photo. However, my work in sampling fisheries, combined with experiences and techniques gleaned from competitive angling, have shown that other water types often hold a majority of the trout when conditions are right. (PHOTO BY MARK OLSEN)

Just because it's cold outside does not mean you should stay at home. This surprise steelhead ate a size 16 pearl Lite Brite Perdigon in 36-degree water while I was targeting trout. It certainly put a flex in the 10-foot-6-inch, 3-weight Cortland rod I was fishing.

When the temperature reaches the mid-40s, *Baetis* mayflies can be a common sight on trout rivers. Be prepared with nymphs and dry flies to imitate them, and get ready for some fun.

to fishing shallower and faster water. Thankfully, this changed later on when I learned about long-leader Euro-nymphing strategies. Nowadays, my catch rates and enjoyment on the same stretch of river are much higher during warmer temperatures than they used to be.

Hopefully, the information on trout physiology above has convinced you of the need to adjust your strategy based on water temperatures. What specific guidelines should you follow? I adapt my approach based on the temperature strata below.

All anglers recognize pools as holding water. Their depth and slower currents provide refuge from overhead predators and energy conservation. These characteristics make pools especially good places to fish during cold temperatures, but other water types may be more profitable as temperatures climb and trout seek greater feeding opportunities. In this photo, Pat Weiss nets a nice rainbow on a January day.

From 32 to 35 degrees, I don't expect much activity; I consider fish caught in these temperatures a bonus, though I have had surprisingly successful days at these temperatures. During these times, I focus on the slowest water I can find and use techniques that present my flies hard on the bottom. I may even make drifts that stall my flies temporarily through the drift to give the trout maximum time to see and intercept my offerings. Flies tied to invert and dressed with bulbous materials, such as eggs, mops, and stoneflies, can be jigged and rolled along the bottom without snagging, except on wood. These flies offer a big-enough meal

Once the water temperature has climbed above 50 degrees, the pockets and riffle seams in this photo will hold trout. Below that temperature I would not expect many fish to be found there, unless there is a hatch of insects.

When the water warms above 50 degrees, or when a hatch develops, riffles are often the best place to find feeding trout that are easily caught. The water in this photo may not look impressive, but it holds plenty of rainbows when the conditions are right.

When temperatures climb into the high 50s and 60s, trout can often be found near the bottom of deep runs where swift water zooms by overhead. A targeted Euro-nymphing presentation to the middle of this run produced nearly a dozen rainbows and a surprise Chinook salmon on an Oregon river with a low density of resident trout. With the temperature in the low 60s in July, this run created prime lies where food and cover were abundant.

that lethargic trout will be swayed to eat them when they find less-conspicuous flies not worth the trouble.

From 36 to 39 degrees, trout activity picks up slightly; there can be good fishing available at this temperature range, especially toward the upper end of the strata. I still focus on slow water, and I find the rear half of pools, runs, and large pockets to be the most productive. If I can't approach these areas without spooking trout, then I will turn to a suspension-nymphing rig to fish as slowly as possible, at a greater distance than what I can when Euro-nymphing.

From 40 to 45 degrees, I expect the fish to spread out just a bit. Instead of focusing only on the rear half of pools and runs, I will spend time focusing on the upper half as well. I will also fish larger pockets in

pocketwater and the heads of pools and runs where there is a riffle transition. I also find bankside eddies to reliably give up fish, particularly if there are brown trout and the eddy has structure they can hold tight to. At these temperatures I will start to consider bringing a dry-fly rod, as there can be good emergences of midges and *Baetis* on many of the rivers I fish.

From 46 to 50 degrees, the trout will start to inhabit shallower water as well. I find a few fish in shallow pockets and riffles at these temperatures, especially if there are mayflies or larger midges hatching.

From 51 to 59 degrees, the magic really starts to happen. These are the temperatures where trout climb into peak metabolic rates, and all but the fastest water is profitable for them to hold in. I love seeing all of the surprising places that fish will hold at these temperatures. Water types from 6-inch-deep riffles to 6-foot-deep runs will produce fish. These are the temperatures where I find fewer fish inhabiting the slower parts of runs and pools. I will still fish these areas, but it is educational how many times I have gone fishless moving through a pool only to find fish stacked at the head and into the riffles or pockets above.

From 60 to 70 degrees, I focus on banks, riffles, and heavy pocketwater, as well as the fastest water in the river that has any sort of place for a trout to hide. Oftentimes, with the correct presentation, it is possible to catch trout underneath water that is fast enough to produce standing waves. In my experience, these lies may hold the largest fish in the river, because they have more mass and power to deal with heavy currents, and they value the security and abundance of food this type of water provides. Most of the time, standing waves or rapids signal there are large rocks and boulders that are disturbing the current upstream. Even in heavy water, wherever there are boulders there is likely to be a current break that a fish can sit in to conserve energy and take advantage of the plethora of food rushing by. Find the boulders in these habitats and fish below them for surprising results.

In addition to a point value for the current temperature, the ambient temperature, or the patterns that surround a given temperature, can be just as important. For instance, if I take a temperature in the winter and my thermometer reads 42 to 45 degrees, I expect to have good fishing, since the temperature has likely climbed from somewhere in the 30s or lower 40s earlier in the day. However, if my thermometer reads 45 degrees in the spring or fall, it may have descended from temperatures closer to 50 degrees or more, depending on recent weather. In this situation I would expect stubborn trout and challenging fishing. While the temperature value is the same, the thermal pattern that surrounds that temperature is important, as a sharp change can shock a trout's system.

In general, if temperatures are trending toward the range of prime metabolic rates, I expect the fish to respond positively and increase their activity. Common examples of when this pattern might occur are a sunny day that warms the water in the cooler months, or a thunderstorm that cools the water in late summer. The reverse is also true. If temperatures trend away from the prime 55- to 65-degree range, I expect the fishing to slow, especially if the temperature change is abrupt.

In cold temperature swings I will often focus on slow, deep water, as I would during the winter. I also will fish as tight to structure as possible, where fish will tend to sulk. Streamers and junk flies, such as eggs, mops, and squirmy worms, are particularly useful during cold swings. If the temperature swing heads the other way, above the trout's prime temperature range, I will focus on shallow broken riffles and pocketwater, where the water is infused with oxygen. Once the temperature reaches 70 degrees, it's time to find cooler water, or head home.

Fish Density

A simple variable that can help to discern what type of water is worth targeting in a river is fish density. Unlike hatchery trout, wild trout grow up in a world of social dominance hierarchy. There are some very interesting scientific studies that demonstrate the tendencies of trout to isolate their lie from other fish. (In short, fish are territorial; they like to have their own space to hold with minimal aggressive interactions from other trout.)

Not all holding lies in a river are created equal. Trout are adept at analyzing which lies will bring them the most food, for the least energetic expenditure, while minimizing their risk from predators. Within a given reach of stream, the largest and most dominant fish will tend to occupy the best lies, and smaller fish will occupy the surrounding, less-profitable lies. Rivers are always limited in the number of profitable lies, which is one of the reasons a portion of each age class succumbs to mortality each year. How, then, does the density of fish factor into your plan on how to cover a certain stretch of river?

There is a reason for the clichéd saying "Variety is the spice of life." One of the best parts of fly fishing for me is fishing new and different waters. There are productive and stable rivers that tend to harbor high numbers of fish, such as many famous tailwaters and spring creeks. There are other rivers that may have a much lower density of fish, but they can produce outsize fish as a result. Many of the rivers on New Zealand's South Island fit the latter category. If you can find out a little about a river before you fish it, in regard to fish density, it can help you plan what water is worth a significant amount of fishing time, and what water you might want to bypass, or make just a few presentations to before moving on.

Many of the rivers in New Zealand are known for having a low density of fish—although the fish available are often of trophy proportions. In these types of rivers, it is often best to focus on fish you can see, or to focus only on the best water with adequate depth, cover, and current speeds appropriate for the water temperature. (PHOTO BY CONNOR MURPHY)

It may seem simplistic, but in a river with a high fish density, the trout will be forced to spread into secondary and tertiary lies. Fish can hold in some surprisingly shallow, fast, or seemingly featureless water, which most anglers will walk by. My home water, Utah's Provo River, is a good example. It is a typical Western tailwater with a very high density of wild trout. Despite being a small river, I have seen density estimates ranging from 3,000 to 8,000 fish per mile from local fisheries biologists, depending on the river stretch and year. When you do the math, that can be more than one fish per linear foot in a river that flows between 100 and 500 cfs for most of the year. That's a lot of fish to squeeze into a river. When I fish there, I plan on covering each nook and cranny that looks like it might hold a fish. I am often surprised at how many fish can be found in a seemingly mediocre piece of water. Unfortunately, I am still surprised at the places I spook fish while wading where I didn't think it was worth presenting a fly.

Most rivers do not produce fish like a hatchery. However, that doesn't mean they are not worth fishing, nor does it mean that you can't catch good numbers of fish in a low-density river. On these types of rivers, your success can be increased by focusing on the best water available instead of covering every conceivable piece of water.

If I'm competing on this type of river, I may still cover a lot of secondary water in hopes of finding a fish or two that other competitors passed over. However, I will usually try to find the best three to five spots within my beat and spend the majority of time rotating between them with different flies and techniques, while allowing rest time for fish to recover if they weren't convinced by previous approaches. This likely isn't the best approach to success outside of a competition.

As long as you have access to a long reach of river, in low-density rivers it's best to plan on covering lots of water, picking the best pieces of water to focus on for the day. It is generally my experience that in prime water, there can still be multiple fish inhabiting a small area in low-density rivers.

For example, on another river near my home, there is a stretch a few miles long that is warm and has highly variable flows and degraded habitat, yet there are still quality fish to be had. When I fish there, I often

My home water, Utah's Provo River, is typical of many Western tailwater rivers. It has a very high density of brown trout, which forces them to spread out into water that can be nondescript or only inches deep, like the pockets and riffles in this photo. Instead of skipping this water, I find fish that are far less pressured and easier to catch than the fish inhabiting the obvious pools and runs, which most anglers target.

Not all rivers are stuffed with trout, but that doesn't mean they aren't worth fishing. I caught this fish in a river not known for a high density of trout. What the river lacks in numbers, it makes up for in big brown trout. When fishing this river, I plan to focus on prime lies, as fishing secondary water generally yields few fish.

cover five times as much water per day as I would on the Provo River. Occasionally I catch a fish in spots I call "maybe water," which might hold a fish, but is just as likely to produce nothing. In contrast, when I reach prime water, I'm usually able to pull multiple fish from an obvious run, pocket, or shelf. The best part is that because there are fewer fish overall, the fish in this river have less competition from other trout. With more-consistent access to prime feeding lies and food, they can attain surprising size.

If no information is available about fish density on a new river, I plan on fishing it like it has a high density of fish. I'll fish a short stretch of water to begin the day, and again later in the day if conditions improve. Based on environmental variables—like water temperature, and my success in the less-prime lies—within an hour or two, I can usually determine whether the river has enough fish to warrant covering all possible water, or to focus on the prime water. Another way I inform these decisions is by trying to spot fish if possible, or by keeping an eye out for spooked fish as I wade up the river. If fish are tumbling off the bank and out of the shallows, it's time to slow down and cover as much likely water as possible. If I only see or catch fish in the best water, then that's where my focus will turn.

Fish Species

An interesting and less-considered part of making a plan, and deciding which water to fish, is what species of fish are in the river. If you fish rivers with different trout species, you may have noticed that they prefer different water types, or different flies and techniques. During graduate school, I read a study by A. J. Gatz et al. (1987) that investigated habitat preferences of brown trout and rainbow trout in rivers where they lived apart (*allopatric*) or together (*sympatric*). In rivers where they were allopatric, the data suggested they preferred similar habitat. However, in sympatric rivers, they often segregated into different habitats to minimize competition and niche overlap. In these rivers, brown trout were found in lower-velocity areas in close proximity to cover. In layman's terms, they preferred slower water near the bank where they could get protection under trees or rocks. Conversely, rainbow trout preferred higher velocities near the *thalweg* (or main center flow) of the river.

My own fishing experiences have followed patterns similar to those found by Gatz and his colleagues. I grew up surrounded by brown trout in the small rivers of Utah. My early fishing experiences demonstrated that though there were definitely brown trout in the obvious pools on rivers, there were as many or more tucked along the bank on the slow sides of current seams, near structure. These types of lies provide safety when they are near a place to hide. Because the main flow of the river tends to push food and particles to where they are deposited along the edges of the river, these locations also produce food. However, they may provide less food per unit of time than the faster zones near the center of the river. As mentioned previously in the study by Naman et al., the food-production zones of the river are generally in the riffles and runs with larger substrate. Therefore, in my opinion, their habitat preferences suggest brown trout are more concerned with conserving energy than with seeking it. When they hold on bankside lies and under or near structure, they exhibit ambush predatory behavior, lying in wait for a meal to come into range of an attack. This is one of the reasons that pounding the banks with streamers from a boat is so popular in brown trout rivers.

My experiences with rainbow trout have demonstrated their predilection for faster water near the center of the river. When I moved to Sacramento back in

This fish exhibited classic brown trout behavior. I caught numerous rainbows from the open water of the run it inhabited. Before I left the run, I fired a bow-and-arrow cast under a branch and tight to the far bank, and was fortunate enough to connect. If you fish rivers with brown trout, do not overlook water tight to the bank and under structure and tree branches. If you do, you may miss an opportunity for your fish of the day, or even worse, the fish of your life.

On a recent trip, I caught several fish along the obvious eddy seam below the foam line in this photo. Just before I left, I saw a tiny disturbance from a rise almost touching the rock in the center of this photo. I made a cast that scraped along the face of the boulder, and it was instantly picked up by a chunky 14-inch brown. It was another in a long line of lessons that have shown me that I still pass up a lot of brown trout holding near the bank.

Over the years I've learned to seek rainbow trout in water I used to think was too fast. This rainbow came from underneath standing waves in a rapid on California's Yuba River. Finding it wasn't a fluke, as many more fish came from similar water during the rest of that day and in future trips. These days, if I'm fishing a river with rainbow trout, I make sure to fish water that may seem too fast, as I'm often surprised at the trout inhabiting it.

2014 to work as a salmon and steelhead biologist, the first river I fished was the Lower Yuba River tailwater. On my first trip, I was catching fish occasionally and enjoying the Yuba River rainbows' reputation for acrobatics when hooked.

When I came upon one fast run, I began fishing the bank sides of seams on both sides of the river. I caught two or three rainbows on both sides of the run, but it was an obvious piece of water, and I thought there should be more fish. Just before I was about to move on, I noticed a slashing rise in the center of the run that was more like a rapid with standing waves. I was surprised there would be fish holding there despite prime water temperatures, let alone that a fish would rise through that type of water. I re-rigged with heavier flies and proceeded to catch six fish from the center of the run, several of which were much larger than the fish I had caught from the margins. The rest of the day I focused on faster water when I came upon it, and was regularly greeted with fish where I would not have expected them.

My experiences on my home rivers have brought similar findings. I have floated one river with my teammate Lance Egan a few times during the past several years. We normally just focus on casting big terrestrial dries to within inches of the bank. The action can be consistent, and the takes are visually exciting. We rarely catch rainbow trout during these floats, yet, when wade fishing, they make up 30 to 50 percent of the catch on most days. The reason we don't catch many rainbows while floating isn't because they don't like terrestrial dries; it's because they tend to inhabit the higher-velocity water near the center of the river—water that is usually targeted by wade anglers.

Interestingly, much of the creel data taken by fisheries biologists across the country suggests much higher rainbow trout catch rates than brown trout catch rates when they inhabit the same water. This pattern is even the case when the brown trout are the dominant fish. Lower catch rates have given brown trout a reputation for being wily or difficult to catch. In my opinion, I don't find brown trout to be drastically more difficult to catch than rainbow trout. I think the reason most anglers catch proportionally more rainbow trout is because they focus on rainbow trout water near the center of the river instead of on brown trout water near the bank.

Naturally, other trout species have their preferences for habitat as well. Like many anglers, I have not had as much experience with brook and cutthroat trout in rivers as I have with rainbow and brown trout. What

experiences I have had suggest that brook trout favor water very similar to brown trout, with even more of a tendency to seek out structure. If I'm fishing a river with brook trout and I can't find them in the obvious riffles or runs, a switch to targeting logs and under boulders and overhanging trees usually brings about a change in fortune. In contrast, I've found cutthroats to frequent open riffles, pools, and runs—the obvious water that most anglers would identify as holding water. Their tendency to be surface-oriented is well known, and earned. Much of the time I see cutthroats suspended in the water column, and when fishing a cutthroat river, I fish dry flies more often than I would elsewhere.

Hatch Activity

There is another key observation to make before you wade into a river, and again periodically throughout the day. Despite my usual excitement, I try to pause on the bank to watch the water for insects, shake some bushes to look for insects that have previously hatched, and watch for rises before I charge into the first likely holding spot. Coupled with information you may be able to glean from hatch charts and talking to local fly

Sometimes the bugs are thick and make their presence known without much observation needed. It's not hard to decide which pattern to choose when there are green drakes crawling inside your fly box. PHOTO BY GILBERT ROWLEY

shops and anglers, these simple acts of observation can help slim down your decisions on fly selection and contribute to your choices on where—and how—to fish.

Before you step into the water when you reach the river, search some streamside grass, willows, or trees, and look on top of the snow if it's wintertime. Recently hatched insects will collect in the riparian vegetation. With a little inspection, you should be able to find insects that will help to guide your decisions. For instance, during the warmer months I like to fish dry-and-dropper rigs on a Euro leader because of the likelihood of raising fish to the dry fly with the warmer water. Oftentimes there is not a hatch in progress when I arrive at the river, but I find that fish are likely to take flies that resemble insects that have hatched or fallen on the water in the last day or two. I can usually narrow my choice of dry fly to fish down to a mayfly, caddis, stonefly, or terrestrial/attractor pattern by spending a minute or two on the bank prior to fishing. Even if you anticipate nymphing to be your primary strategy, seeing some adult insects suggests it would be wise to choose nymphs that represent the larval or pupal stages of the adult insects that you see streamside.

Once you are in the river, it is always wise to keep an eye on the water's surface for hatching insects or rising

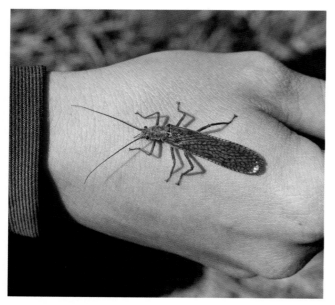

Inspecting streamside grass and sticks is a great way to find out which insects have hatched recently. During a May trip, a quick look in the grass on the banks of the Deschutes River showed it was crawling with salmonflies. It wasn't hard to guess what insect the trout were rising to when the surface flushed like a toilet.

fish. If I see insects hatching, I will switch to a representative fly pattern. If I'm nymphing and I'm unsure what the emerging form of the insect looks like, I will stomach-pump the next fish I catch to see if the fish are eating the nymphs, and examine the shape, size, and color of the natural insects. With this information, it is simple to look in my boxes and try to find a nymph that matches these characteristics.

Hatches can spur trout activity in a way similar to temperature. Often these two variables are connected, and insects begin to hatch as the temperature rises or cools. Remember that insects are also ectothermic creatures, and they receive thermal cues that trigger their behavior, similar to trout. That's why I look for hatch activity when I reach the river, in addition to taking the temperature. If there are few insects hatching or flying around above the river and the water temperature is cold, I search out slow water with depth, where trout find energetic refuge in lean times. If I start to see insects hatching, my strategy usually changes; then I start to focus on the heads of runs or pools and the riffles or pocketwater in between. Remember that these areas are the primary food-production areas of the stream, and the higher velocity moves more food-carrying water volume past a waiting trout than slower water does. Simply put, if there is more food being produced and more of the underwater drift passing by, trout have greater feeding opportunities in riffles and pocketwater than they do in slower water.

If you are trying to plan your fishing day around hatches, it is wise to keep your eye on the weather forecast. Weather can affect the timing and intensity of hatches. Obviously, weather can affect the water temperature, which can spur or deter a hatch. A windy day can kill a hatch altogether by quickly blowing insects off the water. Some insects, like *Baetis* mayflies, prefer to hatch under cloudy, cool, and calm conditions. There is no better day to chase rising trout in the spring or fall than one with a cloud-laden sky and a slight drizzle. Other insects, like many caddis species, hatch better under the ascending warmth of a sunny day.

As part of your plan and fly-fishing learning process, it can pay dividends to learn a bit about the insect community in the river you plan to fish, along with the behavior of each species. Combining this knowledge with the season, the weather forecast, and the water temperature and discharge can help you to predict the probability of a hatch that you need to prepare for.

Riffles and pocketwater are the best food-producing water types in a stream. When insects are hatching, look for fish to hold in surprisingly fast water. The fast chutes on this stream, in California's Sierra Nevada range, held plenty of rainbow trout during a hatch of sulphur-colored mayflies in April.

That probability can help you make decisions, such as whether to bring a second rod to fish dry flies, or whether you should just focus on nymphs and streamers if the conditions for a hatch are poor.

When water temperatures are favorable, trout may inhabit faster water permanently. However, even when water temperatures aren't prime, trout will still react to the increased insect drift caused by a hatch. I routinely run into this behavior on my local rivers, from fall through spring. When I begin fishing in the morning, the temperature is usually cold, and I only occasionally find the odd trout in the fast water while bouncing between slow spots. Later in the day, there is usually a hatch of midges, *Baetis* mayflies, or the occasional caddis. When I see this activity, I broaden my focus and start fishing faster water again. Often, I catch fish where I found none an hour or two earlier.

I have tried to use this pattern to my benefit during competitions, with good results. One tournament that has been very kind to me over the years is the America Cup International Fly Fishing Tournament. The America Cup was held in Vail, Colorado, until 2014, and I was

fortunate to win three individual gold medals and one silver medal in the six times I competed.

This tournament took place in September at high elevations in the Colorado Rockies. The September weather there is often cold in the mornings, warming to pleasant sunny afternoons. The cold nights tend to chill the water in the rivers, but the sunny days warm the water and produce different conditions between the morning and afternoon sessions. During the morning sessions of this tournament, I always followed my protocol of taking the temperature and looking for hatches prior to my sessions. Much of the time the water was from 43 to 48 degrees before a morning session, with few bugs hatching. When I would fish pocketwater and riffles during the first half of these sessions, I caught few fish, and spent too much time fishing fruitless water.

However, as these sessions progressed, the water would warm a few degrees and a *Baetis* and/or caddis hatch would usually start in the last hour of the session. If I returned to the faster water I fished early in the session, I usually caught fish where I had previously drawn a blank. After observing this pattern in the first few America Cup tournaments I fished in, during morning sessions in later tournaments I began to focus on slower water for the first one and a half to two hours, where I was confident I would find fish. As each session progressed, if bugs began to hatch, I switched to fishing the faster water in my remaining time. This strategy increased my efficiency and led to consistent results. It's a strategy that has translated well to other rivers with similar conditions.

Obviously, one of the best results of an insect hatch is the opportunity to fish dry flies. If there are rising fish, I watch the riseforms and look for any adult insects that disappear into them. There are lots of books by authors such as Marinaro, Swisher, Borger, and Hughes (see bibliography), and others detailing dry-fly fishing strategies and what to look for in riseforms. If you search out these volumes, you will find descriptions of all manner of riseform variations.

Plenty of anglers have dedicated much of their angling career to decoding trout rises and the messages

they send about which stage of an insect to fish. I can't claim to be a part of this group; when I'm in competitions, the need to make quick decisions about rising fish often prevents the careful study and decoding of each rise. However, there are a few types of rises that signal different choices for me. To keep it simple, I ask myself two questions: 1) Did the trout's snout break the surface? and 2) Was the rise gentle, or aggressive and splashy?

Early in a midge or mayfly hatch, it is common to see gentle dimple rises. There may not be much surface disturbance associated with these riseforms, and many anglers may miss them altogether, especially in slightly riffled water. The key diagnostic feature of these rises is that the trout's snout does not break the surface. Dimpling rises signal that the trout is taking insects in the emerging stage before they have broken through the surface film and molted into their adult stage. When I see these rises I opt for a fly pattern such as a Shuttlecock Emerger, which will protrude through the surface film and represent an insect that is going through the

When I fished this run in the morning during December 2017, I only found fish in the slower water, on the far left bank and in the tailout near the top of this photo. However, I returned in the afternoon to a hatch of midges and caught five brown trout and a couple of whitefish from the faster water below a shelf in the center of the photo. By fishing different water as the day progressed, I capitalized on the locations the fish shifted to when the hatch increased their feeding opportunities.

One of my favorite tournaments over the years has been the America Cup International Fly Fishing Tournament. This photo comes from my final session on the Blue River in 2012. A successful strategy during this tournament and others has been planning which water types to focus on at different times in my sessions, based on water temperature and hatch activity. (PHOTO BY JULIA OLSEN)

emergence process and is stuck in the film. If I struggle to get the fish to rise to a dry fly, I fish an adult version of the insect with an unweighted nymph on a short dropper. The nymph will only sink a few inches below the surface, but breaking that barrier can provoke confident responses from cagey fish.

While trout may daintily take midge pupae and small mayfly emergers, their reaction can be different with other insects. During warmer temperatures and hatches of larger insects, rises can be splashy and ferocious. Caddis and larger mayflies are quick mobile swimmers. Their speed and agility prompt a more-aggressive predatory response from trout than the languid ascension of smaller mayflies and midge pupae. Trout rise through the column quickly to capture these insects. Even if they intercept the emerging insect before it reaches the surface, the trout's momentum can carry them close enough to the surface to make a disturbance. These disturbances can look like boiling swirls if the trout stops a bit farther down, or they can throw a splash if the trout stops just below the surface.

If I see aggressive rises but no trout snout, my first thought is to look for large mayflies or caddis that are starting to hatch. If I can identify the source of the trout's feeding excitement, then the same formula of matching shape, size, and color applies. With these types of insects, a typical dead drift may not fully match their behavior. If dead drifts don't produce the desired response from fish, I add jigging motions and/or swings to my drift to imitate their mobility as well.

When trout eat insects flush with the water's surface, their snouts or bodies may break the surface. There are few scenes in fly fishing that get my heart pumping more than the classic head/dorsal/tail rise. These riseforms are particularly common in flat water. They form when trout ascend confidently and their swimming velocity and angle carries their momentum more horizontally than vertically. Typically, I see these riseforms associated with insects the trout feel confident are not going to fly away. Examples are spent mayfly spinners or terrestrials that are flush in the surface film and immobile. If you see this type of rise, closely inspect the surface for insects sitting flush on the water and pick a pattern that appropriately represents what you find.

When trout take hatched adult insects, their snouts break the plane of the water's surface. These rises are hard to miss and leave impressions in my mind that return in dream form. They can be accompanied by a bubble left on the surface after the rise. These bubbles are produced by a gulp of air that the trout intakes when it closes its mouth around an insect while above the water.

I have seen these types of rises to single adult midges, midge clusters, and spent post-egg-laying caddis. However, most anglers associate this type of rise with mayfly duns. Trout rise in this manner when pursuing prey that has wings or a part of its body above the surface film of the water. Insects in this stage are generally more mobile, so the trout adjust their rise-form to surround the prey item with their mouth to reduce its chances of escape. Regardless, when I see a snout break the surface, I start looking for adult insects on the water and searching for a pattern to represent it. If I'm fortunate, I try to spot a natural insect drifting toward the location of the last rise from a trout. If the insect is eaten when it reaches the trout, it confirms which insect I should look for more closely to find a suitable imitation.

The last broad category of rise I look for is an aggressive leaping rise. This type of rise may look like a dolphin celebrating life by leaping through the air. Unlike dolphins, however, trout don't have the luxury of expending energy and exposing their location to predators without justification. This type of rise usually signals the pursuit of a highly mobile insect, such as caddis pupae, or a baitfish. The trout builds up enough momentum during the chase that it clears the water. I have also seen trout do backflips over ovipositing (egg-laying) caddis, as well as the odd unlucky mouse crossing the river. Though it may catch you off guard in the excitement, when you see a trout clear the water, try to backtrack its trajectory when exiting the water. This will give you an approximate location to which you can present your flies to try and catch the trout.

If you take the time before stepping into the water to watch for hatching insects and rising trout, your odds of having a successful day will improve. However,

If you see trout leaping from the water, mark their position and reverse their trajectory to pinpoint where you should target your presentation. It is likely they were chasing a mobile insect or baitfish. Or, if you're lucky, they might be cartwheeling over your mouse pattern like this bull trout. (PHOTO BY GILBERT ROWLEY)

When trout rise with protruding snouts, it is usually a sign they are eating hatched adult insects. In this photo, a Green River brown trout is taking advantage of the numerous midge adults sitting on the surface. If this scene doesn't make you want to run out the door with a dry-fly rod in hand, I don't know what will. (PHOTO BY RYAN KELLY)

don't fall victim to complacency while you are in the river and catching fish. Environmental conditions can change over time, and hatches can start and end seemingly within minutes. The angler who keenly observes these changes will be able to adapt to them and continue being successful. The angler who doesn't may be left wondering why their magic fly is suddenly receiving no attention.

Let me provide a real-world example that was critical to my success during the 2015 World Fly Fishing Championship in Bosnia. In my first session, I arrived at a beat on the Sana River—one that our team had agreed none of us wanted when we first walked the river during practice. There was a small section of riffles and a couple of pockets at the bottom, but it was largely a medium-depth to shallow flat glide with few features. I spent most of my setup time watching this flat, hoping for rises. I knew that to be very successful here I needed a hatch and rising fish. There were a few sporadic rises before the session, and I noticed a few size 18-20 gray/olive mayflies flying around. To imitate them I tied on a Pliva Shuttlecock Emerger to begin the session.

The first few undisturbed fish I cast to took the fly, but the next refused it. I was still seeing the occasional small mayfly, but the hatch never gained any steam. During practice, the fish had reacted well to small CDC Ant patterns when there was no visible hatch. I opted for the Ant, and was rewarded with a couple more fish in the net, and on my scorecard.

The next fish I cast to ignored the Ant. There were a few caddis dancing around by this point, so I put a CDC Caddis on my leader and quickly caught the fish. To keep things interesting, the next rising fish refused the caddis. Upon closer inspection I saw a few size 16 yellow mayflies beginning to emerge, and one of them disappeared in the swirl of fish I had cast to. I switched to a yellow CDC Comparadun and promptly caught the grayling that had passed over my caddis pattern. At this point I had covered most of the water in the upper half of my beat, and the remaining rises were very sporadic. I decided to head to the fast water at the bottom of my beat to try and catch a few fish on nymphs while I let the fish on the flat rest.

When I returned to the flat I looked for rises again. Near the top I watched a trout take a caddis adult. I switched back to the CDC Caddis in response. Deep water in the center prevented me from wading close to the fish, so I was left with a 45- to 50-foot cast with

My first session during the 2015 World Fly Fishing Championship on the Sana River in Bosnia landed me on a challenging flat. With local rules that only allowed one fly, I knew fishing dry flies to rising fish would bring my best chance of success. By observing the progression of hatches and changing flies to target individual fish, I was able to secure a second place in the session, on my way to an individual bronze medal.

I watched the last fish I caught during my session on the Sana River in Bosnia eat a Danica mayfly with gusto. The closest pattern I had in my box was a size 10 CDC Green Drake Comparadun. As you can see from the Danica resting on the glasses of Fly Fishing Team USA captain Bret Bishop, the drake pattern was too small and the wrong color, but thankfully the brown trout still found it worth eating.

a wall of bankside vegetation behind me. It took a few steeple casts over the vegetation to get the right lane, but the brown trout took the caddis with the proper drift and location.

A few minutes later a fish rose about 10 feet upstream of the prior fish. I presented my caddis to it with no result. As I contemplated what to try next, a large (~size 6) yellow Danica mayfly fluttered by the fish, and it broke halfway out of the water to try and eat it. I had seen a few Danica during practice, and it was the last fly on my tying list the night before. Unfortunately, I hadn't tied any in the interest of getting at

least a few hours of sleep. As I sat there cursing that decision, I sifted through my dry-fly box, trying to decide which pattern to try. The closest imitation I had was a size 10 CDC Green Drake Comparadun. Thankfully, the brown trout decided it was close enough and took the fly.

I ended up with 12 fish and a second place in the session, on a beat that I was scared to fish before I started. The rest of the tournament, that beat averaged 4 fish per session and 19th place. This session gave me a jump start to a tournament that brought my first individual and team medal at a World Fly Fishing Championship. There were lots of variables that helped me succeed, but observation throughout the session was a critical component. By continually watching for hatching insects, rises, and which insect each fish rose to, I was able to make necessary fly changes. Of the seven fish I caught on dry flies during the session, I fished four dry flies to catch them. I could have stuck with the same fly and tried to find fish that were willing to eat it, but I was more successful because of the observations I made, which prompted adaptation for each fish when needed.

Putting It All Together

In this chapter, I have covered a list of the variables I observe to help me make a plan before I enter the river, as well as throughout the day as conditions change. Based on these variables, most of the time I am able to devise a strategy to help me be successful on the day, whether I'm fishing for fun or about to start a competition session. These variables include water clarity, water temperature, fish density, fish species, and hatch activity.

If you're wondering how to put all of these variables together in a practical way, keep reading, as I will provide concrete examples of how to put decisions into practice with the case studies in the following chapters. In addition, I will add some suggestions on fly selection in chapter 11.

CHAPTER 2

In water types with complex currents, such as pocketwater, flies spaced widely apart may land in currents heading in different directions. To achieve a better drift, space your nymphs only 10 to 15 inches apart to make it easier to land them in the same vein of current. Alternatively, fish just one fly, as I did when fishing the white water around the boulders in this section of the Vltava River in the Czech Republic.

Gear and Rigging

Over time, the typical competitor amasses enough gear to empty out a large bank account. Most anglers do not have the need and/or funds for such an arsenal. However, one thing I have learned many times over the years is that, just like with any job, the right fly-fishing tool for the right job can make a big difference. Accordingly, I tend to be a splitter—aiming for one specific tool for a job—instead of a lumper, who seeks a hybrid tool that can do lots of things, but not necessarily as well as a tool designed specifically for the job. This has led me to design or adopt specific leaders and use specific rods and lines for different techniques, where other anglers might prefer to use a hybrid leader or one rod for multiple tasks.

You will need to make your own decisions about gear and rigging to best suit your own style, mind-set, budget, and other considerations. Truth be told, I'm willing to invest a lot more time and effort into rigging multiple rods and rigs for competitions than I am for a regular day out on the water. However, anytime I find myself struggling a bit or passing by water that the rig I'm fishing does not fish well, I find it useful to be prepared to swap rigs or techniques. Often a change in presentation will make all the difference between struggling to catch a few fish and staying consistent.

In this chapter, I will discuss leaders, rigging, and my preferred gear for the techniques I'll be addressing throughout the rest of the book. Competition anglers are often labeled as Euro-nymphers. In fact, I could outfit a fly shop if I had ten bucks for every time someone asked me what it's like to be on the "National Czech-Nymphing Team." However, I don't remember a single successful tournament where I Euro-nymphed 100 percent of the time. To be successful in a competition, or just on your home water, it pays to adapt your methods to individual situations.

European-Nymphing

Basic leader and rigging

Since I first tried long, French-style leaders for Euro-nymphing back in 2007, all of my experimentation has shown that variations on this theme provide a larger radius of presentation, more delicate presentation, better strike detection, and better drifts than shorter-leader, Czech/Polish leader styles. Depending upon the specific use, I vary the makeup of my leader to attain certain properties along the spectrum of what I need.

In general, the basic characteristics of an ideal all-around Euro-nymphing leader include:

- a long, small diameter and low-mass butt section that will reduce drift-killing sag when held off the water;
- a stiff butt-section material that will turn over a range of nymph weights despite the small diameter;
- a sighter built of bright material that provides visual cues for strike detection and drift awareness; and
- a taper that transfers enough energy to allow for tuck casting, but will also allow a delicate presentation.

It took me quite a few seasons to decide on the Euro-nymphing leader formulas I like the most. After lots of manipulation and testing over the first few years of practicing this method, I decided I liked to avoid tippet knots in the butt section of my leader if possible. Because the leader exits the rod with every cast and there is very little mass to shoot line toward my target, I try to avoid knots that catch even a little bit in my guides. Resistance in the guides can result in needing an extra false cast to reach your target, or it can cause inaccuracy in fly placement.

It may seem crazy, but catching two fish at once is not all that uncommon when Euro-nymphing. This photo shows a double of brown trout I caught during the filming of *Modern Nymphing: European-Inspired Techniques.* (PHOTO BY GILBERT ROWLEY)

I have tried several commercially tapered French, Czech, or other Euro-nymphing leaders. My experience with most of them is that their butt sections are too thick and lead to a lot of sag between the rod tip and the point where the leader enters the water. The taper is also long and ends in too fine a diameter of material; this results in the leader turning over, losing much of the energy. I also find them difficult to tuck-cast for increased sink rate.

If you are a beginning Euro-nympher, start with one simple formula while you get used to casting and fishing the rig. If you're fishing with a thin Euro-nymphing fly line, the basic formula starts with 10 to 12 feet of 20-pound-test Maxima Chameleon butt section. If not, then double or triple the butt-section length. This will result in fly line staying on your reel, where it will not lead to drift and strike-detection-killing sag in between your hand and the first stripping guide, in between the rest of your guides, or out your rod tip. After the butt section, the rest of the formula is 3 feet of transition material > 18 inches of sighter material with a tippet ring > 1.5 to 6 feet of tippet (depending on river depth and speed) from the ring to the first or only fly > 24 to 28 inches of tippet for each additional fly. I always

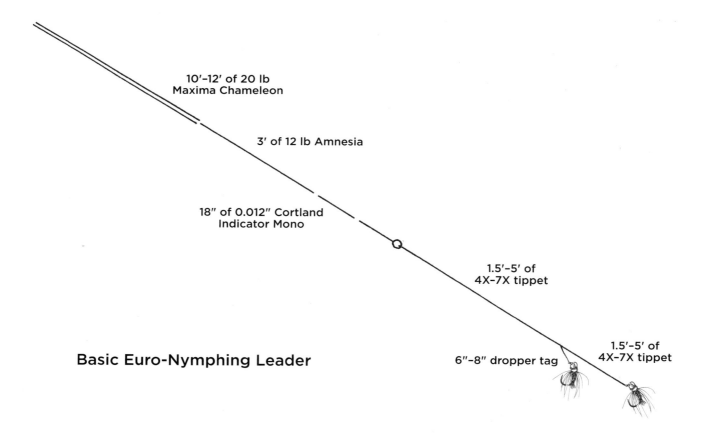

10'–12' of 20 lb
Maxima Chameleon

3' of 12 lb Amnesia

18" of 0.012" Cortland
Indicator Mono

1.5'–5' of
4X–7X tippet

Basic Euro-Nymphing Leader

6"–8" dropper tag

1.5'–5' of
4X–7X tippet

STEP 1

TAG END   STANDING END

STANDING END
This is the line leading
back to rod/reel

TAG END
This is the end of the
fishing line

Lay lines in opposing directions (side by side)

STEP 2

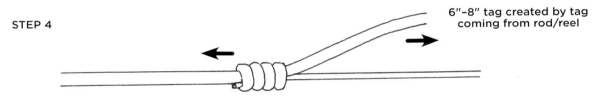

STEP 3

Grab the tag end of the larger-diameter line and the
other line and make three wraps inside the loop.

STEP 4

6"–8" tag created by tag
coming from rod/reel

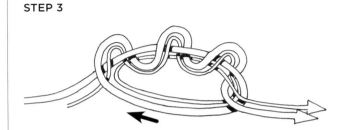

Creating a dropper tag is easy to do. First, tie a surgeon's knot 6 to 8 inches up the tippet already attached to the leader. While closing the knot, if you are right-handed, keep the knot lightly pinched between your left thumb and index finger while pulling on the dropper tag and added tippet with your right hand. This will lengthen the dropper-tag side of the knot.

One trick to add visibility to your sighter is adding a backing barrel. Simply tie a uni knot in the backing around the leader and slide it down into your tippet knot. You can trim the tags flush or leave them for extra visibility. See troutbitten.com for more details.
(PHOTO BY DOMENICK SWENTOSKY)

fish the shortest length of tippet that I can from the tippet ring to the first fly while still attaining the necessary depth. Shorter tippet promotes better drifts and increased strike detection. Later in this chapter, I will cover situations that suit one, two, or three fly rigs.

To make your sighter more visible, try adding extra blood knots, or leaving 1- to 2-inch-long tags on one or more of your tippet knots. The tags and blood knots will grab paste-type floatant when applied, which creates mini suspenders in your sighter. You can also attach bright-colored fly-line backing above a tippet knot by tying a uni knot around the leader and sliding it down until it jams into a tippet knot. Similar to the sighter tippet knots, you can leave a short tag of the backing to enhance visibility. However, check the rules if you enter any competitions to see if extra knots and long tags are allowed.

I fish all of my flies on dropper tags. To create a dropper tag, the tippet added for each additional fly is tied 6 to 8 inches up the tippet already attached to the tippet ring. I use a triple surgeon's or Orvis tippet knot. The waste material creates a long tag facing the terminal end of the leader (away from the rod) that can be used as a dropper tag for your nymphs. If you make a dropper from the tag pointing toward your rod, it will cut back through the knot when pulled on, and strength will be greatly reduced.

While tying the knot, lightly pinch the loop of the knot in one hand and pull the dropper tag and point fly tippet with the other hand until the loop is small and ready to cinch. Then cinch both sides of the knot. This will lengthen the tags for both flies while keeping the waste on the other side of the knot short. Do not use a blood knot for making the tag because it will fold in half and fail from the pressure created by a fighting fish or a snag.

Most fly anglers look at the 18- to 20-plus-foot length of the typical Euro-nymphing leader and give up before they even start. Given that most of us have difficulty casting longer leaders, it's easy to understand why. However, with the right rod, the right leader design, and some practice to make adjustments, casting Euro-nymphing leaders is not difficult. So why should you use a grotesquely long Euro-nymphing leader? The answer can be summed up in one word: sag.

Try to visualize (or better yet, actually try it on the water) a typical short tapered leader attached to a regular fly line exiting the tip of your rod and held off the water with a high-stick presentation. What you will see is that the fly line displays a drooping arc that drops sharply toward the water before turning horizontally toward your target. Because fly line and thick leader butt sections have a lot of mass, gravity pulls them downward and then horizontally toward their point of attachment at the tip.

Why is line/leader sag a problem? The first reason is strike detection. The downward arc in the fly line creates slack that deadens the tactile feel of a strike. In addition, the extra mass of the fly line has higher inertia that must be overcome in order for the fly line and leader to move enough for a take to be seen visually.

The second reason is reduced radius of presentation. Sag forces the fly line to slide horizontally across the

When fly line, or a thick leader butt section, protrudes beyond the rod tip, gravity forces the line to sag down and across, toward and under the rod tip. This downward arc reduces the radius within which you can fish nymphs while holding the line off the water, and creates strike-detection-killing slack.

Look closely at the right side of this photo and you will see the long colored sighter elevated above the water. The reduced mass of the long, thin Euro-nymphing leader allowed Pat Weiss to hold his entire leader off the water without inducing sag and drag on his rig.

water, toward the rod tip. When your fly line and leader move, your flies follow in tow. Therefore, if you cast them into a narrow seam through which you planned to dead-drift them, they are likely to slide laterally across the current back toward you, and out of your target seam. This induces drag and eliminates your attempts to imitate natural insects with a dead drift. The only way to avoid this fate is to wade closer to your target and fish under your rod tip. The obvious pitfall to that strategy is that the close proximity makes it more likely you will spook fish in your target lie; in addition, there may be water that is too deep or fast to allow you to wade close enough.

Given their low mass, long, thin Euro-nymphing-style leaders help to avoid the sag-induced issues covered above. Because of the viscous nature of water, nymphs drifting through the column resist being moved from their path of drift. The resistance from the flies allows Euro-nymphing leaders to come as close to levitating as possible when held off the water, especially if thinner butt sections are used. The result is a connection to your flies that is much more direct than when a sagging fly line is used. This more-direct connection provides increased strike detection.

The radius of proper presentation also increases, because your leader does not sag enough to pull your flies laterally across the river. The capability to fish farther away allows you to stay far enough from the fish to either get under their cone of vision, or to appear small enough within it that you look less threatening—which means you're less likely to spook the fish. Because a spooked fish is a missed fish, you have more chances to present your flies to willing trout when fishing a Euro-nymphing leader as compared to a high-stick nymphing presentation with a short leader and fly line.

The basic Euro-nymphing leader formula above still has enough mass and stiffness that I can turn over streamers and dry-and-dropper rigs with accuracy, and use tuck casts to drive my flies to depth. These characteristics make it a great all-around leader to cover lots of situations on small- to medium-size rivers. However, there is enough mass in the 20-pound-test butt section to make it sag when it's fished 12 to 18 feet past the rod tip. This decreases the fishable area when making up-and-across presentations.

If I know I'll mainly be fishing broken water with up-and-across presentations, while holding my leader and sighter off the water, I choose thinner leader formulas that will resist sag more easily when fished at distance. Butt sections in the 10- to 12-pound range are great for these situations; however, it's important to note that they don't have as much stiffness or mass to transfer energy, which makes pinpoint-accurate casting more difficult—especially if you're not used to the slower turnover timing of Euro-nymphing casts.

Common rigging questions

FLY SPACING

I'm sometimes asked, "Why do you space your flies so far apart?" The simple answer is that FIPS-Mouche rules dictate that flies must be 50 cm (~20 inches) apart from eye to eye when hanging vertically. Before I began competing, I often spaced my flies much closer together. However, there is a phenomenon that suggests this strategy wasn't always a good one. That phenomenon is the double.

It is fairly common to hook two fish at once while Euro-nymphing, but this only happens if flies are spaced a sufficient distance apart so that separate fish have the opportunity to inspect and eat or reject your fly. Spacing your flies allows you to cover a broader range of the column. Because fish may be belly to the bottom, or suspended, if there are enough food items passing by—and your flies are spaced properly—each drift potentially puts a fly within close proximity of more fish. If you show your flies to more fish, you will naturally catch more—sometimes even simultaneously.

However, in waters with complex currents, it can be difficult to fit flies spaced widely apart into the same seam of current. For example, picture fishing pocketwater with small boulders strewn everywhere. Currents in this type of water change rapidly with longitude or latitude across the river. The fish-holding targets in front of or behind boulders may be small enough to make it difficult to cast and land both flies within them, even with advanced casting ability. Given the myriad of different speeds and directions of current in this type of habitat, if one fly lands in one current and the other fly in another, it is impossible to attain a quality drift, and less fish will be caught. In these types of situations, assuming you don't need to follow competition rules, it is best to fish your flies closer together so you can land and drift them in the same seam of current. Alternatively, I often cut the nymph on my dropper tag off in these situations and fish a single fly, until I reach alternative water types where multiple flies are more beneficial again.

Let's follow this train of reasoning a bit further. Depending on where you are fishing, the number of flies you can fish may be determined by local rules. Where allowed, I will fish one, two, or three nymphs, depending on the situation. What determines my decision? Let's cover each possibility below.

Fishing one fly creates one unit of mass and one point of tension on the end of your Euro-nymphing leader. When there are multiple units of mass, they can swing and fight each other through the air while casting. When the cast comes to a stop toward your target, the flies have built up momentum, but not necessarily in the same direction. This leads to casting inaccuracy, as the flies try to continue their individual trajectories. With only one fly, casting is at its most accurate.

A similar problem can occur with strike detection and drift. With multiple flies, during the drift there is the potential for the separate weights to cause a hinge in the leader where the dropper tag(s) is attached. If a fish eats the point fly, this hinge needs to straighten before the take will be registered on the sighter. This can delay detection and cause fish to reject the fly before the take is registered. Therefore, for the ultimate in strike detection, one fly is best.

The last reason to use one fly is simple. A lot of times I fish riffles and pockets that are only 6 to 18 inches deep. When fishing such shallow water, it is difficult to avoid constant sagging when fishing with two flies. If my flies are the FIPS-Mouche–legal 50 cm distance apart, the point fly will snag bottom if they separate vertically in the drift at all. I don't need extra weight in this water anyway, so I will usually rig just one nymph, or remove additional nymphs, when I fish shallow riffles and pockets.

While there are some drawbacks, as covered above, there are also obvious benefits to fishing two flies. I would venture that most competitors, including myself, spend the majority of their time Euro-nymphing with two flies. For a given water depth and speed, you will need a certain weight to attain the proper depth and drift. With two flies, the weight can be spread between them. Dividing the weight allows you to fish smaller flies, which the fish often prefer, without tying them out of proportion to add extra weight. This can be particularly helpful in tailwaters. In small-fly situations, I will often fish a size 18-20 fly in conjunction with a larger and heavier pattern. With only one nymph, you may need a very large bead and/or a lot of lead wire on a large hook to achieve the same amount of weight.

Though it was only inches deep, I spotted and then caught a brown trout from the pocket against the willows in this photo. I switched to one nymph to target the fish, as a two-nymph rig would have snagged bottom instantly.

Fishing two flies allows you to sort through patterns in your fly box twice as fast to see which fly fish are favoring on a given day. Then again, if you're like Pat Weiss in this photo, you just pick a nymph and make the fish eat it!

Fishing two flies allows you to test different patterns. While one fly may be the "right fly" on any given day, it can be helpful to be able to sort through patterns to find what the fish prefer most. With two flies, you can do the sorting twice as fast. A common strategy employed is pulling fish to your rig with an attractor fly. If the fish doesn't choose to eat the attractor nymph, you can combine it with an imitative nymph to seal the deal.

When I need maximum weight for deep and heavy water, I turn to a three-nymph rig. With three flies, I have one more location to add weight or test patterns. A situation where I often use three flies is when targeting steelhead. I normally find steelhead in deep and/or heavy water. When combined with larger tippet that decreases sink rate, I tend to need more weight than I would in most trout situations. However, three-nymph rigs take the drawbacks of the two-nymph rig one step further. They are less accurate, harder to fit into tight locations, and prone to tangling if you aren't used to casting them. That's why if I'm fishing for trout, I only fish three nymphs about 5 percent of the time, when I encounter very deep and fast water.

When Euro-nymphing for steelhead, I fish heavier tippet and deeper water than I often do for trout. These changes call for extra weight, so I turn to three-nymph rigs when needed.

PLACEMENT OF HEAVIER FLY

Another rigging question I am commonly asked is, "Should I place my heavier fly on the point or the dropper?" The best answer I can give is to think visually about how your rig will drift based on each configuration. If you place the heavier fly on the point, the point fly will sink below the dropper fly and the leader will approximate a vertical line, assuming that your leader angle from your rod tip is also vertical. This configuration provides the best connection to both/all flies in your rig. It also provides the best strike detection, in my experience.

However, having weight concentrated at the end of the rig makes it more difficult to cast than having weight closer to the rod tip. Moreover, this configuration will put the nymph(s) on the dropper(s) above the point fly in the water column. This can be beneficial in deep runs or pools when fish are suspended and the upper fly can give the illusion of an insect in the process of emergence. Furthermore, some point flies, such as mops, eggs, and stoneflies, can slither along the bottom, avoiding most snags when tied to invert. Fishing them this way will stall the lighter fly on the dropper in the current. It seems counterintuitive that this would work, because it's certainly not a dead drift.

However, at times it can work very well, especially on fish that have seen repeated dead-drift presentations. If you have ever experienced a fish grabbing your dropper fly while your point fly has been snagged, you've seen this tactic work, even if unintentionally.

If you are rigging in the opposite fashion, with the heavier fly on the dropper, the dropper fly will sink faster than the lighter fly on the point. This results in your flies spreading out more horizontally in the drift. As mentioned above, a bit of a hinge forms in the leader at the dropper tie-in point, which can reduce strike detection. However, if you don't want to remove the dropper fly, fishing the heavier fly on the dropper can be beneficial in shallow riffles, where there simply isn't enough water column to spread the flies out vertically. Furthermore, when trout are bellied up to the bottom, your best chance of presenting both of your flies in the taking zone is with the heaviest fly on the dropper. And if you subscribe to the common attractor-first theory, then you can show a trout the larger/flashier/heavier nymph first by tying it on the dropper. The point fly can then be a smaller, more-imitative fly, with the purpose of sealing the deal after the attractor dropper has pulled the fish's attention to the area.

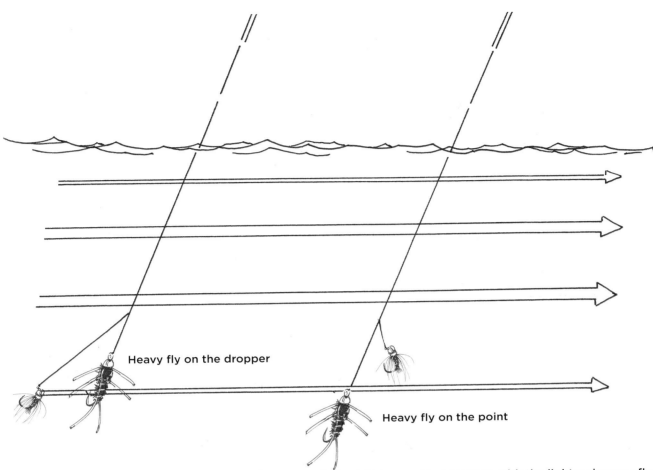

Rigging with the heaviest fly on the point will force your rig to drift in a vertical manner, with the lighter dropper fly higher in the column. Attaching your heaviest fly on the dropper will align your rig more horizontally, with both flies riding low in the column.

DROPPER TAGS

I often get questions about why I fish a dropper tag instead of an inline method of rigging for multiple flies. Until I began fishing in FIPS-Mouche–governed competitions, I rigged my multi-fly setups the same way as most American fly anglers. If I wanted to add a second fly, I would either tie tippet to the bend of the hook (aka kiwi-style) or the eye of the first fly. However, FIPS-Mouche rules mandate that the leader must be one continuous section of monofilament (unless a tippet ring is added). If more than one fly is fished, additional flies must be tied to a dropper tag off the main leader. At first this seemed like a nuisance restriction to me, and I did not appreciate having to change my rigging tactics to stay legal. However, within a short time, I began to realize some benefits to having a dropper tag, and now I happily fish with dropper tags, whether or not I'm fishing in competitions.

The benefits of dropper tags include:

- Changes to upper flies can be made with one knot instead of two.
- The fly can hinge and move to suggest natural movement in the drift when attached via a dropper tag. If it is tied inline, the movement is restricted by the tippet added for the fly (or flies) on the terminal end.
- Tippet attached to the bend of the hook or eye of the fly can block a fish's mouth from encompassing the hook point and lead to missed or foul-hooked fish. Most dry-and-dropper anglers have experienced this—when fish rise to their dry fly, but are flossed and hooked on the nymph below the dry.

Dropper tags make switching between single, multiple, and varied rigs very easy. For example, I often switch between single- and double-nymph rigs when I pass from shallow riffles or complex pocketwater to deeper runs or pools, and so forth. A simple removal or

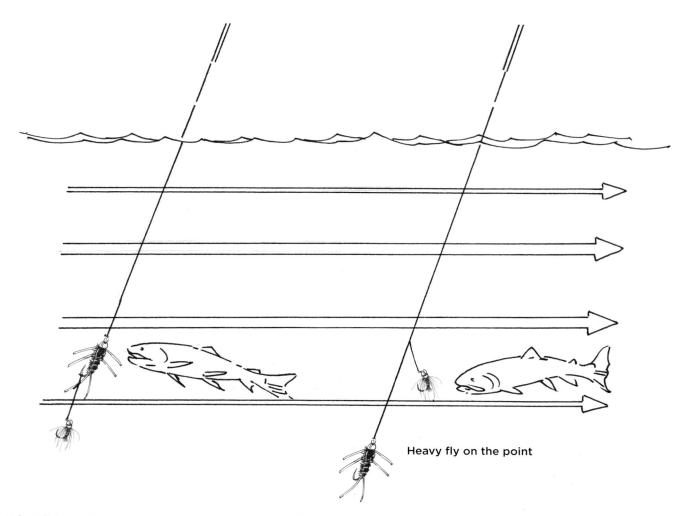

Heavy fly on the point

When fishing with your flies on dropper tags, your fly has freedom of movement in the currents, and the trout can take the full fly in its mouth, leading to more-consistent hookups. When tying the point fly directly to the upper fly, the upper fly's movement is constrained by its connection to the point fly. The added tippet also blocks the trout's mouth from surrounding the fly, which leads to more missed or foul-hooked fish.

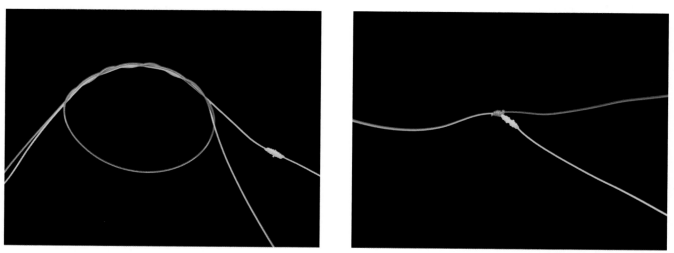

To create an easy dropper tag with a uni knot, with 12 inches of tippet, wrap around the main tippet and then around the tag material five times. Wet and cinch the uni knot and slide it down to the preexisting tippet knot. Trim the dropper tag to length and you're set to go.

addition of a nymph to the dropper tag accomplishes this task. Another common change I make is from a dry-and-dropper rig to a single- or double-nymph rig. In either scenario it would require multiple knots to achieve a re-rigging, when one knot will accomplish the same task with a dropper tag.

Obviously, dropper tags provide only so many fly changes before the tag becomes too short to use. There are a couple of strategies to get the most out of a tag or to add a new one without fully re-rigging. With practice, most knots can be tied with drastically less waste material than most anglers end up with. For example, the loops on a typical blood knot or clinch knot can be pulled on during the tightening of the knot to change the amount of waste material created by the knot. Furthermore, practicing the length of tippet you start your knots with—and just practicing knots in general—will help you to tie knots with less waste, which will give you more fly changes per dropper tag. As a result of lots of practice, most of my knots from tippet to fly result in $\frac{1}{16}$ to $\frac{1}{4}$ inch of waste.

If the rest of your tippet remains fairly intact and you don't want to re-rig your entire tippet section, it is possible to add a new tag with a uni knot. Simply tie the uni knot above the original tippet knot with a long waste tag facing toward the point fly. Moisten and tighten the knot slightly before sliding the uni knot down to the original tippet knot. Once the uni knot is jammed into the tippet knot, pull on the long tag with your fingers and on the short tag with a hemostat.

Alternative Rigging

I am commonly asked what I would do differently if I didn't have to follow FIPS-Mouche rules. The short answer is, not much. There are plenty of opinions out there from high-level fly anglers about beaded versus non-beaded flies and rigs with or without split shot. As with any information, I suggest you try out recommendations for yourself to see what works best for you.

For me, if I were to quit competing today, I think I would stick with tungsten-bead flies and the rigging described above, at least 80 to 90 percent of the time. Weighted flies provide tension and increased strike detection. The beads provide a trigger point that can be varied to learn what color fish find most attractive. Beaded flies also let me probe tiny pockets and shallow riffles, where it's difficult to fit multiple flies and split shot. Therefore, most of the time I don't

find competition rigs to be a hindrance. In fact, I feel very fortunate to have been forced to fish a different way—a method that I've come to find more effective and rewarding the majority of the time.

The one exception where I might change to unweighted flies is during the winter on tailwaters, where micro-size midges are sometimes called for. Most anglers would be surprised to discover how many fish they could catch on tailwaters using larger tungsten bead flies. Indeed, a lot of anglers have sent me photos of the fish they've caught Euro-nymphing the famous tailwaters of the Western United States with large nymphs. When midges are called for, most of the time I find I can still be successful with a size 20 tungsten bead fly tied short on the shank to approximate a size 22 fly. However, no method is the best choice 100 percent of the time. Maybe you find yourself reaching for a micro nymph, or you want to try Euro-nymphing but aren't ready to make the plunge and buy or tie a swath of tungsten nymphs. If this describes your situation, try the rigs below.

The simplest way to rig unweighted flies with split shot is how I learned when I first started nymph fishing. To adjust it to a Euro leader, add 2 to 5 feet of tippet to your tippet ring/sighter. Using a blood or surgeon's knot, add 12 to 15 inches more tippet and attach your first fly. Then add 12 to 15 inches more tippet either to the eye or the bend of the hook on the first fly and attach your second fly on the other end. Place split shot above the tippet knot to prevent them from sliding down into your flies.

The other common way to rig with split shot is known as a bounce rig or drop-shot rig. To rig this way, add 2 to 5 feet of tippet to your tippet ring/sighter. Add 18 to 24 inches of tippet, tied 6 to 8 inches up the previous tippet, to create a dropper tag. You can stop there for a one-fly rig, or add another 18 to 24 inches of tippet in the same way for a second fly. For either rigging, tie an overhand knot at the end of the tippet. Place split shot above this knot to prevent them from sliding off. The split shot will be at the end of the leader, with the nymphs on dropper tags above.

I am asked about the drop-shot rig during nearly every interview or presentation I do. You'll find plenty of proponents for this rig, as it's a good way to avoid constant snagging. There are some drawbacks, however. Non-beaded nymphs do not have sufficient weight to prop themselves away from the leader during the drift. This leads to their tags twisting around the main leader, until it resembles a fly with two pieces of

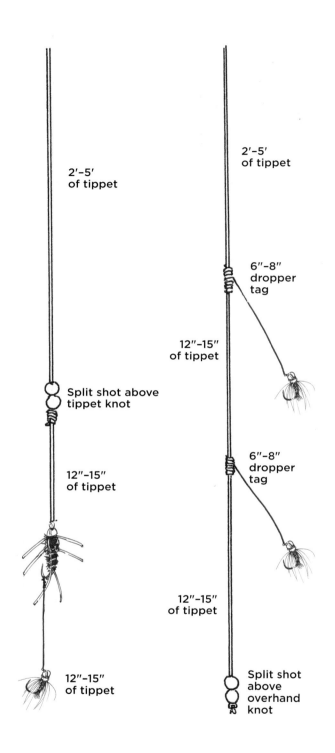

Above left: Create a simple nymph rig by placing split shot above a leader knot to prevent them from sliding into the nymphs tied in tandem below.

Above right: Create a drop-shot rig by adding two dropper tags for your nymphs. On the final piece of tippet, add an overhand knot and place split shot above the knot.

tippet attached. It's also hard to fish this rig in shallow water. If you target a shallow riffle, your nymphs are likely to be high in the column or above the surface, unless you have a very shallow leader angle. Lastly, your point of tension is to the split shot. Though the tags are short, their inherent slack must be removed before a strike is registered, which can lead to a few missed takes, especially in slow water.

Different Types of Sighters

If you happened to miss it above, a sighter is simply Euro-nymphing's version of a strike indicator. There are lots of different types on the market these days. The simplest form of sighter is just colored monofilament that is built into your leader. Lots of companies—including Cortland, Umpqua, Rio, Orvis, and Hanak—make dyed monofilament specially designed for this purpose. These materials are usually dyed with two or three alternating colors in hopes that one or more will be visible in whatever light conditions you may face on the water that day. Cortland also makes opaque white and super yellow sighter mono. The white material can be nice when fish are really spooky.

In addition to dyed monofilament, there are plenty of other sighter types available out there. Common types include the curly q/coiled sighter, paint-drop sighters, and furled/backing sighters. Most of these sighters are illegal in FIPS-Mouche competitions, where the rules require leaders made only of monofilament, with no floating or sinking additions to the leader. However, if you want to play around with them, I'll cover their pros and cons below.

These days we are fortunate to have a lot of options available for sighter material. From different colors to different sizes, there is a material to fit any rig you choose.

The curly q or coiled sighter is simply monofilament sighter material that has been formed into a spiral shape. It became famous a while back through a magazine article written by Charles Jardine. In my opinion, the curly q is a niche-use sighter. It is definitely more visible than a straight monofilament sighter. Because of the repeated spiral contacts with the water, it will float a bit more weight for a longer distance than a straight monofilament sighter. Curly q sighters also land very delicately on the water. However, curly q sighters dig into the surface when picked up for a backcast, which can create fish-spooking surface disturbance. The spirals form a hinge in the leader that can hinder casting accuracy. Furthermore, the increased surface area of the curly q leader can catch more air during breezy conditions. As such, I rarely use curly q sighters, although they can still be useful with long upstream casts into slow, shallow flats.

If you want to try a curly q sighter, several manufacturers sell them premade, including Umpqua. You can also make your own by winding sighter material around a small-diameter cylinder, like a straw or wood dowel. Secure the sighter to the cylinder and drop it in some boiling water. Then transfer it to ice water and freeze it overnight to set the coils into the leader.

A unique sighter that showed up several years ago was the glue- or paint-drop sighter. This is just a regular monofilament sighter with drops of bright-colored glue or paint added to the monofilament. The drops add visibility to the sighter, and can add flotation when greased. Their main drawback is added mass, which can increase the sag on the sighter when held off the water. They also tend to come off if the sighter is stripped into the rod guides. As with the curly q sighters, there are several commercially available versions. You can make your own with T-shirt paint as well.

One other type of common sighter is one made of fly-line backing or stiffer braided nylon. These sighters are highly visible, and they float well when greased with paste floatant; one Sybai model even has a foam cylinder inside to increase flotation. They are well designed for upstream fishing with a floated sighter in flat water. However, they have a lot more mass than a traditional monofilament sighter. When held off the water, they will sag until they touch the water, unless you compensate by fishing a lot of extra weight. As such, they make a poor sighter choice for traditional across-the-river Euro-nymphing presentations, where the sighter is held off the water.

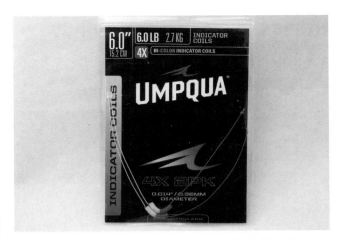

The curly q sighter is more buoyant and visible than a straight monofilament sighter. However, it catches more wind and can make a bit of commotion on the surface of the water with a backcast.

Glue- or paint-drop sighters are a good option if you need some extra visibility.

Braided sighters are good for upstream fishing when floating the sighter; however, they have a lot more mass than monofilament sighters, so they will sag when fished up and across.

Other Leaders and Methods

As I will cover in later chapters, there are circumstances where a typical suspension/strike-indicator or dry-and-dropper rig can be more effective than a straight Euro-nymphing rig. The standard thin (20-pound butt section) leader I detailed above can work just fine for these situations, as it can move back and forth between Euro-nymphing and suspension nymphing quite easily with a few rigging and casting adjustments. The main difference is the rigging beyond the sighter.

Modular Euro-nymphing leader

A modular Euro-nymphing leader provides a framework within which you can switch between single nymph, double nymph, dry double dropper, dry-and-dropper, and streamers. If I have to fish one rod for the day and I expect to do a lot of changing, this is the leader I will fish. The formula is similar to the basic Euro-nymphing leader described previously, but with additional tippet below the sighter before the ring. The formula is as follows: 10 to 12 feet of 20-pound-test Maxima Chameleon > 3 feet of 12-pound amnesia > 18 inches of 0.012-inch bicolor sighter > 12 inches of 3X tippet > tippet ring > 1.5 to 6 feet of tippet to first nymph > 24 to 28 inches of tippet to the second nymph. Again, use the shortest tippet possible, while still attaining appropriate depth, to promote a better drift and increased strike detection.

A few simple changes provide lots of options with this leader. To create a dry-double-dropper rig, I add 6 inches of tippet to the tippet ring, to which I can attach a dry fly. Because the ring and sighter are separated by a foot of tippet, fish will still eat the dry fly, especially if the sighter is held off the water. To switch back to a straight nymphing rig, I simply remove the dry-fly tag at the tippet ring, which can be reattached later if desired. To make a single-nymph rig, I remove the nymph on the dropper. For a dry and single dropper, I add a dry fly to the dropper tag, where I would normally have a second nymph. To switch the leader to a streamer rig, I chop the tippet at the tippet ring and spool my nymph-rig tippet onto a Loon rigging foam. I construct the streamer rig the same way as a nymph rig but I increase the tippet size to between 2X and 4X.

When floating the sighter or fishing a dry-and-dropper with this leader, it is important to grease the leader all the way down through the sighter and the last several inches of tippet before the dry fly. This will allow

Using several Loon rigging foams, I can swap between different rigs on a modular Euro-nymphing leader. Before using the rigging foams, I cut a slit in the rim with a pair of fly-tying scissors. To spool the rig on the foam, I stick the fly (or flies) into the foam, winding tippet around the spool. When I get to the last turn, I slide the tippet into the slit in the foam to keep it from unraveling. You can see the slit between the flies in this photo. It's also easy to build rigs this way ahead of time, at home.

quick liftoff from the water or mending without moving the dry fly and nymph. Tangling with this rig can be an issue, so be sure to use an oval-shaped casting stroke (see chapter 3) to track the flies around the rod and avoid midair collisions.

Hybrid dry-and-dropper leader

Much of the time, instead of choosing one rod to cover all of my bases, I take multiple rods in order to use leaders built specifically for individual techniques. I use this hybrid dry-and-dropper formula as a dedicated leader for short- to medium-range dry-and-dropper fishing. The thicker-tapered butt section will sag a bit more at distance with the leader off the water. The positive trade-off is that it will turn over a bushy dry with a light nymph (or nymphs) a bit easier. If I plan to switch back and forth regularly between nymphing and dry-and-dropper techniques, then I will stick with the modular Euro-nymphing leader described above.

The hybrid dry-and-dropper leader formula is 4.5 feet of 25-pound Maxima Chameleon > 4.5 feet of 20-pound Chameleon > 18 inches of 15-pound Chameleon > 18 inches of 12-pound Chameleon > 18 inches of 0.012- to 0.014-inch bicolor or opaque white sighter material > 12 to 18 inches of 3X tippet > tippet

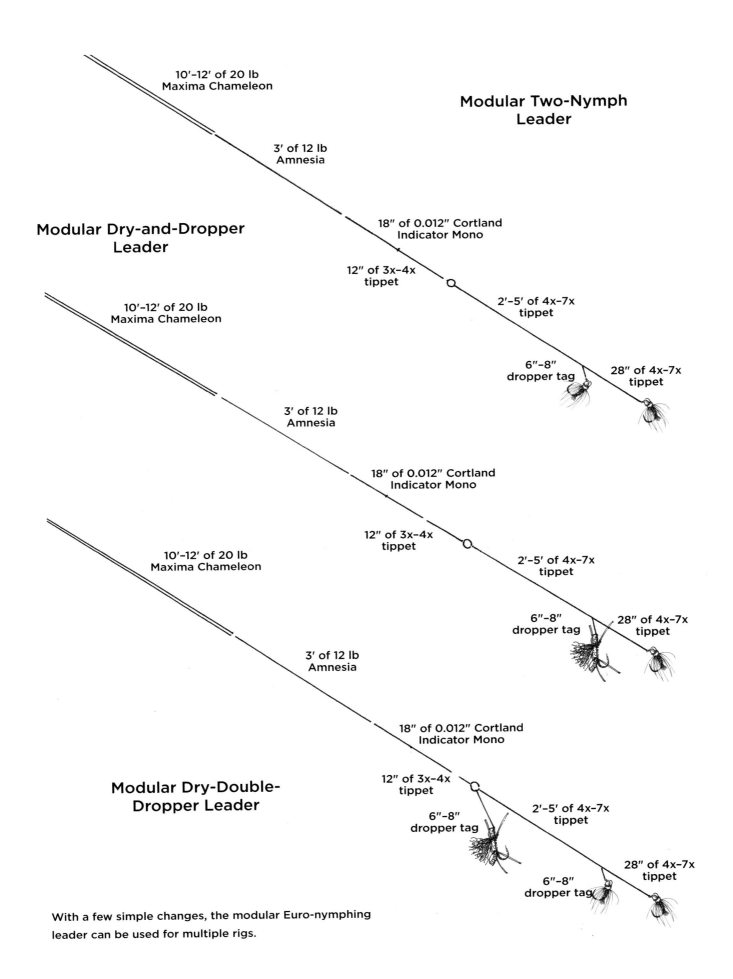

Modular Two-Nymph Leader

10'–12' of 20 lb Maxima Chameleon

3' of 12 lb Amnesia

18" of 0.012" Cortland Indicator Mono

12" of 3x–4x tippet

2'–5' of 4x–7x tippet

6"–8" dropper tag

28" of 4x–7x tippet

Modular Dry-and-Dropper Leader

10'–12' of 20 lb Maxima Chameleon

3' of 12 lb Amnesia

18" of 0.012" Cortland Indicator Mono

12" of 3x–4x tippet

2'–5' of 4x–7x tippet

6"–8" dropper tag

28" of 4x–7x tippet

10'–12' of 20 lb Maxima Chameleon

3' of 12 lb Amnesia

18" of 0.012" Cortland Indicator Mono

12" of 3x–4x tippet

2'–5' of 4x–7x tippet

6"–8" dropper tag

28" of 4x–7x tippet

Modular Dry-Double-Dropper Leader

12" of 3x–4x tippet

6"–8" dropper tag

6"–8" dropper tag

2'–5' of 4x–7x tippet

28" of 4x–7x tippet

With a few simple changes, the modular Euro-nymphing leader can be used for multiple rigs.

ring. Add 2 to 4 feet of 4X to 7X tippet to the tippet ring for the first fly, and 28 inches of 4X to 7X for the point fly. Remember to tie the second section of tippet 6 to 8 inches up the first section with a triple surgeon's or Orvis tippet knot to create a tag for your dropper fly.

Hybrid Dorsey indicator leader

If you're not fishing in a competition, you may find it helpful to fish a suspension device/strike indicator other than a dry fly in flat water. As written about by Domenick Swentosky, a Pat Dorsey–style yarn indicator works well when attached to a modular Euro-nymphing leader or to the hybrid dry-and-dropper leader. The Dorsey indicator lands much more gently than bobber- or cork-style strike indicators. It also lifts off the water with less disturbance, so it's less likely to spook fish. The volume of yarn can be tailored to the amount of weight you need to suspend.

To make a Dorsey leader, cut a small clump of macramé yarn from 1 to 2 inches long. Using fly-tying thread, bind the center together with 15 to 20 wraps and whip-finish. To attach the indicator, thread a loop of the leader four to five times through a ⁵⁄₁₆-inch medium-strength orthodontic rubber band. Insert the indicator into the loop and pull the leader tight so it rests on the tying-thread-reinforced section of the yarn. The tippet/leader can be slid through the indicator to change depths. Just make sure to do it slowly and possibly underwater to avoid a friction burn on the tippet. For a how-to video and further details on the Dorsey indicator, see troutbitten.com.

A Pat Dorsey–style yarn indicator is easy to add and subtract from your leader to switch from suspending nymphs to a straight Euro-nymphing rig. (PHOTO BY DOMENICK SWENTOSKY)

Micro-thin Euro-nymphing leader

After back-to-back team wins at the world championships for the Spanish team in 2015 and 2016 (and a long history of previous success), my Fly Fishing Team USA mates and I have discussed rigging and tactics with several Spanish anglers, including Pablo Castro Pinos and David Arcay Fernandez. I have also discussed rigging with French angler Julien Daguillanes, the 2016 individual world champion. What my teammates and I have discovered from talking to these competitors is what I already knew from fishing with my Spanish friend, Luis Esteban Hernandez, when we both lived in California.

Essentially, the Spaniards like micro-thin-diameter nymphing leaders. They build entire leader-butt sections from 3X or 4X tippet, with a sighter at the end, or the entire leader made of sighter material. They fish fairly short (approximately 2 or 3 feet to the first fly), very thin tippet to their flies. Their sighters are typically 4X or 5X diameter and can be raised out of, and lowered into, the water with less drag in the surface currents than thicker sighters create.

While thicker sighters can be dropped in the river to allow for deeper presentations, they do create enough friction to cause noticeably increased drift speeds, also known as drag. Many times, I've experienced drifts where my flies did not touch bottom when my thick sighter was underneath the water. In subsequent drifts, my flies did touch bottom with the sighter out of the water because the drift was able to slow down to allow further descent.

Because thinner sighter reduces interactions with the surface currents, it can be plunged far enough under the water to adjust for depth. In this manner, a shorter section of tippet on a micro-thin Euro-nymphing leader will still allow the flies to get near the bottom in deep and/or swift water. The short tippet section below the sighter also reduces slack, which results in more-immediate strike detection and fewer missed takes. The thin sighter can be difficult to see, however, especially against a whitewater background when fishing high-gradient stretches. Thinner sighter also does not support weight as well when fishing a floated sighter (see chapter 3), so a thicker sighter is more appropriate for that method.

I tried decreasing the butt sections of my Euro-nymphing leaders on my own back in 2011, but I had a hard time getting used to them. When I moved to California in 2014 and fished with my friend Luis

A brown trout from Utah's Green River that fell to nymphs drifted on a micro-thin Euro-nymphing leader.

Luis Esteban Hernandez with a Lower Sacramento River rainbow trout caught using his version of a micro-thin Spanish nymphing leader.

Esteban Hernandez frequently, I tried his leader a few times. It was essentially just one 18- to 20-foot section of Hanak bicolor 0.22 mm or 0.25 mm sighter material with tippet attached to it via a tippet ring. At the time, my casting stroke was too impatient, and I struggled with accuracy because I did not allow the rig to fully turn over behind me. As a result, my flies would come forward still carrying lateral acceleration from swinging around the oval-shaped casting stroke. It frustrated me that they would land inaccurately to one side or the other of my intended target.

In marked contrast to my shortcomings, Luis was very effective with his leader. I could see the potential it held for resisting sag better than a leader with a thicker butt section. He could fish up and across farther away

from the fish than I could, as well as attain depth with nymphs that weighed less than mine. His leader was so light that it seemed to defy gravity, connecting to his flies in a nearly straight line with little to no sag at all.

After the world championship in Colorado in 2016, I decided I needed to revisit the micro-thin Euro-nymphing leader, and I've come to appreciate it. In addition to sag and drift benefits, the tactile connection to your nymphs is greatly increased with a micro-thin leader. With thicker leaders I detect most of my strikes visually by watching the sighter. With the micro-thin leader, I often feel and see the take simultaneously. It sounds crazy, but sometimes I can actually feel the fish bite down on the fly several times. The takes usually feel different than bottom contacts as well. This

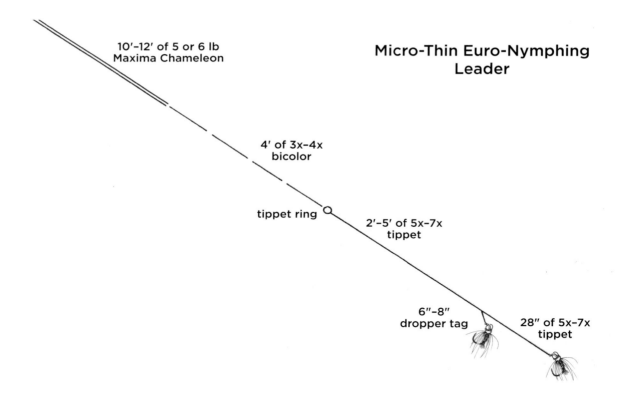

Micro-Thin Euro-Nymphing Leader

10'–12' of 5 or 6 lb Maxima Chameleon

4' of 3x–4x bicolor

tippet ring

2'–5' of 5x–7x tippet

6"–8" dropper tag

28" of 5x–7x tippet

makes differentiating between takes and ticks on the bottom easier.

Despite the cons, the micro-thin Euro-nymphing leader is definitely worth a try if you are already an avid European nymph angler. It is definitely not the leader I would try if you are learning to Euro-nymph, or trying to teach someone else. The unique casting challenges are a setup for failure without the familiarity of casting other, thicker Euro-nymphing leaders beforehand. I've Euro-nymphed for a long time, and it required about three months of dedicated practice for me to become comfortable with it; even so, I'm still less accurate with this technique than I am with other leader formulas.

If you want to try the micro-thin Euro-nymphing leader, I suggest moving down to thinner-diameter leaders in steps. Start with something simple, like adding 16 to 18 feet of 0.012-inch bicolor sighter material to a tippet ring, and then add tippet for your flies. While this leader will show you many of the benefits of going micro, it's still thick enough to have a bit of energy transfer and to float your sighter when needed.

If you go thinner still, I suggest switching back to Maxima Chameleon for a butt section. Its stiffness resists wrapping around the guides on your rod, which can be a constant problem with fine, limp materials. My formula is as follows: 12 feet of 5- or 6-pound Maxima Chameleon > 4 feet of 3X - 4X bicolor sighter material > tippet ring > 1.5 to 5 feet of 5X to 7X tippet > 2 feet

of 5X to 7X tippet tied 6 inches up the preceding tippet section to form the dropper tag.

Streamer leaders and rigs

My approach to streamer fishing is simple. I typically fish one of three ways:

1) When I'm fishing small- to medium-size rivers, I usually fish weighted streamers on a Euro-nymphing leader. I start with the basic 20-pound butt-section Euro-nymphing leader, or the modular Euro-nymphing leader described above.

2) For smaller rivers and shallower water, I normally rig just one streamer, which allows accurate work under trees and structure.

3) If I face deep pools and runs, I will rig for the option of fishing two streamers.

Depending on the size of fish I expect and the size of streamer I'll be using, for a one-fly rig I usually add 4 to 7 feet of 2X to 4X tippet from the tippet ring to my streamer.

As with nymphs, I use the smallest tippet I feel comfortable with to increase sink rate and improve movement during the drift. If I need to add a second streamer, I simply add 30 inches more tippet in the same manner as my nymph rig, to add a tag for the streamer on the dropper. If I want to hedge my bets, I tie a nymph on the top dropper and a streamer on the

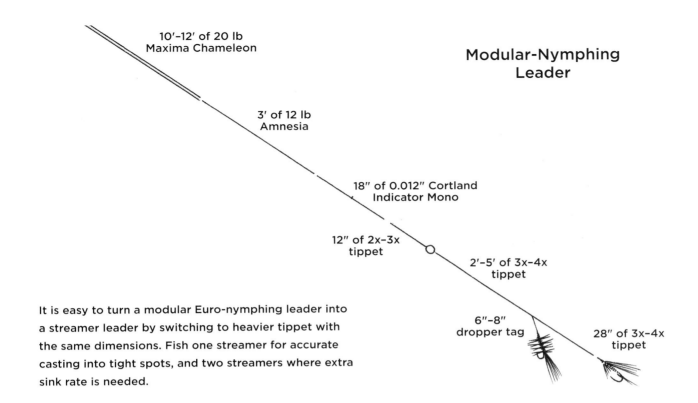

Modular-Nymphing Leader

10'–12' of 20 lb
Maxima Chameleon

3' of 12 lb
Amnesia

18" of 0.012" Cortland
Indicator Mono

12" of 2x–3x
tippet

2'–5' of 3x–4x
tippet

6"–8"
dropper tag

28" of 3x–4x
tippet

It is easy to turn a modular Euro-nymphing leader into a streamer leader by switching to heavier tippet with the same dimensions. Fish one streamer for accurate casting into tight spots, and two streamers where extra sink rate is needed.

A brown trout caught when casting to the bank with a floating line and one of Charles Card's four-eyed Woolly Buggers.

bottom to see if the trout favor one over the other on that day. It is easy to switch back to a single streamer rig when needed by chopping off the dropper fly.

There are times when I need to cover a larger area of shallow water or rapid-fire streamers to the bank from a boat while using a floating line. In these situations, I use a standard commercial 9-foot leader tapered to 2X tippet with a heavily weighted streamer. When I encounter consistently deep water, I will add more 2X or 3X tippet to my leader. The extra length can be

difficult to cast with a heavily weighted streamer, but it's worth it when it puts the streamer in the strike zone for longer and leads to more fish. While this rig doesn't fish as well as the Euro-nymphing streamer route when fishing through disparate currents, the mending capability of the line at least allows for adjustments during the retrieve, to speed up or slow down the streamer.

The last way I fish streamers is tailored to long glides and runs. In these water types, there is a lot of water to cover that is similar in speed and depth. I prefer to

I have dozens of lines in different sink rates and designs that I use for lakes. I find that these lines cross over well for fishing streamers in large rivers, which eliminates my need to add even more clutter to my fishing room.

make long casts with sinking lines that will get my fly to depth and hold it there. For this rig, I find that my sinking lines from lakes cross over well without having to add to my line arsenal. I typically use lines with sink rates in intermediate, type 3, 5, or 7, depending on the depth and speed of the river. The type 7 line will result in a lot of snags if the water is not deep or swift, so I use it only in unique deepwater situations.

The leader on this rig is very simple: I start with 2 feet of 10- or 12-pound Maxima Chameleon and add a tippet ring. To the other side of the ring I add 2 or 3 feet of 0X to 3X tippet. I often fish two streamers with this rig, since I'm usually concerned with covering swaths of water and not with picking small pockets. For the second streamer, I add 3 to 4 feet more tippet and create a dropper tag in the same manner as with my nymphs.

Dry Flies

In recent years I have tried a lot of leaders in order to sort through what I do and do not like in a dry-fly leader. Much of the time, I find myself targeting rising fish, where a delicate presentation is critical. To achieve this end, the leader needs to be long and without an overly thick or stiff butt section, so that casting energy is dissipated in a controlled manner. Most standard trout tapers in commercial leaders have butt sections that are very thick, which leads to hard turnover of the fly. These can be good when working hoppers or other large dry flies, but not when you are trying to land an emerger in flat water with no disturbance.

For several years, I used commercially available spring creek/delicate presentation taper leaders, and they worked well, especially with added tippet. The

A nicely kyped Oregon brown trout caught on a Pliva Shuttlecock Emerger attached to a long Spanish-style dry-fly leader.

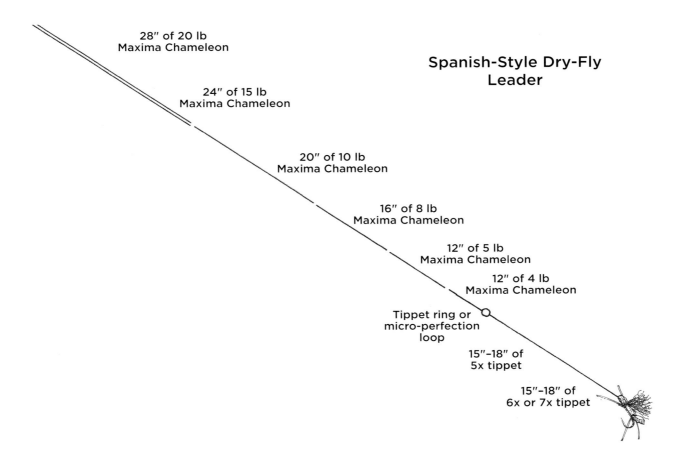

28" of 20 lb
Maxima Chameleon

24" of 15 lb
Maxima Chameleon

**Spanish-Style Dry-Fly
Leader**

20" of 10 lb
Maxima Chameleon

16" of 8 lb
Maxima Chameleon

12" of 5 lb
Maxima Chameleon

12" of 4 lb
Maxima Chameleon

Tippet ring or
micro-perfection
loop

15"–18" of
5x tippet

15"–18" of
6x or 7x tippet

George Harvey dry-fly leader is another good option. Recently, my Spanish friend Eduardo González Ferreiro shared a leader formula with me, which came from several of his friends who compete on the Spanish circuit. It has become my primary leader for delicate dry-fly presentations.

Eduardo's leader formula is as follows: The butt section is tied from Maxima Chameleon. The butt formula is 28 inches of 20-pound > 24 inches of 15-pound > 20 inches of 10-pound > 16 inches of 8-pound > 12 inches of 5-pound > 12 inches of 4-pound > a tippet ring or a micro surgeon's loop. After the butt section, Eduardo uses either a short or long tippet section, depending on the size of dry fly, the type of water, and how spooky the trout are.

For the short tippet formula, add 30 to 35 inches of tippet to the ring/loop. This can be straight 5X or 6X. If I'm going all the way to 7X, I add 15 inches of 5X and 15 inches of 7X.

For the long tippet, Eduardo uses over 9.5 feet of tippet. This creates a 20-foot leader. I haven't found a need for that long of a dry-fly leader yet, but I have extended the tippet up to 6 to 7.5 feet a few times. I suggest experimenting with the length of tippet until you are comfortable casting the leader, and also

achieving an accurate and delicate presentation. (Note: Eduardo boils the butt section of his leader to increase the suppleness. I've tried it both boiled and unboiled. The difference is small enough that I usually forgo the process.)

Strike-indicator/suspension leader

Before I began competing, I was a dyed-in-the-wool strike-indicator nymph angler. I tied my own leaders to create specific turnover characteristics. I also preferred flat portions of leaders where I could attach an indicator without it sliding down the leader onto a thinner portion of the taper. FIPS-Mouche rules prohibit adding floating devices to leaders, but it's easy to incorporate a floating dry-fly substitute. Most of the time on smaller rivers, I find I can cover my bases well with a modular Euro-nymphing leader if I need to fish a dry-and-dropper or attach a suspension device. However, on larger rivers, I still find a shorter leader with a traditional fly line and strike-indicator leader useful, as I did on the Vefsna River in Norway (described in chapter 1).

The formula I use for my suspension/indicator leader is as follows: For the butt section, which again is made from Maxima Chameleon, 24 inches of 25-pound > 18 inches of 20-pound > 18 inches of 15-pound > 12

In flat clear water, increasing the radius of your presentation with a delicate-landing suspension rig is often the best way to avoid spooking trout. (PHOTO BY CHARLIE CARD)

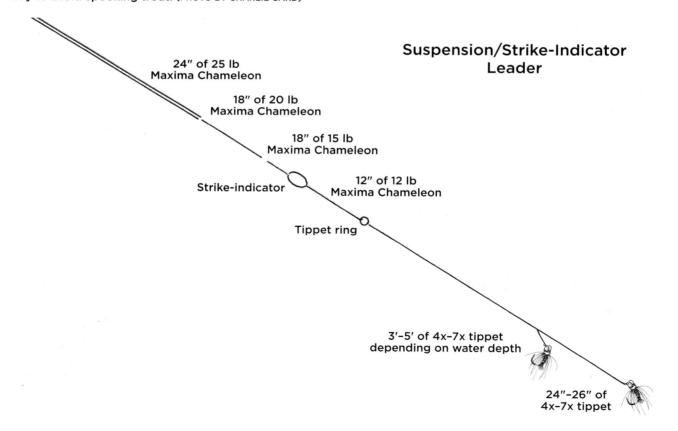

Suspension/Strike-Indicator Leader

24" of 25 lb
Maxima Chameleon

18" of 20 lb
Maxima Chameleon

18" of 15 lb
Maxima Chameleon

Strike-indicator

12" of 12 lb
Maxima Chameleon

Tippet ring

3'–5' of 4x-7x tippet
depending on water depth

24"–26" of
4x-7x tippet

inches of 12-pound > tippet ring. The indicator is usually placed between 3 to 5 feet from the tip of the fly line, depending on the depth of the water. Depending on the depth and velocity of the water, for the tippet I add 2 to 5 feet of 4X to 7X to my first fly, and another 24 to 26 inches for the second fly, again tied up the previous tippet to create a dropper tag. If I'm fishing a dry-and-dropper rig, I will shorten the last two sections of Chameleon to 12 inches in length. I will add 12 inches of 3X tippet before the tippet ring, and then tie a 6-inch tag of tippet to the ring for the dry fly. This will space the dry fly from the brown-colored Chameleon so the fish are more likely to still take the dry fly.

Many anglers place their indicator so close to their fly line that it moves with each mend. If the indicator moves, then the fly moves. That's why I prefer a longer leader, where the indicator can be distanced from the fly line in order to allow mending without moving it. I try to avoid having too much of the butt section below the indicator, as this will increase the downstream drag forces by catching higher-velocity water in the upper column.

Tippet Material

I am always struck by how many people get their feathers ruffled when the topic of tippet material is raised. There may not be another piece of fly-fishing gear that generates more brand loyalty or disdain. The amazing thing is, you could poll a group of 10 high-level anglers and you would get plenty of diverse opinions on favorite brands and material. It's no different with competitive anglers. I've asked world champions from many countries and received many varied responses regarding brand, and nylon versus fluorocarbon. The truth is, these days we're blessed with infinitely better material than the catgut tippet our forefathers fished. This still doesn't stop the squabbles over tippet, however, especially on social media.

Since the release of fluorocarbon, a great debate has ensued between anglers on whether fluorocarbon is better than nylon, and vice versa. Considerable marketing has been focused on convincing anglers that the more-expensive fluorocarbon will improve their fishing. The fly-fishing industry has also published test results and reviews that need to be analyzed carefully, as they can sometimes be pseudoscientific.

While many anglers have decided they prefer fluorocarbon over nylon, they're not willing to pay the higher price for materials designated as fly-fishing tippet in a fly shop. Instead, they buy a large spool of fluorocarbon spinning line that matches the same tensile-strength rating and feel they have gotten a bargain. I believe this is a mistake, and let me explain why.

Diameter is a crucial component of drift, as it relates to drag. If you want to do some complex physics calculations, investigate the drag coefficient as it relates to cylinders of different diameters. In short, what you'll find is that drag is directly related to diameter. As the diameter of a cylinder increases, the drag created by a fluid flowing past also increases.

How does this relate to tippet? Tippet is simply a flexible cylinder that extends into the water. The thinner it is, the less drag your flies will experience from currents that drag tippet in other parts of the column. In addition, thinner tippet is less stiff and will allow

Regardless of the material, fly-fishing tippet is light years better than it was just a few decades ago. These days it's possible to land fish quickly and consistently on light tippet and light rods. This stout rainbow trout was subdued without any issue while fishing 7X tippet and a 2-weight rod.

your flies to move more naturally, both on and under the water's surface.

Let's return to the tippet customer example above. He goes to a fishing store and buys a 200-yard spool of 6-pound fluorocarbon for $20. He walks away happy that he only spent $5 more than he would have at a fly shop, but received a 200-yard spool of line instead of a 30-yard spool. What he doesn't notice is that the diameter of his 6-pound-test line is 0.008 inches, or 3X. The same company sells 3X fluorocarbon tippet for fly fishing reported at 9.2-pound-test. That's a 53 percent increase over the same diameter of line marketed to spinning anglers. At the same time, a different company sells a 50-yard spool of nylon 3X tippet rated at 9.5 pounds. It is a bit more expensive than the fluorocarbon spinning line, but much less expensive than the fluorocarbon fly-fishing tippet. So, which is the best choice?

If you value budget above all else, you may choose the fluorocarbon spinning line. In addition, fluorocarbon has a lower index of refraction, which means it's supposed to be invisible, right? Not necessarily. I've looked at fluorocarbon and nylon while snorkeling underwater, and both are still visible. There are properties to fluorocarbon and nylon that make them both desirable in various situations. However, in the end, what really makes the most difference to your drift and your catch rate is fishing the finest-diameter tippet you can still feel comfortable with, regardless of the material. Therefore, when doing your own research, don't get caught up in the dogma from one source or another. If your budget only allows nylon, that's fine. If you prefer fluorocarbon and are willing to spring for premium tippet, that's great. Just make sure you are choosing a material with a high

When you purchase tippet material, buy the best material you can afford and have confidence in, whether it's nylon or fluorocarbon. You will get higher breaking strain per diameter from fly-fishing tippet than from a bulk spool of spin fishing line.

strength-to-diameter ratio, and let your own opinions form based on performance on the water.

Rods

If there is another hot button topic in fly fishing, it's fly rods. From graphite to cane to fiberglass and beyond, we all have our favorites, and there are a lot of great rods available on the market these days. Like cars, lots of people get caught up in the status symbol one rod may bring over another. If you fit into that category and it makes your fly-fishing experience better, that's fine. Because my gear choices can help or hurt my performance in competitions, I take them seriously, and base them on performance above all else. I am always looking for the next improvement in a rod that will give me a slight edge over a previous model. I also believe in choosing purpose-built rods that are designed for specific uses and techniques. That's how I will divide my recommendations below. You may not have the budget or need for rods based on each nuance in technique, so take my recommendations and adjust them to your own circumstances.

Euro-nymphing fly rods

Most major manufacturers have rods targeted to Euro-nymphing anglers. This has been the case abroad for over a decade, but is a relatively recent phenomenon in the United States. As materials have become lighter and designs smarter, it has become easier for rod manufacturers to build long rods that are still light and enjoyable to fish with. However, I've had the opportunity to fish a lot of rods designed for Euro-nymphing. Many of them are well designed, but others are not. To help you sort through the growing body of rod choices available, the characteristics I look for are found below.

The all-around Euro-nymphing rod is typically a 10-foot to 10-foot-6-inch 3-weight. Rods 10 feet and longer provide extra reach, which will help distance you from the fish you are targeting. They make casting long Euro-nymphing leaders much easier, because the rod tip travels a longer stroke without alteration in the hand. They also cast and mend lightweight suspension/indicator rigs well. In addition, the extra length provides additional leverage while fighting fish. So even though you're fishing a 3-weight rod, you can land fish more like you are fishing a 5-weight.

To fish comfortably, the rod must be built light enough to still balance in the hand without an overly

A Colorado brown trout caught using a Cortland rod that is purpose-built for Euro-nymphing.

heavy reel. Your hand is the fulcrum of your fly-rod lever, and the weight should balance in the cork, where you hold the rod. This reduces the force required to start and stop the rod during casts and hook sets, which results in reduced fatigue and more connections with fish, because your reaction time is quickened. If the balance point is in front of the cork, you will have to flex your forearm through the drift in order to keep the rod elevated, and it will require more energy to start and stop the rod. Many of the best rods feature down-locking reel seats to help shift the balance point into the cork.

A general-purpose Euro-nymphing rod should feature a fairly fast blank for casting accuracy and loop manipulation. However, it must have a soft-enough tip to protect tippet, flex with fish head shakes during the fight, and load when casting very light rigs. I look for the rod to be fairly stiff through two-thirds of the blank, with a progressively softer tip beyond. I also look for the tip to quickly return to its original position after stopping the rod. If the tip dampens slowly, it will continue to shake after stopping the rod, which means your casting accuracy will suffer. As of this writing, most of the rods I fish are made by Thomas & Thomas

and Cortland, but I have fished—and sell—many other fine rods in my online shop. More companies continue to jump into the Euro-nymphing market as well.

When fishing fine tippet, lighter-weight rods will provide even more cushion. I currently have 10-foot-plus-length rods in 0 and 2 weights from Cortland, Thomas & Thomas, and Maxia. These rods are excellent at protecting the finest tippets, and as long as I don't expect outsize fish, they are wonderful tools in technical situations. These rods provide extra cushion that helps to absorb head shakes from boisterous fish so they can help more fish come to the net. However, they do lack leverage to turn larger fish in heavy water. If you fish a lot of small- to medium-size rivers with correspondingly sized fish, a lighter rod in this category will likely suit you.

There are times when you may need to turn to larger rods as well. I have had a lot of feedback from customers who live—or have fished—in New Zealand in recent months. They find a lot of success Euro-nymphing the water other anglers pass by because they cannot spot fish in it. For situations where trophy-size trout are the target, a 10- to 11-foot 4- or 5-weight rod is ideal. There are fewer purpose-built Euro-nymphing rods in these lengths and weights, but there are some good ones, such as the Thomas & Thomas 10-foot-8-inch 4-weight Contact Nymph. If you expect to do more indicator nymphing but want a rod with enough length that it can Euro-nymph in a pinch, then rods in the 9-foot-6-inch to 10-foot 4-weight range make for a good crossover option.

I have also done a lot of Euro-nymphing for steelhead over the years. Depending on the size of the fish I expect, I use 10-foot rods in 6- to 8-weight. It is more difficult for rod manufacturers to design well-balanced longer rods in higher line weights, but a few have been successful, usually in premium-priced models. When

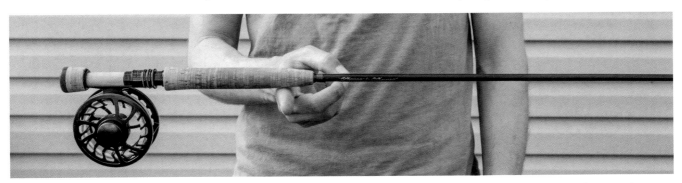

A Euro-nymphing rod balanced in the cork reduces arm and shoulder fatigue and makes a day of fishing much more enjoyable.

When Euro-nymphing for steelhead, I typically fish 10-foot, 6- to 8-weight rods to provide extra fish-fighting leverage. Choose a rod in this range wisely, though, as long, higher-line-weight rods can be burdensome to fish all day if they are not designed with light materials and components.

looking for a Euro-nymphing rod to target larger fish, make sure the rod will still balance in the cork, as the likelihood of fatigue with these rods is higher.

Dry-fly rods

When fishing dry flies, casting control during the stroke is paramount. Many Euro-nymphing rods also make sufficient dry-fly rods. If you want one rod to handle both techniques, then a 10-foot 3-weight is a good model to look for. However, most of the time I favor a fairly fast-action 9-foot 3-weight if I'm only fishing dry flies. The softer tip at this line weight still protects fine tippet, especially with hook-setting practice. The shorter rod makes loop control a little easier for more deliberately accurate delivery, but the 9-foot length is still long enough to mend or reach-cast over tricky currents. There are lots of companies that make excellent rods in this model range, so let your budget and research be your guide.

Streamer rods

As mentioned earlier, much of the time I fish small- to medium-size streamers interchangeably with a standard Euro-nymphing leader and rod. When I need to throw longer casts with floating or sinking line rigs and heavier streamers, I opt for heavier-weight rods. For

When it comes to fly rods, I tend to be a splitter rather than a lumper. I enjoy fishing rods purpose-built for specific techniques, so no performance is compromised. I also prefer to have multiple rigs ready when I can to avoid re-rigging each time I want to switch methods. This photo shows a typical nymph, dry-and-dropper, and dry-fly rod lineup for me.

"Normal" fly lines sag between the hand and guides, which kills drifts and tactile strike detection. Micro-thin Euro-nymphing fly lines have far less mass and exhibit much less sag.

me, the 10-foot 6-weight rods I fish on lakes make nice crossover streamer rods on the river. The extra length helps to keep backcasts above riparian brush or the water's surface. It also makes single-hand spey casting easier when needed. Additionally, it's nice to have the extra leverage when picking up long sections of line to recast, especially from a boat. The rods I regularly fish for this purpose are made by Thomas & Thomas, Sage, and Cortland.

Fly Lines

Euro-nymphing fly lines

Several years back, FIPS-Mouche instituted two rules:
1) The maximum length of leader to be used is twice the length of the rod.
2) Fly lines must be at least 0.022 inches in diameter.

Before these rules were put in place, many competitors were using leaders long enough to allow the fly line to stay on the reel. Thankfully, fly-line companies soon adapted to these rules at the request of competitors, and created fly lines specific to Euro-nymphing.

At first, I felt like these rules were a hindrance. Over time, however, I came to appreciate handling fly line while stripping in slack, setting the hook, and fighting fish. Especially when I experimented with thinner

butt sections and micro-thin leaders, I found it difficult to pinch the leader without it slipping. Excessive coils of slack butt section can be prone to tangles as well. Euro-nymphing fly lines are helpful in this regard. I have fewer accidental slips—on hook sets or during the fight—that can lead to missed fish when using a Euro-nymphing fly line. I still prefer to fish leaders around the competition legal length limit, to keep the line inside the rod, because Euro-nymphing fly lines still sag more than thin butt sections when fished beyond the rod tip.

Obviously, Euro-nymphing lines can still get tangled. However, tangles are usually caused by the line twisting after repeated casting over the same shoulder. Casting downstream and retrieving line through pinched fingers will usually take care of this issue.

I have fished Euro-nymphing fly lines from four or five manufacturers. They all do the job well, but several companies' lines have been very fragile. The most durable of the lines I've tried has been the Cortland Competition Nymph line. I usually fish the level braided-core version, but they make a mono-core model that also works well.

Regardless of the Euro-line you choose, it's crucial to join your leader with a smooth connection. Loop-to-loops will catch in your guides every time and stop your casts short. Nail knots and needle nail knots are

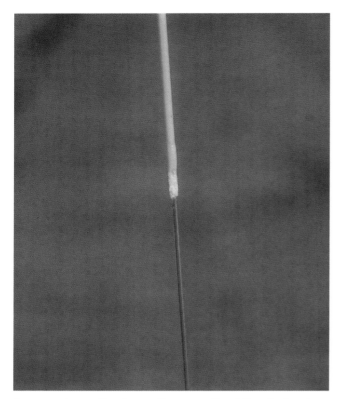

A superglue splice forms the smoothest line-to-leader connection for braided-core fly lines. Try the superglue splice on an old fly line and run it through your rod's guides. You will quickly see why I ditched loop-to-loop connections long ago.

better, but still not quite smooth enough for my taste. With a braided-core line, I prefer a superglue splice that slides through the guides as if nothing is there. With mono-core lines I prefer to strip the coating on the last 2 to 3 inches of line and tie a blood knot to the leader. I do not have space to cover these connections here in the text. However, you can find video tutorials for them on my Tactical Fly Fisher YouTube channel. Just make sure you rough up the tip of the leader for a superglue splice with a hook file or sandpaper beforehand, so it will stick better to the superglue.

Dry-fly lines

At least when fishing smaller dry flies, delicacy is the name of the game. As such, I steer clear of the short, heavy, all-purpose lines that are often designed a half-line-weight-heavy to load today's fast-actioned rods. Instead, because I use a rod and leader purpose-built for dry-fly fishing, I prefer a line that is also designed for the purpose. Cortland's Finesse Trout line, Rio's Trout LT, and Scientific Anglers' Amplitude and Wavelength Trout lines are all appropriate for the task.

To increase delicacy, I have been fishing 2-weight lines on my 3-weight rod for the last year or so. If you have problems with proper loop formation, line speed, and casting timing and turnover, then stick with the designated line weight for your rod. However, lining down a weight allows midair adjustments to quick, snappy dry-fly casts that are less likely to lead to tailing loops. When combined with a long, light leader, extremely delicate finesse presentations are possible, which will lead to fewer spooked fish when your fly crashes down on their heads.

Streamer lines

There are lots of good streamer lines out there these days. Because I Euro-nymph streamers more often than fish them on a long line, I have mostly used my lake fly lines to cross over, to avoid purchasing several other lines and reels. Integrated shooting-head lines such as Airflo's Forty Plus and Cortland's FO-Tech lines work really well as crossover lines. They have sufficient mass in the head to turn over larger streamers, and long casts are easy to shoot if you've reached the running line. A variety of sink rates, from floating to type 9, are available in these lines. This allows you to adjust for your presentation depth depending on the speed and depth of the water, and whether you are fishing streamers with or without much weight.

Suspension/indicator nymphing lines

Fly-line companies make lines purpose-built for indicator nymphing, with lots of mass near the tip to help turn over large indicators and lots of weight. If you fish this style a lot, you will likely find these lines useful. Most of the time, I'm Euro-nymphing in heavy water, and I turn to suspension rigs for smooth flats and pools where I cannot approach fish without spooking them. I rarely need exceptionally heavy rigs in this type of water, so I prefer lines with a less-aggressive taper.

Ease of mending and roll-casting is crucial to a good suspension rig line. With most short-headed, all-purpose, weight-forward lines, once you have more than 30 feet of line out, you are forced to mend with running line that does not carry energy through the head of the line. That's why I prefer either long-belly or double-taper fly lines for suspension nymph rigs. For years I've used the Scientific Anglers Mastery Expert Distance taper. Other fly lines on the market that fit this category include the Rio Gold Tournament and Cortland Omniverse.

Reels

It's hard to go wrong with most of the reels on the market these days. When I was a kid, I dealt with reels featuring tiny arbors, inconsistent drag engagement, and scraping spools. It is amazing how many reel companies have joined the fray in the fly-fishing industry in recent years. Unless you are heading to the salt, most reels will certainly take care of the everyday trout angler's needs.

There are a few characteristics I look for in a reel. I prefer larger arbors to increase the retrieve speed when I have a fish running at me. Large arbors also hold line in bigger coils, which reduces memory of the line and leader. In addition, they maintain more-consistent drag pressure than a small arbor reel, when lots of line is removed from the spool. I also prefer machined reels, since they are less likely to crack or bend if I take a fall and ruin a day of fishing. Lastly, especially with rods 10 feet and longer, it is important to match the weight of the reel to the rod to ensure it balances in the cork. Many of today's premium machined reels are so light that they don't balance well with longer rods, so be sure to seek advice from a fly shop or test the rod balance yourself when purchasing a new reel.

Most reels will work just fine for typical trout-fishing situations. I look for reels with a large arbor that balance in the cork with the rod I am using. A smooth, reliable drag is also important, particularly if you run into larger fish, like the steelhead in this photo.

CHAPTER 3

If possible, it's always wise to learn and compare techniques on water with a dense population of trout. If you have a target-rich environment, the fish will confirm that you are fishing correctly and help you sort out where and when different techniques are more successful than others. You can always move to waters with fewer and larger trout once you've honed your skills and bolstered your confidence.

Euro-Nymphing: A Competitive Breakthrough

n 2007, after my first season of competing with Fly Fishing Team USA, my teammate Lance Egan returned from his trip to the world championship in Finland with a book by Karel Krivanec, entitled *Czech Nymph and Other Related Fly Fishing Methods*. Most techniques referenced in the book were being phased out in the world championships around that time, being replaced by updated methods.

We were not one of the better international teams at the time, and our nymphing techniques reflected the short-leader approach originally thought of as Czech or Polish nymphing—the same techniques at the heart of Krivanec's book. However, hidden within a couple of its pages were some leader formulas for French nymphing leaders, which represented a drastic departure from the rigs we were using.

During that period, our team had circulated footage from a Japanese documentary about the 2004 world championship in Slovakia. Being the observant and intuitive angler that he is, Lance realized that the better anglers in the footage were fishing the French-style leaders referenced in Krivanec's book. He began to experiment with their use on our home waters in Utah, and was astounded at the results.

After about a month of fishing the new technique, Lance asked if I would like to go on a trip to a creek to play around with the French leader and compare it with other methods we would normally use on that stream—mainly upstream dry-fly and dry/nymph-dropper methods. Lance isn't the type of person who tends toward hyperbole, so I took him seriously when he said he thought he'd stumbled upon something that would "blow my mind." Whenever I think back to this day, a day I label the "H Creek Experiment," I marvel at the way it changed the way I fish rivers. I only wish I would have thought of something similar myself, or that I'd been taught these techniques earlier in my fishing career.

Our friend and future teammate Kurt Finlayson joined us for the trip, and there was a buzz in the car as we realized the learning that might be ahead of us.

The small stream we tackled on that day is known for a dense population of smallish brown trout. Typically, they eat dries and nymph droppers just fine, so most anglers have little reason to alter their approach from these well-known tactics. However, Lance had fished a French leader rig on this stream several times prior to our outing, and he was surprised at how much higher his catch rates were with this technique as compared to dries and dry-and-dropper rigs.

Based on Lance's experience, our goal for the day was to repeatedly fish each rig in series through different water types and locations and analyze how each performed. The planned quasi experiment was for one of us to fish a dry fly through each run/riffle/pool we came to, followed by another fishing a dry-and-dropper rig and another fishing a French-leader nymph rig. This would let us fish from the top of the water to the bottom in progression and help us to understand how

Trying to inspire an osmotic love for literature and fly fishing in my son Levi, just after he was born in 2013.

Brian Simmons holds his sighter off the water while using an up-and-across Euro-nymphing approach in this Oregon river.

Dead drifts are easy to accomplish with good Euro-nymphing technique. In addition, lots of unorthodox alterations to drifts can be made, which convince pressured fish to eat. Here Josh Graffam works a run on the River Vah in Slovakia during practice for the 2017 World Fly Fishing Championship. In addition to our team, anglers from 29 other countries had been practicing on this short stretch of water for days before this photo was taken. Even so, Josh was still able to pull several fish from this run with Euro-nymphing techniques.

trout reacted to each rig after they had been pressured. A pattern quickly emerged in each location, where the dry fly would catch one to three fish; the dry-and-dropper, another one to three fish; and the French-leader nymph rig, about as many as the previous two techniques combined.

At the beginning of the day, we used a unique technique that worked well for the quick-reacting small brown trout we were targeting. In his book Krivanec mentions that French anglers often use this rig by casting upstream and setting their hook after their flies had drifted for a count of two to three. This technique was devised to take advantage of quick-striking trout before the widespread use of sighter material, which made takes easier to see. Based on our results, it became quite clear that there were definite reasons why certain countries were repeatedly dominating the world championships. Simply put, they were using more-advanced techniques.

In the weeks following the H Creek Experiment, I continued similar testing. I visited reaches of stream that I fished often and compared the dry-and-dropper rigs that I typically fished with the new French nymphing method. The results were comparable to our first day afield. In many instances I caught twice as many fish the second time through as I had the first.

That September I ended up having a monthlong gap between moving back from guiding in southern Colorado and heading to the US National Fly Fishing Championship in Boulder. I fished 32 out of 37 days in an effort to try and learn as much about the new technique as I could. It was a pivotal time for me.

What makes Euro-nymphing so uniquely effective? When boiled down to its simplest terms, I believe that attaining a convincingly natural drift and detecting strikes are the two most crucial variables in successful nymph fishing. You won't convince many trout to eat your fly if it is drifting in an abnormal way that rings the "This is not food" alarm bell. Much of the time a dead drift is the best approach, but other times an induced take or swung presentation can also convince trout that your fly is food. When properly executed by the angler, Euro-nymphing techniques provide consistent dead drifts in a variety of complex currents, with the added capability of easily introducing mobility into the drift.

However, it doesn't matter how many fish eat your fly if you don't realize they have taken it. Euro-nymphing excels at strike detection. This is especially true in water types—such as pocketwater and rocky runs—where turbulent currents create challenging conditions for attaining a dead drift, maintaining strike detecting tension with your flies while fishing a suspension-style strike indicator.

Want more reasoning? The following two sections list the pros and cons of each method.

Pros of Euro-Nymphing versus Suspension/Strike-Indicator Nymphing

Euro-nymphing provides improved strike detection via a direct connection to your flies. When suspension-nymphing with a strike indicator, your rig must sink

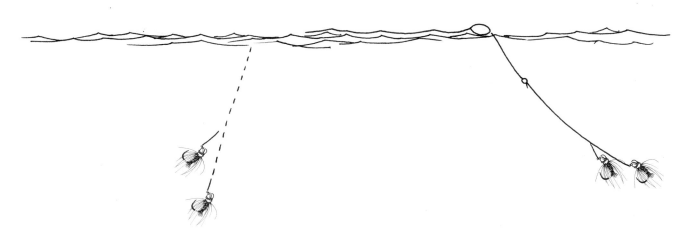

Euro-nymphing rigs provide a more-direct connection to your flies, which promotes more control over your drift and better strike detection. Strike-indicator rigs require mending to manage slack line on the water, and thus reduce your connection to your flies, which in turn reduces control and strike detection.

and attain tension to register a strike, and your indicator must land in the same seam of current as your flies in order to maintain a good drift and strike detection. Often there is slack between the indicator and the flies, which reduces strike detection; in addition, the flies usually land in seams of current moving at different speeds or in different directions than your indicator. This induces drag and/or kills your strike detection.

No mending is required when Euro-nymphing. This means you're always ready to set the hook. Constant mending with an indicator rig creates times when it's difficult to quickly set the hook before the fish has expelled your fly.

Strike indicators act like a kite in the surface currents, pulling your rig at a different speed and/or direction than the bottom currents, where your flies are. If you have ever watched Wendell Ozefovich's *Underwater World of Trout* video series, read Jason Randall's book *Moving Water*, or studied hydrology, you know that the currents we see on the surface of the river do not necessarily reflect the speed or direction of the currents on the bottom, where you're typically trying to drift your nymphs. When Euro-nymphing, only tippet is on or in the water, so there is less surface area to create drag from surface currents that do not have the same speed or direction as where your flies are drifting. Better drifts bring you more fish, especially in complex water types with fast current speeds, and turbulence, where good drifts are hard to attain. This is most evident in pocketwater (as you will see in chapter 5).

Indicators make large surface disturbances on the water when they land, are mended, and when setting

Have you ever been caught off guard by a fish taking your nymphs while mending with a strike indicator? I know I have. When Euro-nymphing there is no mending required, and you can always be ready to quickly set the hook when the need arises. (PHOTO BY MARK OLSEN)

Even when floating the sighter, Euro-nymphing leaders lift off the water gently, allowing you to fish smooth water with less risk of spooking trout. Imagine how different this photo might look if there was a bobber-style strike indicator ripping across the water's surface.

Fish hooked on strike-indicator rigs are often hooked at a downstream angle on a rig with a lot of inherent slack that creates delayed hook sets. Because of better hooking angles, less slack, and a shorter distance to the fish at the beginning of the fight, a greater proportion of fish can be landed when Euro-nymphing.

Imagine covering all of the water types in this photo, from the smooth pool at the bottom to the shallow broken riffles and pockets above. Could you fish all of it well with a strike indicator and nymphs? You can with a Euro-nymphing rig.

the hook. Long-leader Euro-nymphing rigs land light on the water and come off when setting the hook with much less disturbance than a strike indicator. Less surface disturbance = less spooked fish, especially in shallow or smooth-surfaced water where fish are prone to spooking.

Euro-nymphing provides a better fish-hooked-to-landed ratio due to less slack in the system, more strikes coming at close range, and fewer strikes coming downstream. Strike-indicator rigs provide longer drifts, but much of the first half of each drift is inefficient while your rig sinks and tracks into line before attaining tension and strike detection. Therefore, most strikes end up in the latter half of your drift when fishing a strike indicator. This creates inferior hooking angles because the fly is pulled out of the mouth when the

hook is set. Furthermore, the downstream angle, and the increased distance to fish, allows them to get the upper hand early on in the fight, which leads to more lost fish.

The versatility of a Euro-nymphing rig allows you to fish water types from inches to many feet deep without constantly changing your rig. With a Euro-nymphing rig, you control the depth your flies reach by allowing more or less leader to enter the water, changing the angle of your sighter during the drift, and manipulating your cast to cause it to enter vertically or horizontally. A quick fly change adjusts your weight and further manipulates your depth control. There is no need to move an indicator and repeatedly remove or attach split shot to adjust for the myriad of depths and current speeds you may encounter on the river.

It is easy to move flies for an induced take with a lift of the rod when Euro-nymphing. This can be deadly during insect emergences or after fish have seen repeated dead drifts. I've had many experiences where I have caught fish while dead-drifting through a lie and then followed with just as many fish on drifts with an induced take. When fishing a strike indicator, it must be moved on the surface to move your flies below. This causes surface disturbance, and can track your indicator laterally across the river into seams of current different from those where your flies are drifting, which induces drag through the rest of your drift.

Cons of Euro-nymphing versus suspension/strike-indicator nymphing

Indicators allow a greater radius of presentation. When the water is smooth, clear, and/or deep, it can be difficult to get close to fish without spooking them. In these situations, an indicator or dry fly that can suspend your nymphs at distance is a better choice for effective fishing.

Indicators suspend flies evenly and can provide better drifts in slow water with a uniform depth. On long and slow drifts when Euro-nymphing, your shoulder may fatigue after a while and your rig may shake a bit, which results in unnatural movement during the drift. If I encounter this type of water while fishing, I will often switch my dropper tag to a dry fly, or add a dropper near my sighter to attach a dry fly (modular Euro-nymphing leader from chapter 2). This allows me to switch back and forth between suspending my nymphs at distance and traditional Euro-nymphing as the water types change.

It is difficult to build enough weight into flies smaller than a size 18 or 20, to fish them at depth. This can be a bit of a limitation if the trout are focusing on midges or very small mayflies. To attain depths of more than a few feet with micro flies, a larger fly must be fished on the rig in addition to the small fly (or flies).

Euro-nymphing can be a physically demanding technique. Aggressive wading may be required to approach fishing lies, and strong shoulder-stabilizing muscles are needed to hold repeated drifts with a smooth extended high rod. Thankfully these challenges can be overcome with practice and training, but it can require some effort from anglers used to less-strenuous fishing.

In the years since 2007, I have tried to develop a system that combines the best aspects of the different styles of Euro-nymphing in ways that work best for me. This has included working on leaders, casts, angles, presentations, and as many variables as possible to achieve the best success I can. However, I have also realized that Euro-nymphing has its limitations, and other rigs and techniques are often called for. In the right situations and water types that call for dry flies or a suspension-rig approach, I have also found ways to resurrect the dry-and-dropper rigs I previously fished, coupled with a European long-leader format. Still in other situations, a dry-fly-only, wet-fly, or streamer approach is most appropriate.

By broadening my technical skill set, I am now able to target each piece of water I find in front of me with an appropriate strategy. This has certainly been helpful at competitions where I have drawn beats that have been typified by inches-deep riffles to 30-foot-deep stagnant pools and everything in between. It is also helpful to any angler wishing to make the most out of the entirety of any river he/she encounters rather than just hitting the highlights that are fished time and again by the majority of anglers.

Executing Euro-Nymphing Methods

There are a lot of other great books available to teach the finer points of fishing dry flies, indicator-nymph rigs, and streamers at distance. While I will periodically reference how I fish these methods in the rest of the book, there isn't enough space to provide in-depth instructions, and much I could write would be redundant.

There is a growing body of literature that references Euro-nymphing, including George Daniel's *Dynamic Nymphing* and Jason Randall's *Nymphing Masters*. However, I still find there is a lot of misunderstanding regarding implementation of the method when I talk to other anglers. While the finer points of Euro-nymphing deserve an entire book, in the rest of this chapter I hope to give you enough details to provide some basic Euro-nymphing instruction. I will also include more details in the chapters on water types. You may find it helpful to combine your learning from this chapter with instruction from the videos *Modern Nymphing: European-Inspired Techniques* and *Modern Nymphing Elevated:*

Beyond the Basics, which Gilbert Rowley, Lance Egan, and I have released in the past several years.

In my mind, the best way to break down how to fish a Euro-nymphing rig is by the angle between your position and your target water. Depending upon which zone you fish, the adjustments you need to make to your rig and how you fish it will differ. Below I will cover how to fish the rig upstream, up and across, and down and across.

Fishing Upstream

Fishing a Euro rig upstream is the best approach when the probability of spooking trout is high. Casting upstream from a downstream position, you can stay within the blind spot in a trout's vision, which exists directly behind them. However, Euro-nymphing upstream is the most difficult way to fish the rig. It requires longer casts, and the strikes are harder to see when the sighter is coming toward you instead of drifting laterally. Therefore, I generally do not teach upstream methods to beginners; instead, I will opt for a dry-and-dropper on a modular Euro-nymphing leader to lessen the degree of difficulty. So, if you are new to Euro-nymphing, do not be discouraged if you find fishing upstream difficult to begin with. It will become easier with experience.

When Euro-nymphing upstream, you can fish with your sighter off the water or greased and floating on the water. Let's cover both in turn.

When fishing broken water, you will need to fish with your sighter elevated off the water. The sighter will

Fishing upstream is the easiest way to stay out of the view of trout. However, it is also the most challenging way to Euro-nymph. Approach to within 20 feet of your target lie to begin with, and then work upstream.

If you are fishing broken water, stop your rod high enough that your cast turns over with your sighter above the water, as seen in this photo. Adjust the elevation of where you stop your sighter to manipulate how deep your flies can sink.

not float for long if the surface is agitated, and it will create drag on your flies below if it sinks. Depending on the diameter of the leader you are fishing, and its resulting mass, it is usually possible to hold the sighter off the water for up to 12 to 20 feet beyond your rod tip. Broken water is generally very approachable, so getting even closer is usually not a problem.

To fish upstream with the sighter off the water, approach to within 15 to 20 feet of your target lie. Make a cast upstream with the rod arm extended and the rod stopped at head height or higher. If you stop the rod lower, the sighter will touch the water.

Cast far enough above your target so that your flies sink near to the bottom by the time they reach where you expect a fish to be. This distance can vary from as little as 18 inches to approaching 6 to 8 feet above the fish, depending on the depth and speed of the water and the weight of your flies on the rig. If more sinking distance is needed, it is best to try an up-and-across approach.

I prefer to start my casts short and extend subsequent casts farther upstream to ensure that I work from shallow to deep. I would rather have my nymph(s) drift over potential fish than hook bottom before reaching them. Not only will fish be less likely to see flies drifting below them, but hooking bottom also leads to setting the hook, which can spook fish that are close by.

Managing slack

One of the biggest challenges for beginning Euro-nymphers is slack management. When fishing upstream, your rig will be drifting toward you and slack will steadily accumulate. If you are close enough to your target, you may be able to lift the rod tip high enough to remove the slack. However, do not raise the rod diagonally to the side, as this will pull the flies laterally and hamper their drift. Instead, leave the rod pointed in the direction of the sighter as you raise the tip to retrieve slack.

Before you retrieve slack, always ensure that the fly line is pinched against the rod grip by the middle finger of your right hand. The line hand should always retrieve slack below your rod hand so that you never lose control of the line during the drift. Step 1 of the hand-twist retrieve: Pinch the fly line between your thumb and index finger on your line hand.

Step 2: Rotate the back of your hand toward you by pivoting the wrist, and then slightly extend the middle through pinkie fingers on your line hand.

Step 3: Curl your fingers over the line and rotate your palm toward your chest.

Step 4: While your fingers are curling over the line, simultaneously let go of the line with your thumb and index finger. Once your wrist is rotated and your other fingers are fully curled, pinch up the line with your thumb and index finger again and you are back to step 1. Each hand twist should crawl up the line 5 to 6 inches. With practice it can be done quickly and smoothly.

At longer distances, leave your rod in an extended and elevated position while retrieving slack line. When most of the drift is over and the remaining slack is minimal, raise the rod tip near the end of the drift to remove the rest of the slack, and you will be in position to make the backcast and repeat. Slack can be retrieved by stripping in line, but I prefer using a hand-twist retrieve when possible, as the slack retrieval is smoother and less likely to influence the drift with the rod hand. Most anglers have a hard time isolating the movements of their line hand and their rod hand. If your rod hand moves when you strip in slack, your sighter will move, which means your flies will move unnaturally during the drift.

Detecting strikes and setting the hook

During the drift, if you notice any hesitation, twitch (especially moving away from you), or abnormal angle change in the sighter, set the hook. Although there is

the potential to spook fish with repeated hook sets, I always share the following advice with anglers: "It's better to set than be sorry," and "Hook sets are free, so use them." When fishing up and across, the sighter is presented in profile and travels from upstream to downstream. Because the sighter is coming toward you and not showing its profile, takes are harder to see when fishing upstream. Repeat my hook-set mantras if necessary, and be ready to react if the sighter signals any deviation of the drift. You will never know if the sighter moved because of a fish if you don't set the hook.

Because you have a fairly tight line when Euro-nymphing, typically accompanied by a long rod, it does not take much effort to set the hook. A small flick of the wrist will move the flies fast enough and far enough to penetrate the hook, especially if you are diligent about sharpening hook points. If you miss the fish or the sighter moved because your flies touched

When Euro-nymphing, a quick wrist flick is all that is needed to set the hook with a long rod and not much slack. Set the hook downstream to pull the fly back into the fish's mouth for the best chance of hooking. A hook set that is low and parallel to the water will keep your flies in the water and out of the trees if the hook set is turned into a backcast.

Right: To float the sighter, make sure you apply a paste-type floatant, such as Loon Outdoors Payette Paste. Notice the extra blood knots in the sighter in this photo. They can act like mini suspension devices that grab a little more floatant to increase buoyancy. However, don't plan on using extra blood knots if you fish in competitions, as they are currently not legal under FIPS-Mouche rules.

the bottom, simply allow your hook set to turn into a backcast, and you can get right back to fishing.

Floating the sighter

Now let's look at why and how to fish upstream with a floated sighter. In smooth currents and clear shallow water, you will likely need to approach target lies from 20 to 30-plus feet downstream. At these distances, the leader will sag back toward you if you try to hold the sighter off the water. The sag will speed up the drift of your nymphs and create downstream drag.

To avoid the sag, lay the sighter on the water and allow it to float. When greased with a paste-style floatant, the floated sighter ends up acting like a weak suspension device. Thicker sighter material will float more weight, and vice versa. Other sighter types, like braided sighters and curly q's, can increase the buoyancy further and allow you to float heavier nymphs for a longer distance, but I avoid using them unless I only plan to fish water where I am floating the sighter.

With a basic or modular Euro-nymphing leader and a 0.012-inch sighter, it is possible to float up to a two-nymph rig with 2.3 mm and 2.8 mm tungsten nymphs for most short- to medium-length drifts (3 to 8 feet). Lighter-weight rigs will obviously float more easily. Also keep in mind that shorter tippet will increase the

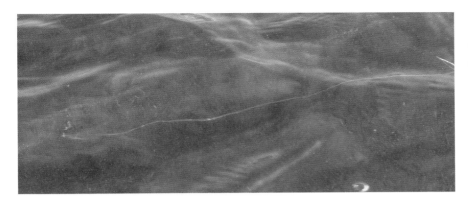

If your sighter sinks, stops drifting, or tightens, set the hook! Takes on a floated sighter are subtle if you are not used to spotting them, so remember that it's better to set than be sorry.

A sighter that has been greased will float on the water like a weak suspension device. If you have trouble seeing the sighter on the water, try adding extra blood knots and leaving long tag ends on a tippet knot to increase visibility.

Once the sighter is near vertical under the rod tip, it's time to recast if there has not yet been a reason to set the hook.

downward vertical force of the sinking nymphs and sink your sighter more easily. Longer tippet shallows out this angle and results in less vertical and more upstream horizontal force from the sinking nymphs.

Fishing the floated sighter is pretty basic at its core. If you have fished a dry-and-dropper upstream, then you should be able to float the sighter without issue. Simply cast far enough above your target to allow your rig sufficient time to sink near to the bottom by the end of your drift. Adjust your casting length and the weight of your rig as needed to increase or decrease the depth

of your flies. If your sighter tightens, stops, or sinks abruptly, then set the hook.

When fishing a floated sighter, it should move a little slower than the surface of the water. You will need to retrieve slack smoothly at the pace of the water where your nymph(s) is drifting, not where your sighter is drifting. Retrieve too fast, and you will drag your flies downstream. Retrieve too slow, and your sighter will take on a serpentine shape and drag will ensue.

Once the sighter has reached a point just upstream of your rod tip, terminate the drift and cast again. If

The up-and-across drift is the most basic drift in Euro-nymphing. Depending on the amount of line you cast, your drifts can be very short, or up to 30 to 35 feet in length.

you allow it to go farther, your leader will invert under the rod tip and affect your drift. You will also be covering water close enough to your position that any trout inhabiting it will have likely spooked already.

Keep the rod tip extended and at chest level or higher during the drift to hold your leader off the water. During most drifts, only your sighter should be floating on the water. If you allow the rest of the leader to lay on the water, it will grab the faster surface currents and lead to downstream drag. It is also critical to land your sighter in the same seam of current as your flies. If you land your sighter to the left or right of your flies, it will likely travel in water that is faster or slower than where your flies lands. These differences can be difficult to spot in smooth water, where differences in current are not obvious on the surface.

Fishing Up and Across

When most anglers think of Euro-nymphing, they picture the up-and-across approach. The basic drift for this zone starts with a cast made diagonally upstream and across the river. These casts can be very short, or up to around 30 feet long. The drift can be as short as 2 feet in a tight pocket, or 30 to 35 feet long in pools or runs where the water stays consistently deep. When deciding where and how long to make your drift, always look for snags above and below the water and shorten your drifts to avoid them.

The oval cast

The basic Euro-nymphing casting stroke is built on an oval. This stroke clears the flies around the rod tip and maintains tension. With tension you can control where your flies land. Without tension your flies can change direction abruptly, like a tuber being pulled behind a boat. This scenario leads to loss of control and inaccuracy.

Unlike most traditional fly casts, oval-casting a Euro-nymphing rig should involve a lot of pivot at the wrist. In fact, for many shorter casts I make the cast entirely with the wrist, with very little arm movement. The oval cast will track the flies under the rod tip as they exit the water and over the top of the rod on the forward cast. This keeps tungsten beads from colliding with your rod.

The steps to the oval cast are as follows:

Make a sweeping backcast low and parallel to the water. Most people under-power their backcast, so ensure you use sufficient energy to get your fly and leader moving quickly.

As the leader and fly are turning over, raise the rod tip diagonally behind your head by pivoting the wrist and raising the elbow.

Once you have felt the weight of the nymph(s) straighten behind you, make the forward cast with a controlled rod stop. A short 6- to 12-inch haul on the forward cast can improve turnover.

The elevation where you stop your rod on the forward cast is critical to starting the drift in fishing position, with the sighter held off the water. Notice the position at which Pat Weiss has stopped his rod in this photo; look closely, and you will see his yellow sighter held off the water on the left side.

At the end of the cast, the rod is usually stopped high enough to keep the sighter just barely off the water. If the sighter is stopped too high, the flies will not have enough tippet to sink, and the sighter can be hard to see when it's not silhouetted against the water. If the sighter is allowed to touch the water, it can be difficult to raise back up off the water without the rig jumping upward when the sighter breaks the surface tension. This motion lifts your flies early in the drift when they should be sinking.

When you make your final forward cast, stop with your arm extended and the hand raised to between chest and head height. This position will increase the radius you can drift and keep the sighter in the proper position.

Many anglers struggle to be exact with the elevation of their rod stop because they involve their torso in the cast. When you bend or twist at the waist, the casting stroke will continue too far because of the built-up momentum. This causes the rod tip to slice across the body or drop lower than desired. Neither situation allows control of the leader during turnover, and sets up the beginning of the drift for failure. Remember that fly-casting should not be an ab workout, so stop doing crunches during your casting stroke! Especially when making short casts with a Euro-nymphing rig, the arm and wrist provide all the power you'll need to turn the rig over, as long as the rod is loaded and comes to a stop at the end of the stroke to unload the stored energy.

Twisting your torso during the cast leads to the rod tip moving across the lane of your cast. This is a recipe for poor turnover and inaccuracy. Keep your shoulders squared to the target and you will improve your casting accuracy and consistency.

This may be one of the most common casting mistakes in fly fishing. Bending back and forth at the torso gives the illusion that you are putting more power into your cast, while in reality, it's just wasted energy, and leads to the rod being stopped too low on the forward- and backcast. Whether you are Euro-nymphing or not, keep your torso still and focus on making the cast only with your arm and wrist. Your casting performance will be much more consistent and require far less effort.

The Drift

Once the cast has been made, be ready to lift the rod tip or retrieve line and manage slack. With shorter casts, lifting the rod tip and moving it downstream may be all that is needed to manage slack. On longer casts, your line will need to be retrieved by stripping or a hand twist. The more upstream your cast is, the more slack you will need to retrieve. Casts that are made farther across the river drift mostly parallel to your position, and therefore, less slack needs to be retrieved.

I mentioned this point earlier but it's worth repeating, because it's critical, and most beginning Euro-nymphers struggle with it. When retrieving slack, you need to keep your rod hand and rod tip steady. If you

When Euro-nymphing up and across, there is tension between your rod tip and your flies. Any movement of the rod tip will therefore be transferred down the leader to your flies. Many beginning Euro-nymphers struggle to be steady with the rod tip at the beginning of the drift, while retrieving slack, and their rod tip bounces along an undulating path, as shown by the red arrow in this photo. Focus on making a smooth, arc-shaped drift, like the one shown by the green arrow, and you will make better presentations and catch more fish.

fumble for the line or your line retrieval leads to your rod hand moving, your rod tip will move as well, which in turn causes your sighter to move. If your sighter moves, then your flies are moving too. Not only will they look unnatural in this situation, but your movements will also kill their descent.

While retrieving slack, I normally leave my rod tip pointed at the sighter and elevate the rod until the sighter tracks vertically underneath. Once the sighter has reached this angle, I track the sighter downstream with the rod tip until it is just beyond 45 degrees downstream. At this point the sighter will take on a downstream angle and the flies will begin to ascend through the column. Obviously, I will set the hook earlier in the drift if needed, or make a backcast earlier if the drift

approaches a rock or snag. If the water is a fairly consistent depth during the drift, I leave the sighter near the water's surface throughout. If it shallows out near the end of the drift, I will lift the sighter to avoid my flies constantly hooking the bottom during the drift.

At the end of the drift, I lower the rod tip to feed slack and extend the drift by a few feet. Usually I leave the rod extended out over the river slightly to allow the flies to ascend without tracking across the drift. A lot of takes come as the nymphs start to ascend through the column, when they resemble emerging insects.

When Euro-nymphing, be willing to move your feet. My teammate Lance Egan describes the Euro-nymphing drift as an elongated U. I refer to the same principle as "fishing the hammock." During the drift your

To begin your up-and-across drift, cast upstream of your target lie with enough distance to allow time for your nymphs to sink. Stop the rod high and retrieve slack smoothly if needed. (PHOTO BY MARK OLSEN)

As the sighter begins to drift downstream, elevate the rod tip and allow the sighter to reach a more-vertical angle under the rod tip. If you move the rod downstream, the sighter angle will stay shallow, and the maximum depth your flies can reach will decrease. (PHOTO BY MARK OLSEN)

Through the middle of the drift, track the sighter downstream with the rod tip. Keep the sighter near vertical and avoid any rod movements that will move it unnaturally out of its path. (PHOTO BY MARK OLSEN)

As the sighter passes downstream of your rod, lower your rod tip to provide enough slack to allow the drift to continue for a few feet before swinging your flies up. (PHOTO BY MARK OLSEN)

Euro-nymphing drifts take the shape of a hammock underwater. Different fish may prefer your flies sinking on the drop, drifting through the center, or swinging up at the end of the drift. In order to cover a long run or pool, you must be willing to move your feet to shift the path of the hammock-shaped drift around to new fish and new water.

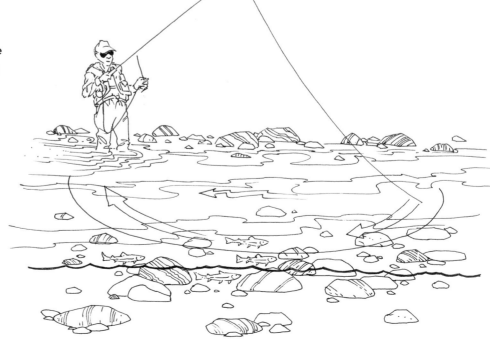

nymphs will track the basic shape of a hammock. They sink in the first one-third of the drift, are at their deepest during the center one-third, and begin to ascend in the last one-third of the drift. In order to fully cover a piece of water, your feet need to move upstream and/or across repeatedly to shift the different points of the drift to new water. Each fish is an individual and may be more susceptible to the drift at different points of the hammock. Sometimes a half step one way or another is all that is needed to bring your flies a few inches closer to a fish and convince it to eat. If you fish like your feet are buried in concrete, you will be much less successful.

Sighter angles

One of the fundamental Euro-nymphing concepts to understand is the role your sighter angle plays in how your flies drift. If you try to execute a dead drift, the sighter angle will naturally progress from a shallow upstream angle at the beginning of the drift, to a near-vertical angle in the center, to a shallow downstream angle at the end. However, intentionally manipulating your sighter angle during the drift can change its behavior.

Each angler tends to develop his/her own style over time. Some anglers, like my friend Lance Egan, focus on casts that tend toward more quartering-upstream than across. Casts that are made diagonally from 5 to 30 feet upstream and 5 to 12 feet across fit into this zone. Drifting this zone creates pros and cons that lie between fishing upstream and fishing up and across.

Fishing at a quartering-upstream angle has the benefit of allowing you to stay downstream of most of your target fish, but also allows a longer drift with the sighter off the water—though not as long as casting more diagonally across the river.

Most drifts made at this angle terminate when the flies have drifted to a position that is even with your feet—in other words, when your rod is about perpendicular to the river currents. Because the cast is not made very far across the river, if you allow the rig to drift past your position, it will drift through water where fish have likely been spooked. In addition, if your rod is extended out over the river, it will track a lateral arc over the river and force your flies to trace across the currents when they reach below your position.

Because the drift focuses mainly on water that is still upstream, the sighter tends to stay at a shallower angle, which can give the appearance that the flies are being led downstream faster than the current. However, to achieve the best drift when quartering upstream, the rod is still moved downstream at the approximate speed of the water where the flies are drifting. What provides most of the tension for strike detection is the

Fishing quartering-upstream mixes the benefits and challenges of fishing upstream, or up and across. You can stay below the fish using a quartering-upstream presentation and spook less of them. However, your drifts will be shorter, and downstream drifts with nymphs ascending through the column are not possible.

Each angler forms his or her own style. Lance Egan tends to focus more on quartering-upstream drifts instead of up-and-across presentations. As a result, his sighter stays at a shallower angle during the drift because the cast is terminated before the sighter reaches under the rod tip.

If his impressive competition history wasn't enough, maybe this brown trout will convince you that Lance knows how to catch fish. Lance and I have formed different nymphing styles over the years, yet we are both successful on the water. Don't be afraid to experiment with your own techniques; just make sure you get in touch with me to share your secrets!

weight of the leader creating a slight amount of sag, which pulls slightly on the flies and maintains contact.

Because the leader does not reach a vertical angle when fishing quartering-upstream, it may be necessary to fish more tippet or fish flies slightly heavier to reach the same depth. For instance, when I'm fishing with Lance, he often has 12 to 24 inches more tippet to his first fly than I do. He uses quartering-upstream casts with a shallower sighter angle during the drift much of the time. He also places his heavier fly on the dropper tag and prefers more tippet to get both flies to depth. I tend to cast more across the river where my sighter can reach a vertical angle during the middle of the drift. Usually, we are both similarly successful, which shows there is room for flexibility in the execution of a proper drift.

Occasionally it can be beneficial to lead the flies slightly faster than the current. Most of the time I use this tactic, with a quartering-upstream cast, to cover water that is shallower than the surrounding water. A typical scenario would be moving from a deep pool into a short shallow riffle and then to a deeper run upstream. I may need the same amount of weight in the pool and run, but I don't want to change flies to fish the riffle for a few casts. Instead, I will make short drifts through the riffle with my sighter tight and at a shallow downstream angle. To reduce the sink rate, I will move the flies slightly faster than the current they reside in. If I need a further reduction in sink rate, I will elevate the sighter above the water as well, until I'm able to drift without repeatedly touching bottom.

Fishing Down and Across

Another sighter-angle trick that can be useful at times is inverting the sighter and extending the length of the downstream drift. I first watched my teammate Pat Weiss do this during practice for the 2013 US National Fly Fishing Championship in Colorado.

We were fishing a mid-depth run on the Roaring Fork River in fairly cold temperatures. He stopped his rod about one-third of the way into his drift and let his flies and sighter travel downstream of his rod. Once the sighter angle had reached a few degrees downstream of his rod, he began moving his rod downstream again occasionally, at a slightly slower pace than the river. When his point fly ticked bottom, he would lift the rig slightly and allow it to continue drifting.

He caught a couple of fish with this method at the time, but it wasn't a silver bullet during practice that day. I wrote it off as another Pat trick, of which there are many, and didn't think much more about it. In the intervening years I've seen times when Pat is able to catch fish that have ignored standard dead-drift presentations using this method, especially in cold water.

He used it very successfully during our case studies in later chapters, which were done in cold January conditions. This type of drift also helped catch some heavily pressured European grayling in Slovakia for our team during the 2017 World Fly Fishing Championship.

Induced takes

Learning to manipulate the angle of your sighter during the drift can drastically increase your versatility and success when Euro-nymphing. Another important trick is learning to induce takes by adding mobility to your drifts. Many times, fish will respond to dead drifts initially but shut down after repeated drifts. A simple 3- to 4-inch jigging motion with the rod tip during the middle and end of the drift can provoke aggressive takes from fish that need some extra convincing.

Let me provide an example. A couple of years back I was fishing the Salmon River in Idaho. The water was exceptionally clear, and I could see several dozen whitefish and trout holding in a rocky run in front of me. I worked the run with standard drifts for a while and landed 10 fish. Then it was like someone flipped a switch, and I made around a dozen drifts without

Pat Weiss is a master of making small, unorthodox adjustments to his rigs and drifts, which produce big results. One adjustment he often makes is stopping the rod midway through the drift to create a long drift with a downstream sighter angle. Sometimes the fish can't leave this drift alone when others fail.

Adding motion to your flies during the drift can convince stubborn fish to eat. Try making a 3- to 4-inch gentle jigging motion with your rod tip midway through a drift when conventional dead drifts are failing.

a take. I could still see the fish, but they were simply ignoring my flies. I knew I either needed to change my flies or add motion to them during the drift. Since it did not require manipulating my rig, I chose the latter.

On the next drift, I waited until my flies had sunk and reached the midpoint of the drift. I gently lifted the rod 3 to 4 inches and dropped it back down to jig the flies up and then immediately allow them to sink again. I caught a fish on my first drift as my flies dropped back to depth, and on many of the drifts thereafter, until I had landed a dozen fish—two more than with standard dead drifts. Most of the time the results are not this drastic, but this experience has served as a solid reminder when I've needed it, to try adding motion to my drifts before I make other changes.

Another benefit of adding the occasional lift during the drift is eliminating vertical drag. In his book *Moving Water: A Fly Fisher's Guide to Currents*, Jason Randall describes vertical drag when fishing a strike-indicator nymph rig. Because of the faster-velocity currents present high in the water column, the leader forms a downstream belly that speeds up your flies and lifts them upward. Jason describes twitching the indicator

upstream during the drift to intentionally lift the flies and straighten the leader. After the twitch, they drop back to depth without tension from the upper part of the leader while the vertical drag is temporarily removed.

When Euro-nymphing, there isn't the added drag-inducing component of the strike indicator. However, vertical drag will still form as the tippet in the upper part of the column is pulled downstream by currents faster than where your nymphs are. One way to reduce vertical drag is by fishing thinner-diameter tippet, which naturally avoids more of the water's dragging force. The other way is using the slight jigging motion I described above.

Similar to what Jason Randall describes when fishing a strike indicator, this up-and-down jigging motion straightens the tippet, removes the vertical drag, and then allows the flies to sink with some momentary slack. This motion has the same effect as making a tuck cast during the middle of your drift. It seems counterintuitive that lifting your nymphs can actually help them get deeper, but, if you try it, you will see that your flies often touch bottom immediately after the small jigging

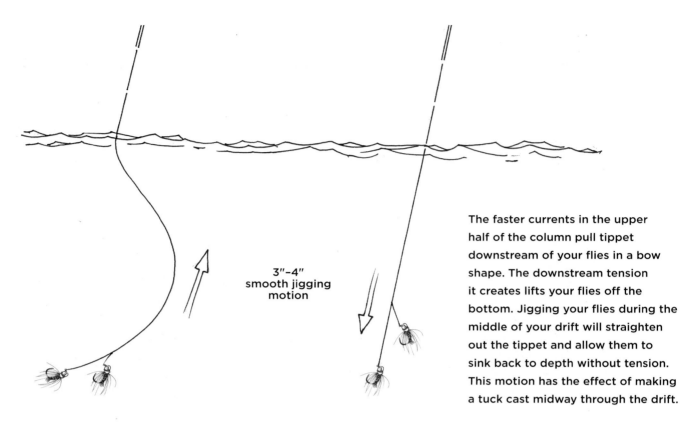

3"–4"
smooth jigging
motion

The faster currents in the upper half of the column pull tippet downstream of your flies in a bow shape. The downstream tension it creates lifts your flies off the bottom. Jigging your flies during the middle of your drift will straighten out the tippet and allow them to sink back to depth without tension. This motion has the effect of making a tuck cast midway through the drift.

motion. This is a clear sign that they are deeper than they were prior to the lift-and-drop motion. However, don't go overboard; keep the motion to a gentle 3 to 4 inches, and only use it once or twice per drift.

Adjusting for depth

One of the most common questions beginning Euro-nymphers ask is, "How do I know when my flies are deep enough?" The most obvious way is if your sighter stops and you set the hook on the bottom and not on a fish. Ideally, you should touch the bottom every three to five drifts in the latter half of your drift. If you are repeatedly touching bottom early in the drift, your flies are below the trout, and you need to adjust your rig for depth, as we will talk about below. Remember that trout are drift feeders and not benthic feeders most of the time, so "bouncing the bottom" constantly with your flies is counterproductive.

However, it is important to get your flies near the bottom on most drifts. In addition to your flies touching the bottom, you can infer their depth from the behavior of your sighter. At the beginning of your drift the sighter will drift close to the speed of the surface current. If you look closely, you will see your sighter slow down, sometimes abruptly, as it progresses to the middle portion of the drift. The sighter will also usually tighten. When this happens, your nymphs have sunk to

the much slower currents near the boundary layer, just above the bottom. If your rig fails to slow down and you never touch bottom where you are fishing, then it's time to make an adjustment to get your flies deeper.

One of the great things about a Euro-nymphing rig is how many ways you can adjust for depth without making changes to your rig. To increase efficiency, I prefer to make changes to my presentation first. If these changes are insufficient to gain the desired change in depth or sink rate, then I will take the time to alter my rig. Here are some ways to alter your depth through presentation:

Change your casting length. To get deeper in the column, cast farther above your target lie to allow more sinking time. To stay shallower, cast shorter to reduce sinking time.

Change your sighter angle. To get deeper, allow the sighter to reach a vertical angle through the middle of the drift. As I mentioned above, you can also add a slight jigging motion once or twice during the drift to reduce vertical drag. To stay shallower, lower the rod tip and provide more downstream tension to lead the flies slightly faster.

Change your sighter elevation. This one is simple. To get deeper, drop the sighter down near the surface of the water. Letting it sink underwater will increase the vertical drag and can actually reduce the maximum depth your flies will reach. To stay

To make a tuck cast, start with a normal backcast, but stop the rod high behind your head. Ensure you have enough energy in the stroke to fully turn over your cast behind you, as the forward stroke needs a lot of rod load to execute properly.

Make a tight-looped forward cast with plenty of energy and line speed. Add a single haul for extra energy if necessary. Aim your rod tip at an imaginary target high over your head and come to a hard rod stop. The high hard stop will turn over your rig abruptly and force it to curve vertically toward the water.

Immediately after the rod stop, extend your arm up and out. This will add some slack to your line to allow it to pile on top of where your flies enter the water. The slack will let your flies sink quickly without tension.

Adjusting for Depth

Staying Shallow	Getting Deep
• Shorter casts near your target	• Cast farther above your target
• Lead flies with shallow sighter angle	• Allow the sighter to get vertical
• Lift sighter higher off the water	• Fish with the end of the sighter just barely out of the water
• Shorten tippet and fish lighter flies	• Remove vertical drag with a jigging motion
• Turn over cast with a horizontal leader entry into the water	• Lengthen tippet and add heavier flies
	• Tuck cast

If you need help remembering strategies for adjusting depth, take a picture of this cheat sheet and stick it in your fishing pack. Take a quick look when you need a reminder.

shallower, raise the sighter above the water during the drift.

Change the entry angle of your flies. To get deeper in the column, stop the rod high with a tuck cast to drive the flies to depth with a vertical entry. To stay shallower, stop the rod lower and allow it to drop as the flies turn over. This will promote full horizontal turnover of your leader and expose the full length of the tippet to the water, which will slow the descent of your flies.

The tuck cast, made famous by George Harvey and Joe Humphreys, forces your fly to enter the water vertically, which drives it to depth. It also stacks your sighter on top of your fly to allow slack for your fly to sink until your sighter moves downstream far enough to gain tension. The steps to the tuck cast are found in the photo sequence on the previous page.

If you've used several of the techniques in the list above and still haven't reached the desired depth, there are two ways to alter your depth by changing your rig:

Change the length of your tippet. To get deeper, add more tippet. To stay shallower, remove tippet.

Change your weight. Obviously, if you add weight you will get deeper, and if you remove weight, you will stay shallower. You can change the weight of your rig by changing the bead size of your nymphs, or changing to nymphs that also have added weight under the body dressing. The other way to change weight is to add or subtract nymphs from your rig.

Dealing with wind

A common challenge when Euro-nymphing is dealing with the wind. Proper drifts are built from a foundation of maintaining control over your leader and sighter. In the wind, they can act like a kite, and all control is lost. Here are some common strategies for dealing with the wind:

Fish heavier flies. The extra weight will counteract some of the force the wind has on your leader and maintain tension for proper drifts and strike detection.

Lower your rod tip to expose less of the leader to the wind. You may also need to lean the rod tip into the wind to keep it from moving the rod and leader uncontrollably. If the wind is coming

If the wind is too strong to attain proper Euro-nymphing drifts, I switch to a dry-and-dropper rig. The dry fly anchors in the surface and resists the push of the wind.

The proof is in the pudding, as they say. The most obvious benefit of streamers on a Euro-nymphing leader is having shots at fish like this bull trout I caught during the filming of *Confluentus: The Merging of All Things.* (PHOTO BY CHRIS CUTLER)

from downstream, this means you will need to lead the flies downstream slightly. If the wind is from upstream, the leader will form a downstream bow shape as you lean your rod upstream into its force.

Fish more upstream than across. When fishing across, the profile of your leader is exposed to the wind, assuming it is blowing from upstream or downstream. By fishing upstream, the leader will be in line with the wind instead of presenting its profile, and less surface area of the leader will be exposed to grab wind like a kite.

If the wind blows hard enough that the above strategies are not enough, use a dry-and-dropper rig or strike indicator to anchor your rig in the water's surface tension.

One last strategy to consider when dealing with the wind is the specific location you fish on a river. If you can find a piece of water where the river bends and flows perpendicular to the wind, the force of the wind will be less than where the river is parallel. If your chosen water has a lot of riparian vegetation or a high

bank as well, then much of the wind will be blocked, and you can find refuge on some very windy days.

Streamers on a Euro-Nymphing Leader

Before I end this chapter, I wanted to quickly mention some benefits of fishing streamers on a Euro-nymphing leader, as well as some basic strategies for doing so.

Many people do not see drag as a significant issue when fishing streamers because most streamer presentations employ a swimming movement rather than a dead drift. This may be the case when fishing broad runs and glides where drastic changes in current speed do not occur from one bank to the other. However, when the line and leader cross multiple speeds of current, many times the streamer is quickly pulled away from the targeted strike zone by drag somewhere else on the rig. This offers only a quick view for potential target fish before the streamer is ripped away at unnatural speed.

Tony Morrissey wanted to try streamers for the first time on a recent trip. He caught trout with dead drifts, but the most successful "retrieve" of the day was a 6- to 12-inch-long lateral upstream jigging motion with the rod tip.

Tony Morrissey's first brown trout on a streamer. Look out, Irish brown trout, as he's coming your way with a new bag of tricks.

Fishing streamers on a Euro-nymphing leader solves this issue in the same way it solves a lot of nymphing issues. Trout are more likely to eat a potential food item if they anticipate gaining more energy than they expend to capture it. Because only the tippet enters the water when the sighter is held above, it is possible to drift streamers through target lies for an extended period of time. Dead drifts or retrieves with a more-natural speed end up resulting in more-committed takes. Furthermore, it is easier to get your streamer to a taking depth and keep it there.

Drifting streamers is not that different from drifting nymphs on a Euro-nymphing leader. The basic dead drift can work, but much of the time I add extra movement. I may start with one or two jigging motions per drift, but experiment with three or four. My typical streamer jigging motion moves the rod tip up and down 6 to 12 inches instead of the smaller movements I employ with nymphs. I overweight most of my streamers to still allow them to sink despite the extra movement.

When a drift approach does not seem to work, I employ lateral motion with the rod tip. For this approach, I make lateral jigging motions with my rod tip that are 6 to 18 inches long. To manage slack, I hand-twist during the retrieve, or I strip line as I'm making the drop of the jigging motion. I experiment with jigging the rod tip upstream to keep my flies dangling in front of trout, as well as pointing the rod downstream to move the streamer laterally across the river.

A big benefit of moving streamers with the rod tip is setting the hook. When stripping streamers, trout often grab in between strips and let go quickly before the next strip can be made or the rod tip can be swept. This results in a lot of missed takes. When moving my flies with the rod, I am always ready to set the hook. Combined with the heightened strike detection of the Euro-nymphing leader, I miss far fewer fish than I do with typical cast-and-retrieve streamer presentations on a "normal" fly line and leader.

CHAPTER 4

There's a lot of potential water to cover in this photo. Deciding which water is most likely to hold fish can be an intimidating process at first. In a large river, look at a small section of water and break it down like it's a small river. Find variations in current speed and depth. Then ask yourself which water will provide food, energy savings, and protection, and you will be on your way to knowing where to predict the best locations for trout to hold.

Energy and Currents: Where and Why Trout Hold

There is a fundamental concept in ecology referred to as an organism's *fitness*. This isn't exactly the same fitness we humans think of when we look at ourselves in the mirror, although it may be related. Rather, ecological fitness is how successful an organism is at passing on its genes. In order for an organism to pass on its genes, it must take in enough energy for maintenance, growth, and production of gametes, while at the same time avoiding becoming prey for another organism.

Optimal foraging theory is an ecological paradigm that describes the behavioral choices organisms make as they seek to maximize their fitness. Essentially, this theory likens these choices to those of an investor running a basic cost–benefit analysis. Like an investor, an organism seeks to maximize its fitness with the least possible cost. The goal is to take in the most energy possible with the least energy expended in capturing it, while simultaneously avoiding death in the process.

How does this theory apply to trout in a river?

Trout living in rivers have a different situation than most other organisms. In order to find food, terrestrial animals must actively seek out locations where food can be found. In contrast, river-dwelling trout live in a medium that brings the food to them, while they hold their station. Most anglers refer to these stations as *trout holding lies*.

The idea of "holding station" may sound a little misleading. Trout are not lazy creatures that live a sedentary life while the river provides them with a steady conveyor belt of food. Their reality is a bit different. Instead of the river acting like a conveyor belt, it's more like a downward-moving escalator that the trout has to climb continually, while the side rails occasionally bring food past. Imagine each potential holding lie as an escalator with a unique incline and speed of travel. The goal for the trout becomes sorting out which escalator delivers the most food to them with the shallowest incline or slowest speed. Faster or steeper

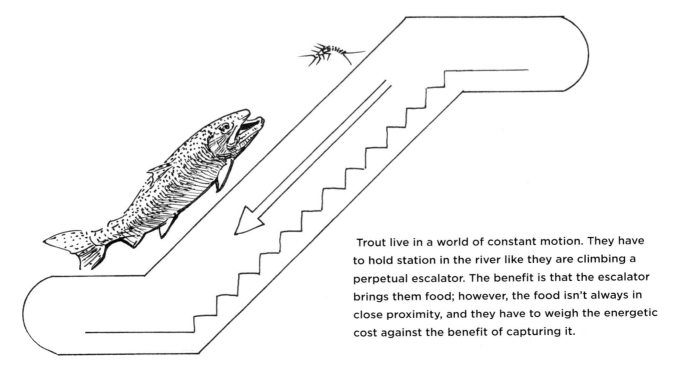

Trout live in a world of constant motion. They have to hold station in the river like they are climbing a perpetual escalator. The benefit is that the escalator brings them food; however, the food isn't always in close proximity, and they have to weigh the energetic cost against the benefit of capturing it.

escalators might deliver more food, but they require more energy to stay in place in order to intercept it. Factor in the trout's safety and its metabolic rate to this cost–benefit analysis, and the equation becomes even more complicated.

Let's leave the escalator analogy behind and head to the river. Imagine you are looking down on the river from directly above, seeing it as a two-dimensional space. Now divide this space into a grid with cells, each one the size required to hold an individual trout. Each of these cells is a potential holding lie, yet most are absent of trout. The reason why is that most of the cells are not energetically profitable. This means that the trout has to expend more energy than it can gain in return for occupying a specific cell. Alternatively, some cells may provide a good energetic return on investment, but they leave the trout more open to predation than a neighboring cell, which may provide less energy profit, but also less risk.

When anglers speak of reading water, we are essentially talking about trying to predict the results of the trout's optimal foraging decisions, which determine their optimal foraging locations. In other words, by looking at the river, where do you think trout are holding? The challenge is that we cannot put ourselves in place of the trout directly. We have to decide which of the potential lies in the river provide the most food for the least energetic cost and risk to the trout. As mentioned in chapter 1, these decisions must be informed by water temperature and hatches, because the energetic profit to the trout changes based on these variables. These decisions can also be informed by changes in sun angle or weather, which can alter how visible trout will be in a certain lie, and thus, how risky it can be for them to hold there.

Right now, you may be thinking, "All of this theory is great, but how do I put it into practice?" Reading water is a lifelong pursuit that takes a lot of practice and trial and error. While it may seem like accomplished anglers decide where to fish based on voodoo, that is not the case. The best anglers and competitors I know have developed a variety of different techniques and approaches to help them find trout in the river. Most of them have honed their abilities by fishing many different types of water during different conditions to see if they can catch fish. The best anglers also tailor their methods to find the best approach for each water type. After all, there may be fish in a certain water type, but if an inappropriate technique is used, the angler may

incorrectly assume it does not hold fish. Over the years, these anglers identify locations in the river where they do and do not catch fish under a variety of observed conditions.

The challenge for most anglers is learning where and when trout hold without spending years in the process of learning. The real gateway to shortening this learning curve is learning why they hold in certain places. I've already given you the broad answer above. Trout hold where they can attain the most energy for the least energy expenditure, as long as these locations do not subject them to overly high predation risk. So how do you as an angler learn where and when these locations exist? Let's examine a couple of quick principles.

Rivers: A Dynamic Waterscape of Currents

Currents flowing in a river are never equal from one bank to another, nor are they equal from the bottom to the top. During my years as a fisheries biologist, I routinely made velocity measurements for habitat surveys. When I lowered a water velocimeter from the surface to the streambed, I usually found the fastest water in the upper two-thirds of the water column, and much slower water near the bed of the river. In faster and deeper water, this difference was most drastic. In these water types, the velocity in the center of the flow often

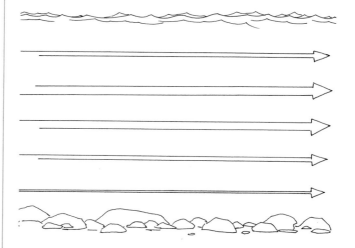

From the surface to the substrate, currents in a river are very different. In a typical situation without excessive turbulence, the fastest currents are in the top two-thirds of the river. Near the bottom there is a layer of water that can be up to four times slower than the fastest current in the upper column.

measured up to four times as fast as the current near the bottom of the river. The reason for this difference is friction.

Water near the bottom and sides of the river comes in contact with the river substrate. This substrate causes friction and slows the water nearest to it. Because water is a fluid, molecules only inches away can slide past with much less interaction at a higher velocity. Trout search out slowed currents to reduce how hard they must swim to stay in place. Naturally, this makes the bottom of the river the easiest place for them to reside. Here, they can draft in the slowed flow similar to how race cars draft behind each other to minimize air friction.

The size of the river substrate (i.e., its roughness) influences the velocity differential between layers of current. The smaller the substrate, the smoother the bed of the river, meaning that less friction force will be applied to the water moving past. On the other hand, rough riverbeds with large substrate have a more-drastic slowing effect on the water. Therefore, even in water that appears to be very fast, there will often be a layer near the bottom of the river where the current velocity is drastically less; thus, trout can hold there with minimal energy expenditure.

In addition to friction, changes in depth are another source of slowed flow and energy savings for trout. Picture a rock on the bank of a river that protrudes into the current and causes a recirculating eddy, as current that is deflected around the rock fills the space downstream of the rock with a spinning vortex or eddy. Now rotate that mental picture on its side to the middle of a riffle in the streambed. The same situation occurs when depths change in the river.

This principle was driven home to me while we were filming *Modern Nymphing Elevated* in August 2017. I was sitting on the bank of the river eating an apple while Lance Egan was being filmed. There was a small stream joining the river where I was sitting. Its bed was made up of silt originating from a beaver pond that it flowed out of. The current had formed small ridges in the silt with peaks and valleys traversing perpendicular to the flow. I watched little bits of sticks and vegetation flow along. After passing a ridge of silt, they usually were suctioned into the space downstream of the ridge. Sometimes they churned and spun repeatedly behind the ridge. I realized they were caught in vertical eddies just as floating debris gets trapped in eddies on the bank of the river.

Biologists and hydrologists use instruments to measure the velocity of the water at different locations in the column and across the stream. During my years as a fisheries biologist, I always found it interesting to watch the velocity readings change from the surface to the substrate. (PHOTO BY KYLE HORVATH)

Snow fences have the same effect as depth changes in a river. On the upslope and downslope, areas of slowed current and vortices form, which lead to sediments being deposited on the riverbed like snow. If sediment is deposited, food will be, too. If there is food, the trout will follow.

When depths plunge below a shelf in the river, or rocks protrude upward from the streambed, there is an expansion of space on the downstream side. Water flowing past must fill the void of expanding space, meaning the current will slow, and possibly recirculate into vortices of swirling current (i.e., vertical eddies). Trout are exceptionally adept at finding and using these vortices to their energetic benefit. Their lateral lines detect vibrations from changing current, and their fins can be finely tilted like an underwater sail to capture the energy of the recirculating current. This allows them to hold station in water that appears exceptionally fast from our vantage point above the surface, but may actually be drastically slower, or even flowing in a reverse direction near the substrate, where the trout hold.

Underwater current differentials are hidden from our view as anglers. Thankfully, with a little inspection, differences in current are much easier to see on the surface of the river. If you scan from bank to bank you will likely see currents in parts of the river that are faster than others. These changes are easier to spot in high-gradient fast water than they are in placid flat

When a rock protrudes out from the bank of a river, a current eddy usually forms to fill the void downstream of the rock. The same situation happens underwater, but the eddy rotates from a horizontal direction to a vertical one. Notice the upstream direction of the flags closest to the river bottom in this photo, from the film *Modern Nymphing: European-Inspired Techniques*. These flags are caught in a vertical eddy behind the large boulder above.

Current seams on the river's surface provide a prediction of the differences in current below. Where differences in current occur, trout can take advantage of slowed current to save energy while the faster current funnels drifting food to them.

water. Many times, currents will show drastically different speeds only inches apart. Most anglers refer to these areas of rapid velocity change as *seams of current*.

Seams of current are hot spots for trout holding lies. Depending upon the velocity, temperature, and hatches, trout may prefer to sit under the fastest current where the most food will flow past them per unit of time. However, much of the time, trout choose to reside on the slow side of a current seam. Here they can conserve swimming energy while waiting for food to drift past. If food drifts by in the faster water, it usually only takes a tilt of a fin to dart into and out of the faster flow to grab it.

Much of reading water becomes a strategy of combining what you see on the surface with what you predict to be below the surface. Each time you visit the river, learn to scan the surface for differences in current. Identify seams where currents of different speeds run adjacent to each other. Then look for changes in depth or underwater obstructions where vertical eddies and differences in current will occur. Further still, evaluate these locations for distance to cover. If you can combine slowed flow with access to faster, food-producing flows and a place to hide, you will have found the ideal trout lie.

In the next few chapters, I will divide the river into common water types. Within each water type, I will provide recommendations on techniques that target each of these water types best. To drive these points home, I provide case studies with real-world examples of implementing tactical strategies for each water type, based on the situation.

CHAPTER 5

There was a nice run below the boulder in this photo that held willing fish. However, I was glad I didn't skip the pocket below the boulder, as it gave up a nice brown trout. When you look at a piece of pocketwater, focus on the pockets instead of the surrounding white water, which can fool you into believing there is no holding water for trout in the area.

Pocketwater

One of the most overlooked and underutilized habitat types within rivers is pocketwater. On my local heavily fished river, and indeed, on many other rivers I have fished, there are well-known bend pools and runs. These locations are often occupied by anglers each time I pass by them. In fact, if I have a particular pool in mind that I want to target, I usually make a beeline for it when I first hit the river in the morning, knowing it won't be open for long. When I'm done fishing that pool, I usually find the other pools and obvious runs in the area occupied by other anglers, so I turn my focus to other water types.

I would say that the vast majority of anglers I run into on my home river focus only on obvious pools and runs. Many of them only fish a certain set of pools on the river where they have had success in the past. It's not just the average Joe weekend warriors that exhibit this pattern. Many of the guides on the river go to the same stretch of water day in and day out. When they secure a known pool for their clients, they regularly stay there, sometimes for the entire rest of their trip.

What's wrong with this picture? Well, nothing for me and the other anglers who are willing to break the mold a little. When guides and other anglers are only willing to fish the obvious water, it leaves large sections of water open to fishing. If I were the client in this scenario, I wouldn't want to pay a guide to park me in the same pool and make the same basic drift over and over for hours. There's not much to learn from this experience, in my opinion.

I look at all of the variations in current on a piece of pocketwater, and my mind instantly jumps to recognizing the myriad of potential trout holding lies. If you are the type of angler that skips pocketwater on your way to the next pool, you are missing out on some exciting fishing.

On my local river, and in many other archetypal mid- to high-gradient trout rivers, there is usually a stretch of pocketwater in between one pool or run and the next. Even though the river is often crowded, it's fairly rare to see an angler make more than a few casts through pocketwater before moving on to the next, more-obvious piece of water. This leaves a lot of open water for the angler willing to tackle it. The trout in these locations are often the easiest to fool with a proper presentation because they have so little time to inspect an offering before it passes by them. Furthermore, trout that are holding in pocketwater are usually there to feed. If the temperatures or conditions are such that they need to switch to energy-conservation mode, they normally opt for deeper, slower water if it is available.

Pocketwater is created by boulders that can be anywhere from the size of a basketball to that of a house in diameter. Essentially, pocketwater is just a riffle with large substrate that creates significant turbulence and very diverse current seams and patterns. While each rock and the hydrodynamic environment it creates are unique, the general form of currents display characteristics that are repeated wherever pocketwater is found. These currents are notably different depending upon whether a boulder protrudes through the surface or has water flowing over its top. Let's look at each situation in detail, and then we will discuss strategies for targeting the resulting holding lies.

Protruding Boulders

When a rock is large enough that the top of it protrudes through the surface of the river, the current displays a repeated pattern with associated identifiable holding lies for fish. On the upstream face of the rock, the water current is temporarily halted before it divides around each side of the boulder. Because water cannot compress like a gas, the molecules colliding with the face of the rock momentarily exert force back upstream before sliding around one side of the rock or another. This momentary stall creates a pressure wave that acts as a cushion that trout can ride. In a way, it is similar to a surfer descending the face of a wave, except that the wave is stationary and the downstream force of the current pushes back on the surfer—or trout, in this case. The interplay of the opposite forces often creates the perfect spot for a trout to hold, where it can expend very little energy to maintain its station. A simple

adjustment from one or more of its fins can capitalize on the forces of current to help it hold in place without constantly moving its caudal fin to sustain its position.

Interestingly, if the lie in front of a boulder has sufficient depth, then the position of greatest cushion for the trout is often near the top of the water column, on the face of the rock. I remember several trips where I first observed this phenomenon, quite a few years back. I had been fishing some local high-gradient canyon streams with high densities of brown trout. As I made my way upriver, working deeper runs, there were quite a few instances where I observed brown trout darting away in my peripheral vision. Upon closer inspection, I noticed most of them were riding the pressure wave on the front faces of boulders.

I started inspecting rocks more closely after that, and regularly saw fish suspended near the surface, upstream of boulders. I began to fish these locations more carefully as a result, adjusting my tactics to ensure that I covered more of the column instead of just near the bottom of the river, especially during times with warmer water temperatures, when I've noticed this phenomenon the most.

Hopefully I have convinced you to stop, observe, and fish the upstream face of boulders. Let's continue moving around the boulder and discuss further holding lies for trout.

Another often-overlooked lie for trout is on the sides of boulders. Most anglers see the eddy behind a protruding boulder and identify it as a likely site for a fish to hold. A smaller subset of anglers recognizes the upstream face of boulders as a potential holding lie, though they often struggle with a strategy to target them. Even fewer anglers realize the potential for trout to hold on the sides of boulders.

You may recall that earlier I wrote about the current-slowing effects of substrate. Even though most of us might not think of the sides of boulders as being like the bottom substrate that slows current near the bed of the river, they can act very similarly, especially when the boulder is large. Oftentimes, if the boulder is somewhat spherical, there is a recess near its terminus at the bottom of the river. This space acts exactly like a miniature undercut bank. These lies are often easy to miss because the surface of the river can be swift and turbulent, hiding the gentler current near the bottom of the boulder.

I first realized there were fish in these locations largely by accident. There were quite a few experiences

Each of the three Deschutes River boulders (one protruding and two submerged) on the lower left side of this photo held a fish on their front face. Do not overlook this type of lie, or you will pass by a lot of willing trout.

I caught four brown trout from the small piece of water in this photo. Two of them were nearly touching the side of the boulder in the center, and another was along the far-right side. Although holding lies on the sides of boulders are usually not obvious, remember that there's always friction in these places, which slows down the current.

There are a lot of crazy currents in this photo, but this pocketwater in a California river produced plenty of trout. The water temperature was 56 degrees, which made the trout willing to spread out into all available lies.

where I was fishing the upstream face of a boulder. I would start a backcast, after drifting a little farther than intended, and hook a trout from the side of the boulder. If I had not been paying attention, I might have thought a fish had followed my flies from the face of the rock and eaten them downstream. However, several times I saw a flash underneath the side of the rock where the trout had been residing, which confirmed its location.

One of the more memorable experiences that remind me of the need to probe these under-boulder lies occurred on a stream on the western slope of California's Sierra Nevada in 2014. The stream is not known for large trout, and indeed, I had mainly been catching 8- to 10-inch rainbows, with the odd brown in the mix. In one rocky run, I crept up and knelt on a boulder to lower my profile. I quickly hooked a small rainbow. As I bent to net the fish, a brown trout, in the 24- to 26-inch range, lunged from under the rock I was kneeling on and made off with my rainbow.

I was left shaking for a couple of minutes, but quickly turned to the thought of how I was going to catch the fish. Unfortunately, I fished an array of streamers and nymphs afterward and was unable to tempt the fish. When I waded out to inspect the far side of the boulder, I could see the boulder extended like a ledge into the river, from the bank, which left the perfect space underneath for an alpha fish to hide.

If you think about it, these types of lies have all the boxes checked for a prime feeding and refuge lie. The recess at the bottom of the boulder creates slowed current that requires less energy to inhabit than the full flow of the river, just inches away. The overhang of the rock, and the turbulent current at the surface, obstructs the view of overhead predators and provides a very safe place to hide. In fact, one of the best ways to find boulders that produce these kinds of lies is to look for a shadow near the base that signals a hole for fish to hide in. Moreover, the constant heavy current surrounding the boulder provides a steady conveyor belt of food items in the drift.

These lies may not always hold fish, however; much depends on the surrounding hydrologic environment. Like riffles, you need to pay attention to the temperature of the water in relation to the velocity and turbulence of the current. Unless the boulder resides in slow current, I generally do not find many fish inhabiting lies on the sides of rocks, unless the temperature is higher than 52 to 54 degrees F. While these lies do offer some slowed current, they do not offer the completely blocked current that lies on the downstream side of the boulder will. Therefore, fish are more likely to inhabit them when their metabolic rates are higher, and they are focusing more on energy consumption than conservation.

Downstream face of boulders

Speaking of the downstream face of boulders, let's investigate this classic trout lie. If a boulder is protruding through the surface and is separated from other boulders, there is a very repeatable set of currents that you must be able to read in order to identify the best places for trout to hold, and to understand where and how to present your flies. There are three separate locations in the currents I pay attention to in this situation, based on the directions of the current.

1) **Y shape**

As the current splits around the boulder, it creates a Y shape. The seams of current that split around both sides of the boulder form the wings of the Y. They begin to merge at the junction of the Y, and

then flow downstream in a single thread of current again.

In between those wings of current there is a void that water must fill. An eddy forms as a result, and the water flows back toward the rock. Depending upon the gradient and velocity of the river and the size of the rock, the eddy may be violently turbulent, or the currents may be relatively placid. In my experience, if the current is churning like a smoothie in a blender, it's rare to catch a fish immediately behind the rock. While there may be a fish tucked under a crevice in the rock, it's exceptionally difficult to get your fly (or flies) to depth with any sort of drift that will convince them to eat, or register a strike. However, if the currents are a bit more docile, it can pay to drift your flies along the seams into the downstream side of the rock.

Where the currents from the wings of the Y merge, there is usually a location where the currents experience opposing forces. Simultaneously, the suctioning force of the eddy behind the rock battles against the overarching downstream force over the direction of each molecule of water. This location may be a boiling-up well that churns with anger, or it may simply be a level spot on the surface, with no clear current direction. In my experience, unless the water velocity is low, it is somewhat rare to find a fish in the middle of the junction. This is likely because a fish inhabiting the space would also be tossed back and forth at the whims of the current.

Downstream of every protruding boulder there is a characteristic Y shape formed by the seams of current. Keep this mental image in your mind when fishing pocketwater, and it will help you to identify important locations to cast and drift to.

2) Center seam

Immediately downstream of the junction in the Y is the most classic of lies for pocketwater trout. Where the currents are coalescing, and begin traveling downstream together, there is a seam in the center that is slower than the faster veins that have split around the rock. Here is the perfect situation for a trout: There is fast water on both sides that constantly conveys food, which can be captured with a flick of a fin. This fast water often exhibits a turbulent surface as well, which obscures the view of overhead predators and offers a feeling of safety. Yet, in between these currents, the seam in the center is often drastically slower than water just inches away on either side. Here a trout can expend very little energy to hold station and capitalize on the culinary opportunities rushing past on either side. Depending on the diameter of the rock upstream and the gradient of the river, this holding lie can be inches or feet in length and width. The smaller the lie, the more likely it is to only have one trout. However, in larger, longer lies of this type, it's not uncommon to catch a half-dozen or more trout if the river has a high density of fish.

3) Downstream gradient check

The best of these types of lies are fortunate enough to have another rock downstream that acts as a gradient check. Here, the cushion on the upstream face of the rock interacts with and pushes back against the currents at the bottom of the Y, coming from the upper rock. This upstream force slows the velocity and increases the depth of the water, like a temporary dam. This situation creates the potential for the holding lie on the upstream face of the downstream rock, as covered previously, in addition to the chance for multiple lies upstream in the seam below the junction of the Y.

All three of these types of lies should be fished thoroughly, as they may have quite a few willing fish.

Submerged Boulders

When a boulder is submerged instead of protruding, water is able to come over the top, which changes the currents downstream. There is still the potential for holding lies on the sides and upstream face of the rock. The main change is the elimination of the eddy on the downstream side of the rock. There are still vortices forming vertical micro eddies on the downstream face

The large protruding rocks form the most obvious pockets in this photo of the Fiplingdalselva River in Norway. However, look closely and you'll see plenty of submerged rocks, which form terraces in the current. Many of these rocks created holding lies for brown trout, especially on their upstream face.

Lance Egan wades through some turbulent water in this photo. Notice that he's wading in a slight squat, with both knees bent. His weight is on the front half of his feet rather than his heels. If he slips in this position, it's easy for him to sit quickly and lower his center of gravity to prevent a fall.

of the rock. However, there is usually not a large suction eddy behind the rock, like there is when the rock is protruding through the surface.

As long as the boulder is large enough that it provides enough of a current break to be attractive to a trout, submerged rocks can be easier to fish than when a macro eddy is formed. The general direction of the currents is downstream and less conflicting. This means that as long as you place your fly (or flies) somewhat accurately in the downstream seam of current, they will not be caught in a suction eddy, which creates a more-difficult situation in which to achieve a dead drift.

The challenge for submerged rocks can be getting your flies to depth quickly downstream of the boulder. The surface currents will be much faster than the currents near the bottom of the river, which are in the slipstream behind the boulder. It can be difficult to reach the taking depth before passing downstream of trout holding behind the boulder. Extra weight and a tuck cast on top—or on the downstream face—of the boulder are often needed to drop your flies near the bottom as quickly as possible.

Strategies for Covering Pocketwater

Earlier I wrote about a local river where the pocketwater is usually devoid of anglers compared to the obvious runs and pools. Why do most anglers leave it alone? In my opinion, there are two key issues for most anglers that prevent them from targeting pocketwater: 1) The large boulders, turbulent currents, and seeming ferocity of the current make pocketwater intimidating to wade compared to other locations; and 2) The complicated currents in pocketwater are difficult to fish with a typical suspension/strike-indicator rig.

Wading pocketwater can be a challenge. However, with a good set of studs in your boots and the proper stance, it can be done. Whenever I encounter challenging wading conditions, I find it helpful to move in a slight squat, with my knees bent and my weight on the balls of my feet and toes. When I feel a slip, I can quickly deepen my squat and bounce back up. Most anglers wade timidly, with their knees locked and their back bent, and their weight on their heels. It's easy to lose your balance and not be able to recover in this stance. If you find yourself in pocketwater with really large boulders, it can be helpful to use a free hand to brace yourself as you move. With an extra point of contact it becomes much easier to avoid a slip and fall.

Now let's examine reason number two, and the characteristics of pocketwater that create challenges for a good presentation with a standard strike-indicator rig. Let's return to the typical midstream boulder in the photo below as an example.

The pocketwater around this boulder is typified by a chaos of currents, and exhibits the archetypal hydraulics produced by a protruding boulder. The currents that rage around both sides of the rock are separated from the slowed currents downstream of the boulder by slipstreams that are only inches wide. Downstream of the rock there is a suction eddy (between the wings of the Y) pulled into the downstream face of the boulder, followed by a turbulent zone (junction of the Y) where the current is pulled both ways, which in turn is followed by currents that are slower than the surrounding currents (tail of the Y), but still proceeding in a downstream direction. This environment creates a lot of challenges for the angler who wants to achieve a natural drift and detect strikes when using a typical strike-indicator rig.

Most anglers rig their strike-indicator setups with many feet between their indicator and the split shot. The split shot produces the sinking tension needed to signal a strike through movement on the indicator

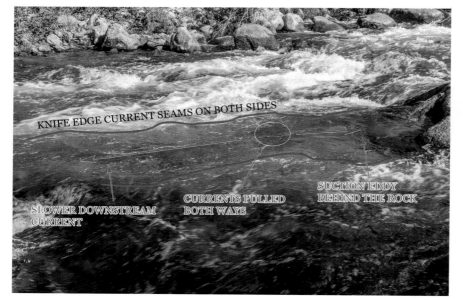

Protruding boulders create repeatable currents downstream. An eddy forms immediately downstream, followed by the junction of the Y, where the currents are pulled both ways. After the currents merge, they flow together at a slower pace in the same direction, but with hard seams on both sides of faster water. The most classic trout lie is just downstream of the junction, but trout can be found wherever they can find a break from the fastest current.

This diagram illustrates some classic problems of fishing strike-indicator rigs in pocketwater. When cast from downstream, the fly lands in the eddy behind the rock, and the indicator lands in the junction where the currents meet and flow both ways.

when a fish takes a fly. The issue is that the distance between the indicator and split shot is usually far too long to be able to fit both the weight/flies and the indicator in currents that are moving in the same direction, at the same speed. If they land in disparate currents—and they usually do—then they fight each other in the drift, meaning a dead drift is out of the question.

Let's examine this with the same rock, specifically. Keep in mind the picture of the river current diagram when interpreting the casting diagrams.

In this common pocketwater scenario, the angler casts an indicator-nymph rig into the pocket below the rock. The fly line, indicator, and fly all land downstream of the rock. However, the fly line lands in current that is traveling downstream, the indicator lands in the junction of the Y where currents are pulled both up- and downstream, and the fly lands in the eddy behind the rock. The fly line is pulled downstream, which moves the indicator downstream as well. Unfortunately, the fly is in eddy current that is going in the opposite direction, and as a result, it's swinging against the current. It does not drift with the current direction and speed in which it resides.

This situation is a drastic example of drag, which prevents the fly from looking natural. In addition, the downstream tension also prevents it from sinking. This creates a trifecta of unintentional circumstances. The fly is dragging, it is too high in the column for a trout to expend the effort to capture it, and strike detection is compromised because any trout that takes the fly

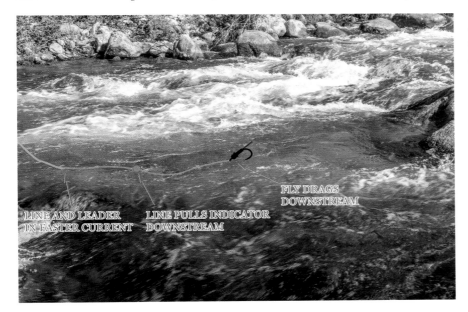

As the drift begins, the fly line pulls the indicator downstream, out of the current junction. The indicator then pulls the fly downstream out of the eddy, in the opposite direction of the current they reside in. This is drag exemplified.

Near the tail end of the drift, the drag continues. Here the indicator is in faster current at the tail of the pocket, but the fly is still in the current junction, being dragged downstream by the indicator.

would be swimming toward the indicator to eat the fly. The trout would have to reverse direction and swim back toward the rock before transmitting a movement to the indicator to signal the strike.

As the drift continues, so does the drag. The fly line drifts into current that continues to speed up as it reaches the tail of the pocket, where gradient and water velocity have increased. This pulls the indicator downstream. By this point the fly is in or near the junction of the Y, where it should be moving slowly—or not much at all—in the currents that are splitting up- and downstream. However, because the indicator is being pulled downstream, it in turn pulls the fly downstream as well, continuing the downstream drag. The fly continues to drift high in the column unless excessive weight is added to counteract the drag.

But what if the angler high-sticks the line off the water; won't this fix the situation? Unfortunately, the mass of the fly line will react to gravity and sag back toward the rod tip, until it reaches a vertical position below the rod tip.

This leaves the angler with two possible strategies to counteract the downstream effect of the current on the fly line: First, the angler could repeatedly mend the line. The problem with this technique is that mending results in excessive disturbance on the water's surface. In addition, the mending motion can increase the reaction time for hook sets, as the angler is often making a mending motion when a fish takes. Alternatively, the angler could wade close enough to the pocket so that his rod tip would be nearly vertical over the indicator, meaning that the line could be high-stuck off of

the water without sagging. The obvious problem with this strategy is that this kind of proximity can lead to spooked fish.

Let's look at a couple of other common fly-placement scenarios that hamper good presentations to pocketwater with an indicator-nymph rig. In the prior scenario, the fly line, indicator, and fly all landed downstream of the rock, but they suffered from the difference in current direction and speed that occurs longitudinally below a pocketwater boulder. Latitudinal current changes can present challenges that are just as detrimental to proper presentation.

In the common scenario depicted in the photo below, the angler has placed the line, leader, and indicator in the pocket downstream of the rock. However, the quartering-upstream casting trajectory has placed the fly in the white water sweeping around the far side of the rock.

Oftentimes anglers don't even realize where their fly has landed, because while they notice where their indicator lands, they often don't look for the splash of where their fly has entered the water. As you can see from the top photo on the next page, in this scenario the indicator and line drift in the speed of water wherein they reside, but the fly is ripped downstream in the current speed where it resides. The fly ends up swinging during the presentation, which again eliminates a dead drift and the possibility for strike detection.

You can try an easy experiment to assess whether this scenario is happening to you. If the water is clear, place a brightly colored large nymph on your rig. Something like an egg or mop fly works well, in fluorescent

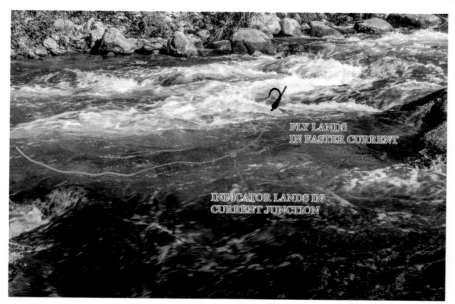

FLY LANDS
IN FASTER CURRENT

INDICATOR LANDS IN
CURRENT JUNCTION

When diagonal casts are made with indicator-nymph rigs, it can be difficult to fit the indicator and fly in the pocket behind the rock. In this classic example, the indicator has landed behind the rock, but the fly has traveled beyond into the fast water outside the pocket.

FLY SWINGS IN FASTER CURRENT
WITH NO STRIKE DETECTION

INDICATOR MOVES IN
SLOWER POCKET CURRENT

If the fly lands outside the pocket and into faster water, it will be ripped downstream while the indicator stays in the slow water behind the pocket. In this scenario, your fly swings downstream like a water-skier behind a boat.

FLY LANDS IN CURRENT
JUNCTION OR EDDY

INDICATOR AND LINE
LAND IN FAST NEAR CURRENT

This diagram depicts the opposite situation of the preceding diagram. Here the fly lands in the pocket behind the rock, but the indicator lands in the faster water outside the pocket. When this happens, the indicator races downstream and pulls the fly downstream, out of the pocket and laterally, into the faster water.

or gaudy colors. Make quite a few casts while watching your fly instead of your indicator. As you watch the fly, pay attention to its velocity, direction, and depth in the water column. It likely will not take many drifts to show that your fly is often not where you may think it is during the drift. This experiment will visually confirm to you how challenging it can be to drift a fly properly with an indicator rig in this type of water.

One last common scenario is shown in the bottom photo above. This situation is essentially the reverse of the scenario. After the cast has been made, the indicator and line land in the faster current that is near to the angler. Because of the casting angle, the fly travels beyond and lands in the slower water in the lee of the rock. The fast current grabs the indicator and fly line and moves them downstream quickly. The fly is quickly pulled out of the current in which it landed and is towed both downstream and across the current until it trails behind the indicator within the same current seam. While tension for strike detection is provided by this movement, the fly is dragged unnaturally and is not allowed to attain depth.

Hopefully from the preceding scenarios, it is clear that there are a lot of challenges to fishing a standard strike-indicator nymphing rig in pocketwater. I believe these challenges reduce the success of most nymph fishermen in pocketwater, and lead to fewer anglers utilizing this type of habitat. In turn, this leads to the often-too-crowded runs and pools we're all familiar with on a lot of pressured rivers.

Yet I've also written about the characteristics that make pocketwater desirable to trout. So how do you overcome the challenges posed by the hydraulic maelstrom in pocketwater? Regardless of the type of flies you choose, the sag- and drag-defeating qualities of the Euro-nymphing leader provide the best strategy. Additionally, these same advantages do not just apply to pocketwater. They apply to any water type with complex currents that can change drastically in speed and direction from bank to bank and top to bottom.

Let's break down the performance characteristics of these two rigs and how they might affect the choices you make regarding method. One of my favorite ways to fish pocketwater is with a dry-and-dropper rig on a Euro-nymphing leader. You're probably thinking, "You just spent the last few paragraphs explaining why a strike-indicator nymphing rig is a poor choice for pocketwater. Isn't a dry-and-dropper the same thing?" Like many questions in life, the answer is, "It depends."

There are four ways that a Euro-leader dry-and-dropper rig overcomes some of the drift pitfalls of the strike-indicator rig.

The first, and most obvious, way is that there is a dry fly that fish are also likely to eat. There are times when the fish just want dry flies, period. I remember a few days' fishing in a river flowing out of Colorado's Front Range during graduate school, when I was experimenting diligently with this rig. During several of these outings, I caught more fish in the same types of water than with a straight Euro-nymphing rig, and 70 percent of the fish ate a Front End Loader Caddis dry. When fish are willing to come to the top, the dry-and-dropper rig can be a big advantage, particularly in shallower pocketwater, where the fish have less distance to travel to intercept a dry fly.

The second way is that most indicator-nymphing rigs have a shorter distance between the dry-and-dropper than between the indicator and split shot/fly. I typically only rig the dry fly 18 to 24 inches above the nymph, whereas many anglers often have 3 to 6 feet in between their indicator and split shot, or nymphs. The shorter distance usually limits the dry-and-dropper rig to being effective in pocketwater that is less than 3 feet, unless the fish are willing to move. However, this shorter distance allows me, especially with some casting adjustments, to place my dry fly and nymph in the same (or nearly the same) direction and speed of currents. By placing both flies in the same speed of current, the potential for the flies fighting each other

Even in January, this rainbow trout decided it wanted a caddis dry fly. I always enjoy seeing fish eat a dry, and will commonly fish a dry-and-dropper rig through pocketwater before turning to a straight Euro-nymphing rig, to drill deeper.

in the drift is minimized and a dead drift is possible. The nymph's drift is still affected by being tethered to the dry fly in the surface currents that are bound to be moving at a different velocity. However, I try to minimize the effect by fishing dry flies that produce as small of a surface footprint as possible while still having the buoyancy to suspend the nymph. By using a smaller dry fly, the surface area of the suspension device is smaller than most indicators, and the effect that the surface currents have on the drift is lessened.

The third way is that the long, light butt section and tippet of the Euro leader allows clean high-sticking off the water. The reduced mass succumbs less to gravity, and the leader can be held off the water at a greater distance. Given the extra high sticking distance afforded by the Euro leader, I can wade close enough to a pocket to be able to fully lift the leader off the water to within inches of the dry fly while simultaneously staying far enough away to avoid spooking trout. This means there is no leader and tippet lying across the river's surface that can be caught in currents of different speed and velocity. This eliminates the need for mending. However, the effect is not maintained with the typical short, tapered leader that most anglers use for dry-and-dropper and indicator-nymph rigs. The relatively massive butt section and fly line sags back toward the rod tip if lifted off the water, which tows the rest of the rig along and sacrifices drift. In order to high-stick effectively with a short tapered leader, the angler usually has to wade too close and cannot avoid spooking fish.

Different sizes and styles of dry flies will have different-size footprints on the water, in addition to different buoyancies. I try to match the buoyancy I need for a given nymph with the correct dry fly. Larger dry flies will grab more surface currents like a large strike indicator, so I fish smaller patterns when possible to achieve better drifts and more-sensitive strike detection.

When fishing a dry-and-dropper, I regularly apply powdered floatant to my dry flies. This way I can fish small dry flies with a small drag footprint and still hold up the weight of a tungsten nymph. (PHOTO BY MARK OLSEN)

The following fourth characteristic is connected with the second and third, above, but worth a separate mention. Because the dropper is short and the leader can be held off the water, the nymph can attain verticality below the dry fly. There is little lateral deviation across the river between the dry fly and nymph, which means they do not cross horizontal current seams. This property allows me to stall this rig and slow down its drift in very narrow seams of current that can be wildly different from the surrounding water. I find this particularly useful along bank-eddy seam lines and in the downstream lee of boulders after the currents have merged.

The other way I typically fish pocketwater is with a straight Euro-nymphing rig, which confronts the hydraulic challenges of pocketwater in an even more productive way when the sighter is held off the water. While I reference European nymphing, understand that the nymphs could easily be replaced by streamers.

Here are four ways that Euro-nymphing overcomes the presentation challenges presented by pocketwater.

First, when fishing pocketwater with the sighter off the water, only tippet enters the water on a Euro-nymphing rig. When fishing an indicator-nymph rig, the indicator, the fly line, and thicker portions of

Euro-nymphing leaders can be lifted off the water to within inches of the dry fly on a dry-and-dropper rig. This removes the drag-causing effects that the currents would have on the leader if it was laid on the water.

When the sighter is held off the water, only tippet penetrates the surface. The angler is then more in control of how the fly drifts instead of relying on a strike indicator as an intermediary.

the leader all enter the water. Their surface areas are much higher than the surface area of a single thread of tippet entering the water, and they catch contrary currents like a kite. With the sighter held off the water when fishing a Euro-nymphing rig, the tippet in the upper column of the water will still catch currents that are moving, contrary to those where the nymph is drifting, but the force is much less than what an indicator, thick butt section, and fly line create. With less force from the currents, the angler can more fully determine the speed and direction of the drift through the angle and amount of tension on the leader.

Second, just as with a dry-and-dropper on the same leader, the long, light butt section of the Euro-nymphing leader resists the dragging effects of sag, particularly with micro-thin formulas. This property means the leader does not have to be fished under the rod tip to prevent the line from sagging back toward the rod and pulling the flies out of the drift. Instead, you can make drifts 10 to 20 feet beyond the rod tip. In addition, the typical 10- to 11-foot-long Euro-nymphing rod provides greater reach and distance from the fish than the traditional 9-foot rod that many anglers would fish.

Third, by altering the path of the rod tip during the drift, it is possible to drift all sides of an eddy. Recall from the indicator-nymphing scenarios above that the nymph will often land in the eddy behind a boulder while the indicator and line land in contrary currents downstream. This makes it nearly impossible to fish the

With a Euro-nymphing rig, it's easy to cast the fly to the far side of an eddy and drift around it to the near side. Simply trace the path with your rod tip during the drift and you can thoroughly cover water that no other rig can.

potential lie on the rear face of the rock with any sort of a decent drift. When Euro-nymphing, it is not difficult to cast to the far seam of the eddy and allow the flies to drift into the rear face of the rock. If the flies reach this point without contacting the rock, then it's possible to continue the drift along the near seam of the river by just switching the direction of the rod-tip path to trace the direction of the currents wherein the flies reside.

And fourth, the contact created by the weight of the nymph(s), and any rod-tip pressure applied, provides much better strike detection in the turbulent currents of pocketwater. Pocketwater trout are often forgiving of poor drifts because of the chaos and velocity of the currents around them. These currents provide the trout little time to make a decision as to whether a fly is food or not. However, it doesn't matter if they take your flies if you fail to register the strike. During my many years of indicator-nymph fishing, although I often saw flashes from fish that had taken my flies in pockets, many times nothing happened on my indicator to confirm that I needed to set the hook. While no method provides perfect strike detection, strike detection is vastly improved when Euro-nymphing, and more takes can be converted into hooked fish.

Much of the time I carry two rods when I'm on the water. In pocketwater, this allows me to swap between a dry-and-dropper and a micro-thin Euro-nymphing leader without having to re-rig. Sometimes it can be cumbersome, however, and I may only want to carry one rod for the day. In this case I usually either pick a micro-thin Euro-nymphing rig, or I opt for a modular Euro-nymphing leader that I can swap back and forth

between a dry-and-dropper rig and a straight nymph rig, simply by changing the fly on the dropper tag.

To help you figure out which way to approach pocketwater, make some observations about the river in general, and then specifically about the section you plan to fish. If you care more about seeing a fish rise to a dry than maximizing catch, the choice is easy. Otherwise, answering a few questions based on the strategies in chapter 1, and cross-referencing the characteristics of the dry-and-dropper versus straight Euro-nymphing rigs, will guide you to the best approach.

These questions include:

- Is the pocketwater over 2 feet deep, or is it shallower?
- Is the water clear, moderately turbid, or stained?
- What is the water temperature? Are there any insects hatching, or any that are in the trees and bushes in the riparian zone?
- Is it windy or fairly calm?
- Do I have one rod that will cover all of my bases, or two that I can rig with separate leaders to cover all potential lies?
- How large are the boulders and the pockets they create?

Based on the answers to these questions, you can decide how to rig appropriately to most effectively cover pocketwater. Let's examine how the issues above might affect your choice of the best rig.

Depth

If the pocketwater is deeper than 2 feet in most places, it will be difficult to reach depths near the bottom with

Good luck reaching the fish in the pockets at the head of this run with a dry-and-dropper rig. Water this deep and heavy is better suited to a Euro-nymphing rig, as Charles Card demonstrated when we fished here.

the dry-and-dropper rig without adding tippet. If you need to add tippet, then the greater distance between the dry and the nymph will begin to create many of the issues that the indicator-nymphing rig suffers from (outlined in the earlier photo diagrams). Therefore, I typically choose to use a straight nymph rig when fishing pocketwater that has a high average depth.

Clarity

Why does the clarity of the water matter? In my experience, the clearer the water, the more likely it is that fish will be willing to rise to a dry fly. In the experience I mentioned earlier, when I first started to fish dry-and-dropper rigs on a Euro leader, the rivers where fish preferred dry flies over nymphs were exceptionally clear, and the river bottom could be spotted in water that was 5 to 10 feet deep or more. Because fish can see farther in clearer water, it only makes sense that they would be more willing to rise to a dry simply because they can see one from a greater distance.

In addition, rivers that are exceptionally clear are usually *oligotrophic*. This means that they have a low

nutrient base and low primary productivity, which is typified by the lack of algae and plant particulates in the drift. If there is low productivity at the base of the food chain, then there will be low productivity in the higher trophic levels as well. As a result, the aquatic macroinvertebrate abundance is likely to be low, and the fish may need to rely more heavily on terrestrial inputs to the stream. In these types of rivers, trout are more likely to take dry flies because they are used to looking to the surface for much of their food. Therefore, if the water has a clarity where I can see 3 feet deep or more, then I will often opt for a dry-and-dropper first. However, if the clarity is less than 3 feet, then the scales may get tipped toward a straight nymph rig, where I can place one or two nymphs more consistently near the bottom, where I anticipate the fish will be.

Temperature and hatches

As outlined in chapter 1, water temperature determines trout metabolic rates. At lower metabolic rates, they usually conserve energy and are unwilling to move very far for food items. The opposite is true at higher

The exceptionally clear water of this western Sierra Nevada river gave the trout a predilection for dry flies. The rainbow trout here loved a Front End Loader Caddis fished dry-and-dropper style on a Euro-nymphing leader.

metabolic rates. If the water temperature is in the 50- to 55-degree F range, or higher, trout are more likely to be willing to move some distance to intercept food. In turn, they are more willing to take a dry fly or travel to intercept a nymph that is not in close proximity. However, if the water temperature is below 50 degrees, then the fish are usually not likely to move to eat a dry fly unless there is a significant hatch of insects occurring, or there happens to be a lot of terrestrials falling in the water.

Wind

If the weather is windy, the scales are tipped in favor of the dry-and-dropper. The dry fly will stick in the surface film and form an anchor for the leader above and a pivot point between the butt section of the leader and the nymph below. With that anchor, the wind is less able to blow uncontrollably around the butt section of the leader. Because the dry fly is a pivot point, some of the leader can be laid on the water and repositioned if necessary, to further control the wind's effect on the leader without having too much of an effect on the drift of the nymph.

Rods

Based on your observations and answers to the questions above, you should be able to choose which leader and rig best fit your pocketwater situation. If you have two rods available, then rig a dry-and-dropper and a Euro-nymphing rig and swap back and forth as necessary.

If you only have one rod to rig for the day, or you're not used to the challenges of casting a micro-thin leader, then use a modular Euro-nymphing leader and start with whichever rig you feel is most appropriate for the conditions. When it comes to choosing a single-versus a double-nymph rig, there are advantages to fishing a single-nymph in pocketwater. Single-nymph rigs provide the best accuracy. They also eliminate the possibility of flies dragging after landing in separate currents. Therefore, especially in shallow pockets with smaller rocks, single-nymph rigs are my first choice. If the rocks are larger and the water is deep and fast, then a double-nymph rig becomes advantageous.

When fishing pockets, I like to work from the tail to the head and from the near seam to the center, and then

The scenery and the trout in these mountains always make it hard to leave, but I'm glad we saved some time and energy to fish some pocketwater on our way home.

the far seam. This progression pulls fish from the rear of the pocket first so that upstream fish are not spooked. It also helps me drift my flies to all possible holding lies. If the water is cold, then I may make repeated drifts (8 to 12 or more) to the same potential lie in a pocket to coax reticent fish into eating. However, if the water is in the prime range (55 to 65 degrees), then I will usually make no more than four or five drifts to a likely lie without moving or changing my rig.

Size of pockets

Depending on the size of the pocket, in good temperatures I may make 10 to 30 drifts in the tail and middle of the pocket, and 5 to 10 casts in the eddy behind the boulder. If the hydraulic conditions suggest that there may be a fish on the side or the front of the boulder as well, then 5 to 10 more drifts are warranted in each location. If a fish can be seen that is not eating, then the whole process may be slowed, and I'll make changes to my rig, my casting location and drift length, and my wading location until I find a combination that works, or the fish is spooked.

Pocketwater Case Study

Now that I have outlined the rigs I typically fish in pocketwater, and the reasoning behind them, let me provide some concrete examples of how I fish pocketwater with photos from a recent summer trip. On our way home from backpacking, my Fly Fishing Team USA mate Glade Gunther and I stopped by a river that I have wanted to fish for a long time, but have always driven by on my way to the trailhead. It is a fairly small river that tumbles from the flanks of a high mountain range in Wyoming. Until it reaches the valley floor, the river is nearly one continuous stretch of pocketwater, with an alluring mix of basketball- to SUV-size boulders that hide trout in lies from obvious to sneaky.

Given the massive snow year the winter before, the river was raging more than flowing through some of the higher-gradient reaches when we fished it in late July. However, although the water was high and the wading was challenging—if not intimidating in places—the conditions were prime for fishing pocketwater. Perhaps because of the higher flows or the absence of more commonly sought-after pools and runs, we saw no other anglers on the river in the entire canyon.

We entered the river at a campground through the only obvious trail in the trees. While we were rigging I took a temperature. The thermometer read 57 degrees; at this temperature, I expected the trout to be spread out into just about all the available holding lies.

I rigged two rods, both with 6X tippet—small enough to minimize drag and increase sink rate, while large enough to land fish easily. The first rod I rigged with a dry-and-dropper on a modular Euro-nymphing leader. On this rod I tied a size 12 Front End Loader Caddis on the dropper tag and a size 14 Blowtorch with a 3 mm inverting tungsten bead on the point. They were hanging approximately 22 inches apart when held vertically.

On the other rod I rigged a micro-thin Euro-nymphing leader with about 4 feet of tippet to a size 16 Lite Brite Perdigon (butano version) with a 2.3 mm tungsten bead on the dropper and about 26 inches of tippet to the size 14 Blowtorch, with a 3 mm inverting tungsten bead tied on the point. This length of tippet allowed me to practice within the fly spacing required by FIPS-Mouche rules. Spacing nymphs closer to 15 to 18 inches apart can be beneficial in pocketwater with smaller rocks because both flies will fit into tighter pockets.

In the first location there was a cluster of boulders on the near side of the river. They formed a large, slowed area of water on their downstream side (location A in the photo on the next page). On the far side of the river there were several in-line, mostly submerged boulders, which created the only slowed vein of current in the surrounding white water. Even though the near-side pocket was formed by a cluster of boulders, if you look at the photo you should be able to see the characteristic hydraulic pattern typified in pockets formed by single boulders. The exception is that a thread of current cuts between the boulders at the head of the pocket, which divides the pocket behind the rocks into two eddies instead of one.

The pocket behind the boulders was deep enough that the double-nymph rig was better suited to it than the dry-and-dropper. The one exception was the tail, which was slow, smooth, and shallow enough that I

Glade Gunther hooks a trout in a beautiful section of pocketwater on a Wyoming river.

The location where we first entered the Wyoming River. Two pockets in this location produced fish (A and B). The numbers mark the locations where trout were hooked. The near-side pocket was the obvious location where most anglers would stop to fish.

began with the dry-and-dropper there. My first cast was along the near-side seam, near the small line of foam at the rear of the pocket. This location was close enough that I lifted all of my leader off the water, except for a few inches of tippet above the dry fly. The initial cast did not entice a fish, so I placed the next cast 18 to 24 inches farther upstream, to allow the nymph a little more time to sink before reaching the back of the pocket. The extra sink time sealed the deal, and as my rig reached location number one in the photo above, my caddis dry sank, signaling that a trout had taken my Blowtorch on the dropper below. A spunky fight with plenty of jumps ensued, and a lovely freestone rainbow in the 13- to 14-inch range came to my net.

I stayed with the dry-and-dropper along the near seam and through the middle of the pocket for about another 10 drifts. The dry fly did not stop again, which suggested that I was likely not deep enough in the pocket to entice any more fish, or to hook bottom. I switched to the double-nymph rig on my other rod. I expected a few more fish from the pocket, and I made repeated drifts up the near seam, in the eddy behind the rock, and along the far seam.

During warmer temperatures, in pockets like this one, I find that the fish are tight to structure and along

seams with heavy current. The structure, combined with the turbulent surface, offer visual protection from overhead predators. This pocket was large and slow enough that I would still expect fish here during colder

In pocketwater you are often rewarded quickly if you make the correct presentation. This is the rainbow that fell to my Blowtorch at location number one in the top photo, on my second drift through the rear of the large pocket. As I write this during the winter, it has me thinking of summer days and my favorite freestone rivers, whose pocketwater is currently locked up in ice.

Trout may not always be big in pocketwater. Much of the satisfaction of pocketwater fishing is pushing the limits of your presentation abilities to where you can make drifts and catch trout from complex water. This trout from location two confirmed that a tuck cast was the right choice to drive my flies to depth early in the drift.

temperatures, but I would anticipate finding them in the slowest central part of the pocket below the rocks, where they expend less energy.

Given that the temperature was prime, at 57 degrees, I was not surprised to catch my last fish in the pocket at location two, where the eddy collided with the seam of current splitting the cluster of boulders at the top of the pocket. My first drift at this location received no response. Thinking that my nymphs had not attained depth early enough in the first drift, I drove a tuck cast against the back face of the large boulder just upstream. The additional sink from the tuck cast provided the extra depth needed to convince another rainbow to eat my Blowtorch as it drifted at location number two.

Most anglers I know would fish this obvious large pocket and move on. However, in my experience, the long narrow pocket on the far side of the river (location B) is the type that often produces gullible trout during summer, and I knew it was worth the effort to reach it. The white water surrounding the pocket is intimidating and might appear too fast to hold trout. However, within the middle of the maelstrom is a narrow band of slower, flatter water created by the partially submerged boulder at the right-hand side of the photo. Immediately downstream of the boulder the water churns, but as the gradient lessens in the left half of the photo, you'll notice the turbulence on the surface is reduced as well.

In order to reach this pocket, I waded out into the larger pocket where I had caught the first two trout.

Most anglers would see a pocket in the midst of white water, such as location B in this photo, and pass by, thinking no fish could reside there. However, when water temperatures climb above 50 degrees, it is worth presenting flies to pockets like those in the photo above. They provide food and cover, and are easy to approach without spooking the fish holding in them. With the proper cast, drift, and weight, fish often come quickly in these types of pockets. I caught trout from locations three and four in the photo with 10 drifts placed carefully between the seams of the surrounding white water.

This trout made me glad I expended the effort to fish pocket B.

Though the water was deep, I was able to benefit from the current break behind the boulders at location A and get close enough to the far pocket to make a good presentation.

Pocket B was quick and turbulent enough to warrant a nymph-only presentation. It was the type that is difficult to land and float a suspending indicator or dry fly, along with nymphs, and maintain any sort of proper presentation. As a result, I left my dry-and-dropper rod in the dugout during my presentations there. I only expected fish from the center line of this pocket because the surrounding seams were too violent for trout to maintain position without excessive swimming. I made my first cast about halfway up the pocket, to give it enough sink time to be at the taking depth near the rear of the pocket.

I focused on making an oval cast with a backcast angled downstream, as close to parallel with the pocket as possible. By lining the backcast up with the length of the pocket and continuing around the oval a quarter stroke, as the flies were turning over, I was able to land both of my nymphs within the narrow lane of slower current below the boulders (see the parallel kick cast in chapter 10). On my first cast a brown trout about 11 inches long ate my Lite Brite Perdigon. I made five to six drifts more at the rear of the pocket, with no further success.

I moved two steps upstream and began casting closer to the rear of the rock, but below the churning current, 1 to 2 feet downstream from its rear face. After a couple of drifts, I switched my dropper nymph from a 2.3 mm to a 2.8 mm bead, to increase the sink rate. I also steepened the angle of entry with my next cast—a tuck cast—and focused on a vertical sighter angle to help increase the depth of my flies. The benefit was immediate, and on my first drift another rainbow ate the Lite Brite Perdigon on the dropper. I decided to move upstream after a few more drifts went unanswered.

As we moved upstream, the river eventually flattened and spread out for a short distance. The pockets in this stretch were shallower and more numerous, and reflected my favorite type of pocketwater to fish during temperatures when fish spread out. The numerous seams and boulders in the area provided lots of places for trout to hold, as is usually the case in this type of water.

We approached this piece of water from downstream to begin. There was a natural rim of submerged rocks at the downstream end on the river left side (lower right side in the photo on the next page). These rocks temporarily reduced the gradient and slowed the water upstream. They also provided hydraulic cushions, which created classic trout lies on their upstream faces. Glade

The second piece of pocketwater we fished during the pocketwater case study. I love fishing shallow pocketwater with midsize boulders, because the number of potential holding lies is so high.

The locations of the pockets and fish caught in the last portion of our case study. The pocket locations are marked with letters, and the locations of caught fish are marked with numbers.

A spunky little brown trout that fell to my dry-and-dropper rig.

and I planned to fish these smaller, less-obvious pockets and then move to the two larger pockets on the far side of the river.

As we approached the submerged rocks, I spotted a fish sitting in front of the rock at location one in the photo. I started with my dry-and-dropper rig and placed my cast a few feet upstream of the fish, careful to land the rig with my leader and sighter off of the water. Two casts in, I caught the foot-long brown trout that I had spotted at location one. It rose and ate my Front End Loader Caddis. Dry flies can work well in lies upstream of boulders, since fish are often suspended in the column and willing to rise.

Glade took the next turn. He was fishing a double-nymph rig on a thicker-formula Euro-nymphing leader. He made upstream casts, but focused on keeping his sighter off the water to reduce drag. It didn't take long before he scored a nice spunky rainbow from location two.

I hopped back in and continued to fish my way upstream on the same side. It is rare that more than one fish will hold on the upstream face of a boulder, so I did not spend too many casts fishing water we had previously covered, from which we'd caught fish. I worked my way up the right side, covering a slight bit of new water with each drift. I placed a cast 2 feet upstream of the rock at location three. As my dry fly began to slide downstream of the rock, it stopped. I set the hook into another brown trout that ate the Blowtorch on the point of the dry-and-dropper rig.

At this point, Glade worked his way over to the faster seam at point B. I expected a fish somewhere in along the edges of the seam, where the water spilled over the flatter pocket upstream at point D. None materialized, though, so he stepped within range of the pocket at point C. Glade started at the downstream near-side corner. He quickly caught a rainbow at location four. For my turn I continued to work back to front. This way, I planned to turn any fish that I hooked downstream away from fish farther up in the pocket, until they had cleared the pocket and could be leveraged across to my position without spooking other fish. It only took a couple of drifts before I caught a smallish brown at position five with my Blowtorch nymph on the dry-and-dropper rig. We were able to take two more turns in this pocket, with two more fish. I switched to my micro-thin leader and double-nymph rig to pick up the fish at location seven, where the turbulence made the dry-and-dropper rig less successful.

If you stop to look at the minutiae, trout are incredibly detailed creatures. This photo is of the caudal peduncle of a pocketwater rainbow. I love seeing the dashed markings of the lateral line and the fine spots on the scales.

The last two fish were hugging the seams, which split around the rock that formed the pocket. The eddy reversing into the rock was violent, and we were not able to catch any fish there. A nearly identical replay occurred in the next pocket upstream at point D. Here we worked from back to front again, and caught three more rainbows and a brown trout.

Throughout these pockets I fished a 3 mm inverting tungsten bead nymph on my dry-and-dropper rig. On my nymph rig I kept the 2.3 mm bead Perdigon on the dropper tag and a 3 mm inverting tungsten bead nymph for my point nymph. Glade fished two nymphs, both with 2.8 mm beads. We did not have to change flies, as the depth differential within and between the pockets was minimal. Adjustments for depth could simply be made by altering the cast entry angle (vertical versus horizontal), the length of the cast and drift, and the angle and elevation of the sighter on the nymph rigs.

It is also important to note that we worked each pocket from back to front, covering the near-side seam, the middle, and then the far-side seam. For the shallow pockets around point A, we approached from downstream and made upstream drifts from 15 to 25 feet away to avoid spooking the trout. For points C and D we used up-and-across presentations to increase the length of our drifts and their maximum potential depth. We stood near point A to fish point C, and used the waveforms in the current around point B to hide our presence from the fish. For point D, we used the same strategy as point C.

Our nymph choices were common patterns we both have confidence in. Neither of us fished especially imitative patterns. Instead, we fished attractor patterns (e.g., the Blowtorch), to ensure that they were seen in the turbulent water, as well as slim, smooth-bodied flies (e.g., the Lite Brite Perdigon), to increase sink rate. When fishing pocketwater, focus on your presentation before worrying about pattern. Fish are forced to make decisions quickly in the turbulent currents, so your pattern will not receive the scrutiny that it might in a slow pool or glide.

Make sure you approach the water in a way that minimizes your chance of spooking fish. Then ensure that you attain a dead drift by landing your flies in the same current and eliminating line lying on the water. Adjust the weight of your flies or your cast, and drift to get your flies to depth quickly, ticking bottom every few casts. Move regularly to cover new micro lies within pockets. Repeatedly casting to the same seam is not going to make a willing fish magically appear. However, make sure your drifts place your nymph(s) in the specific seam of current you are targeting. Trout in pocketwater are willing if they are shown a fly in close proximity, but they usually won't move very far to chase one.

CHAPTER 6

Rita "Rose" Adams fishes some riffles and pockets on a southern Colorado stream. Earlier that summer she taught me that I had been passing up too many riffles with fish.

Riffles

Riffles are overlooked as holding water in a trout stream. They are created when shallow water flows over a high-gradient streambed (0.1 to 0.5 percent or more). The surface of a riffle is characterized by repeated small waves. These waves form because currents are deflected around the substrate. Most often, riffles are dominated by cobblestone-size rocks.

Riffles are usually thought of as the food factory within a stream. Because they are shallow, they receive ample sunlight to power the photosynthetic algae that forms the base of the food web for herbivorous macroinvertebrates. Where there are herbivorous macroinvertebrates, carnivorous macroinvertebrates are sure to follow.

The frequent interstitial spaces, between the cobbles within a riffle, form important locations for insects to live without subjection to most of the water current's violent forces. In fact, macroinvertebrate studies show that the density and diversity of macroinvertebrates is correlated with the frequency of interstices within the substrate. The surface area of interstitial spaces peaks with medium-size cobble, which is often found in riffles. Smaller substrate tends to pack together tightly, leaving few interstices for non-burrowing macroinvertebrates to hide in. Large substrate creates the opposite effect, where the gaps in between substrate are too large to form tight-enough spaces for macroinvertebrates to seek adequate refuge within. Therefore, the abundance of food and hiding places makes riffles high on the list of desirable locations for many of the macroinvertebrates within a stream. If Goldilocks was a bug, she might say the substrate in riffles is "just right."

Despite the food availability within riffles, they are often low on the list of desirable fishing locations for most anglers. The lack of obvious depth and slower holding water convinces many anglers that most fish will be holding in the deeper run/pool below, or the tailout of the run/pool above.

I recently found an example in popular fly-fishing literature, in the story entitled "Wyoming" in John

A brown trout I coaxed from a shallow riffle on a CDC Flying Ant pattern. I crept into a quartering-downstream position and made a 25-foot upstream reach cast to ensure a long-enough dead drift.

This shallow riffle did not appear very fishy at first glance, but that did not stop Lance Egan from catching a brown trout there in December.

Gierach's book, *All Fishermen Are Liars*. In the story Gierach recalls driving past 40 miles of a stream he describes as "a uniform riffle, lacking the obvious pools, plunges, and glides of recognizable trout water." Only when forced back downriver because of a bridge being out did he turn around and head back downstream. After making camp, he and his friend Doug started fishing the river behind camp, without a lot of confidence. However, they both quickly started catching Snake River cutthroats from any small depression within the broad riffles that might have just enough depth to hide a trout. Not only did they catch good numbers of trout, but they also caught outsize trout numbering in the high teens. In fact, they ended up staying an extra day to sample the fishing in a river they originally had little confidence in, after deciding it could qualify as the "longest continuous riffle in North America."

Gierach's experience is not surprising. Riffles can often appear completely uniform at first, with no obvious seams, slicks, or depressions that appear deep or slow enough to hide a trout. I used to largely skip over most faster riffles as well, until one trip I had back in 2007 while fishing with a couple of clients on a tributary of a river in southern Colorado. One of the

clients, Rita "Rose" Adams, was a guide herself, who had fished small brown trout streams in New Mexico and Colorado for years. Her experience taught me a lesson that day.

At one spot in the stream we were fishing, she stopped to make a few casts in a steep riffle. There was no obvious holding water and the gradient was significant. There were not even very many larger rocks to create obvious waveforms on the water. I told her there wouldn't be any fish holding in there, and that it was a waste of time. Thankfully, she ignored my advice and promptly caught a couple of nice brown trout from the riffle. I was surprised, to say the least. Even more surprising, when we crossed the river at the riffle to make our way farther upstream, around 10 more brown trout scattered as we waded through the riffle. Simply put, I was humbled, and I've never forgotten that lesson.

Another defining experience I had occurred later that same year. When I heard, through a Trout Unlimited club, that the local fisheries biologists were looking for a few volunteers to help with an electrofishing survey, I jumped at the chance. It was more than educational, and partially inspired me to pursue my own education in fisheries biology.

We surveyed several sections of a river. The specific reach was chosen in an effort to try and encompass a representative sample of the habitat in the area. I had fished this stretch of river and knew we would find some fish, but I was more than surprised at the outcome. The biologists laid electrical wires powered by generators at the bottom and top of the reach to contain our quarry within the bounds of the survey. We completed a three-pass electrofishing depletion survey. All of the fish were counted and measured before being passed downstream of the reach, until the survey was done.

Using the numbers of fish caught on each pass, the biologists applied a regression specifically for electrofishing surveys that allowed them to estimate the number of fish within the reach. I did not see the final computed estimates, but I wrote down that we netted just over 430 fish within 430 feet of a small river—more than one trout per linear foot. It's important to note that electrofishing depletion surveys rarely capture more than 80 percent of the fish in a reach. Needless to say, I was floored by how many fish were within a single reach of river, in which prior to that day I had caught no more than 20 or 25 fish in any one outing.

In addition to the sheer density of fish we surveyed, I was astonished at where in the river we caught the fish. Because the biologists had been smart enough to not wade through the reach before we did the survey, we were able to see where the fish were holding as they tumbled toward the anodes at the end of our electrofishing wands. There were a few deeper runs and a pool in the reach. However, the majority of the fish we captured came from shallow riffles and tailouts that were 8 to 18 inches deep, and from bankside lies of similar depth.

I was shocked by how many fish I had been walking past when I fished there. The problem was that I did not have a rig or technique that reliably targeted shallow broken water with consistent results. This all changed that same fall when my teammate Lance Egan showed me a French leader and we enacted the H Creek Experiment I wrote about in chapter 3. The versatility and capability of long Euro-nymphing rigs when fishing this water suddenly became deadly apparent.

Contrary to common belief—including mine before the above experiences—riffles are ideal locations for trout to hold and feed during times when the temperatures are warm enough to raise a trout's metabolism

Does this look like a stretch of river that would hold more than one brown trout per linear foot of stream? Well, it certainly did back in 2007, when I participated in my first electrofishing survey in this river.

and generate a higher need for energy intake. While riffles often look fast, exposed, and inhospitable for a trout, the reality can be quite different. The same interstices and "roughness" that create refuge for macroinvertebrates often create current vortices that reduce the energy required for trout to hold station in the current.

However, even though riffles may provide good places for trout to feed, there are times when they will not be occupied by trout. Normally a thermometer, an eye for hatch activity, some prior experience, and a few presentations to successive riffles will let you know whether you are wise to target each riffle, or if your time is better spent targeting slower, deeper, and more-obvious holding water. While trout are adept at saving energy when holding in riffles, they still require more energy and alertness to live and feed there than in a slow pool. Therefore, riffles generally are not good locations to spend much fishing energy on during the colder months, though there are exceptions.

Strategies for Riffles

Hopefully I've convinced you that it's important to fish riffles. Now let's examine how to target them.

Like most water types, choosing how to target riffles typically depends on depth and speed. Most of the time, if a riffle becomes deeper than 24 inches, it has transitioned, or is transitioning, into a run, which I will cover later. Even though riffles are shallow habitat types, it is often best to work shallow to deep in the column and across the riffle if possible. Because trout are usually taking advantage of vortices and slow current near the bottom of the river, they can be reticent to ascend through the column for food unless it presents a significant source of energy.

In slower riffles, trout are often very willing to take dry flies, and these can be great locations to blind-cast with attractor or terrestrial patterns. Furthermore, when you find fish rising in riffles during hatches, they are often some of the easiest fish to raise to your dry fly because the speed of the current and the riffled surface of the water often hide inadequacies in imitation and drift, and only provide fleeting glances at your fly. Because the trout have a split second to decide whether your fly is food or faux, they can be easier to convince than a trout sitting in a slow flat where there is ample time to inspect your offering. When I'm carrying a second rod with me, I will often cast a single dry fly upstream with some sort of slack-inducing cast, such

as a parachute cast or pile cast. Alternatively, as long as the riffle is not overly fast, a shallow dry-and-dropper can be an effective way to try and cover your bases with a dry fly and nymph below.

When fishing a single dry fly, I usually take a quartering-downstream position. By angling a bit to the side of the riffle, I am able to show my fly to possible targets without the fly line and/or leader floating over the fish first. Furthermore, a slight angle to the side provides the best hooking angle. When fishing a dry directly upstream, the trout's mouth and snout may contact the tippet or the thorax section of the dry fly before accessing the hook point. This contact may push the fly out of the way and preclude the trout from closing its jaws around the fly, which results in a missed fish. By taking a bit of an angle to the side of the trout, the tippet will be out of the path of the rise, and the trout will be able to capture the dry fly and close its mouth around it, leading to better hooking rates. If the pace of the water below the riffle increases, it can be difficult to get a drag-free drift even with a slack-inducing cast. In this case it is usually best to approach the riffle from the side, where upstream or downstream reach casts (depending on the speed of water between you and your target) should be sufficient to provide a dead drift.

Regardless of your angle of approach, it is best to get as close to the riffle as you can without spooking the trout. If the surface of the riffle is highly disturbed or the water is turbid, you may be able to approach within 10 to 15 feet without spooking your intended target(s). However, if the water is clear and the surface is only slightly riffled, it may be necessary to fish 25 to 30 feet away, from either a downstream position, or by crawling into position and kneeling to the side of the riffle to keep a low profile. As I mentioned in chapter 1, my basic rule is if I can see the bottom of the riffle clearly, the fish can see me clearly too. I try analyze each riffle I come to from 40 feet or more downstream so that I can choose the best way to approach it without becoming a visual threat to the trout. Remember that riffles are shallow exposed habitats, and only shallow glides make trout feel more exposed to predators. Therefore, caution in approach will always bring better results.

The faster and deeper the riffle, the more likely it is that you will need to bring your flies in close proximity to the fish and near the same vertical plane within the water column. If you are fishing a modular

Euro-nymphing leader, you can work shallow to deep within the riffle by starting with a dry fly on the dropper tag and a nymph on the point. The dry fly will suspend the nymph over the shallow substrate and allow longer drifts through the riffle. It may also be eaten as a nice bonus.

I usually cast a dry-and-dropper rig upstream or quartering across. During the drift I hold the sighter and most of the tippet off the water so that only the dry fly (and possibly a few inches of tippet) are on the water. If the riffle is less than 10 inches deep, I fish 2- to 2.3 mm tungsten bead nymphs. To slow their descent and elongate the drift in shallow water, I make casts that turn over and land horizontally to present maximum tippet surface area to the water. If no fish are caught and I haven't contacted the bottom, I will switch to making tuck casts that drive the nymph to depth. If I still have not caught fish or contacted bottom, I make a switch to a heavier nymph, or I remove the dry fly and opt for two nymphs.

When encountering fast riffles and those 1.5 feet to 2 feet in depth, I find that fishing a Euro-nymphing rig with one or two tungsten nymphs is the most effective way to target them. I typically find myself fishing 2.3 to 2.8 mm beads in this type of water, but may turn to a 3.3 mm bead if necessary.

The best approach for avoiding spooked fish is by fishing upstream or quartering upstream with a greased and floated sighter. Keep your casting distance between 15 and 22 feet, and retrieve slack as your rig floats toward you to maintain a dead drift and strike detection, and to minimize the movement required to set the hook.

If the surface of the riffle is turbulent enough to diminish your view into the water, it will hide your presence, and you should be able to fish across from your target. Once beside the riffle, a typical up-and-across Euro-nymphing presentation is usually very effective.

When Euro-nymphing up and across in riffles, I try to get in contact with my nymphs very early in the drift. Because the water is shallow and swift, fish often take flies with lightning-quick speed. If you allow the nymphs to drift for long without attaining tension, and thereby strike detection, then takes early in the drift will usually be missed, and the fish will be wise to further attempts.

To fish this long riffle, I first made a pass fishing the slow seam where I am standing with a dry-and-dropper rig. I then grabbed a second rod and made subsequent passes in the deeper and faster water with a two-fly Euro-nymphing rig. Both strategies were tailored to the specific water I fished, and both produced trout.

When fishing up and across in riffles, focus on getting tension between your sighter and nymph(s) early in the drift, without affecting the dead drift. Takes can come very quickly in riffles, and will be missed if you have not achieved contact with your flies.

The best way to accomplish early tension in the drift is with a continuation of the oval cast (see chapter 3). While the flies are turning over on the forward stroke of the oval cast, continue the oval around a quarter-turn while also raising the rod tip to an elevated position above chest height. This movement tightens the leader during turnover and creates tension as the flies are entering the water. If they are under tension, even slightly, then strikes can be detected on the sighter.

Based on the first few drifts through a riffle, you should be able to determine whether you are too shallow or too deep. Fish in riffles are always drift feeders that predate on food items that are at or above their eye level. As such, I try to err on the too-light side of the fly-weight spectrum to begin with, because I prefer that my drifts sail over the head of waiting trout rather than under their belly. If you hook the bottom early in the drift, you are either too heavy, or you made your cast too far upstream.

For most riffles, I start with 2 mm to 2.8 mm tungsten beads, and use a single nymph for riffles less than 12 to 15 inches deep. However, often I am fishing heavier nymphs based on greater depth downstream. If I only have a short riffle to fish and I do not want to change flies before the next, deeper piece of water, I will lift my sighter 1 to 2 feet off the water through the drift to hold the flies off the bottom. Additionally, I may lower the rod tip and lead the flies downstream a little faster than the currents at the bottom of the river, which further lifts the nymphs off the bottom.

If I catch fish in the first few drifts, I'm confident that I have my weighting correct. If my nymph(s) sails through the riffle at the speed of the surface current instead of the slower bottom current, and I haven't caught fish, then I know I am too shallow. To increase my depth, I will try casting farther upstream if there is water of sufficient depth, or I will use a tuck cast to drive my flies to depth in a shorter distance. If I still have no interest from fish and I haven't ticked bottom in the downstream one-third of the drift, then I will consider changing to a heavier fly (or flies) to increase depth.

To illustrate where and how to fish riffles, the rest of this chapter contains two case studies. These case studies will help you to sort out where to look for fish in riffles, as well as how to put into practice the methods described above.

Riffle Case Study #1

The first riffle study occurred in July 2017 while fishing a small Utah river. There is ample access on much of the river, and it is regularly fished. This river is not known for high densities of trout, but it does have a reputation for growing larger fish than might be expected.

When I arrived at the river at the end of an access trail, there was an open section of stream with riffles on the river left side, sliding into a slightly deeper run on the river right side. However, the area was not an obviously prime reach, and there were more-desirable-looking runs and pools both up- and downstream. I try not to pass up water, since I often come across poor beats in competitions. I like to be prepared by practicing strategies for fishing them. As a result, I rigged up and started fishing before moving to more-obvious water. I was glad I did, because I ended up catching 10 fish from the stretch, including several outsize brown trout from water that would not be high on the list of most anglers' dream lies for big fish.

The water temperature before I started fishing was 58 degrees F. At this temperature, I expected fish in just about any water that could hold fish. The water was fairly low and clear for this stream. In these conditions I planned on fishing most shallow water locations either from a downstream vantage point or from a kneeling or crouched position, to avoid spooking fish.

Though I caught fish in several places along the reach, there was one specific spot that most anglers would likely pass up. I was fishing at the bottom of the

fairly shallow run at the access point. I picked up half a dozen fish in the tailout, the center of the run, and along an eddy seam on the far bank. I felt good about this success, as the water was open and somewhat featureless (see photo below, top). When I turned to move my way upstream, there were two deeper, swift, short, and narrow riffles on the river right bank (see photo bottom). I eventually caught fish out of the second upstream one after covering several spots along the way. However, these weren't the only holding lies available, and a less-obvious one held the biggest surprise.

The sneaky spot in this reach was a slight depression I could see in the shallow riffle on the river left side of the stream. I identified the depression by the slight color change of lighter-colored rocks arcing around a

The shallow run at the access point: I caught fish at the tailout, in the center, and on the far-side eddy seam.

The riffle that led into the run I started fishing at in this case study.

darker-colored depression (see photo diagram below). The depth change was not drastic or obvious, but I thought it might be enough to slow the current and hold a small trout.

I was fishing the deeper run with a micro-thin Euro-nymphing leader and two medium to lightweight nymphs (2.8 mm and 2.3 mm tungsten beads), with just under 3 feet of tippet to my first nymph and 20 inches to the second. The deepest part of the depression in the riffle was only 12 inches deep, and the current was fairly slow. I likely should have switched to two 2.3 mm beaded nymphs for this water. However, the depression was not an obvious prime lie, and I knew I would need to switch back to a heavier rig for the faster riffles above if I changed. Instead, I decided

to keep my drifts short, with little sink time above the target depression.

I positioned myself about 20 feet downstream from the target. I made one upstream cast to the depression with my flies landing at the lip of the depth change. I held most of my sighter off the water, expecting to make a couple of short drifts and then move on. To my happy surprise, my rig had not drifted more than a foot before it stopped dead. I set the hook, and a lovely brown trout exploded from the water with five continuous tail-walking jumps. I've found jumping is common for fish caught in riffles because they have no deep refuge to escape to, so they take to the air instead. After a spirited fight, I cradled a brown trout about 19 to 20 inches long in the net.

FAST RIFFLED SLOT = SMALL FISH

DEEPER RIFFLE = NO FISH

SLIGHT DEPRESSION = BIG FISH

My flies were too heavy for the shallow water, so I made my cast right at the lip of the depression (see red line at bottom of photo). A big brown ate on the first drift from the slight depression before my flies had even drifted a foot.

Large fish can be found in shallow riffles. This brown trout took a butano-colored Lite Brite Perdigon on my first cast to a slight depression within a riffle.

I caught another large fish just below the white water on the far-right side of this photo. At first glance it looked too fast for its shallow depth to hold a fish. I was glad I stopped to fish it before fishing a seam against the willows at the bottom of the riffle.

This scenario may seem like a fluke that isn't likely to be repeated. However, it happened twice more in the next 50 yards of river.

Just upstream of the previous riffle there was another riffle on the river left bank. This riffle was slightly deeper (~15 to 18 inches), and much faster. A few small rocks within it created a set of standing waves. At first glance, it looked too fast to be a likely holding lie. Trying not to pass by another surprise opportunity, I stopped and tried to look through the water. I found that one of the rocks creating standing waves had a small, flat spot below it. There were also overhanging willow branches in this spot, which I thought might provide proximity to safety to sweeten its desirability as a feeding lie. I decided it was worth a few quick casts, but I was actually more interested in the seam along the willows, near the bottom of the riffle.

I waded into position about 18 to 20 feet away, directly across the river from the riffle. I fished from my knees—not because I was worried about spooking fish under the waves, but because the lower position would help to slide a cast under the overhanging branches of the willows. My plan was to make a helicopter cast (see chapter 10) and place my nymphs about 3 feet upstream of the rock to allow some sink time before hitting the lie. I also made sure to stop the rod high enough to keep the sighter off the water and avoid the drag that would be caused by the water grabbing its thicker diameter.

To my surprise, my sighter stopped on the first drift again! I set the hook downstream and the water exploded in a froth. I knew it was another large fish requiring as much leverage as I could muster without breaking the 6X tippet. I put the deepest upstream-side angled bend I could into the rod to force it away from the willows. Thankfully it bolted downstream instead. I followed, and was able to glide it over into shallow water, where it was easily landed with the Soft Hackle Carrot in its maxillary. It ended up being a brown that was nearly a twin to the prior big fish.

Just upstream of the previous riffle was a slightly rif-fled transition below the tailout to a pool above. It was shallower water, so I decided to cover it with a single dry fly first, and then probe it with the nymph rig if I had no response. This riffle was largely even, with no obvious depressions or structure to focus my approach.

The shallow riffle in the lower half of this photo held a brown trout that ate a CDC Flying Ant with confidence. The pocket downstream of the rock also gave up fish, but by stopping to fish the riffle first, I was rewarded with a memory of the one that got away.

Normally this trout might be the fish of the day. By focusing on water that most anglers might think too shallow or too fast, I was able to hook three trout in this class in only 50 yards of river. Next time you pass by a riffle, don't make the mistake of thinking it's not worth stopping to fish.

Therefore, I decided to move through it steadily, making two or three casts in lanes spaced a foot apart until I had covered most of the likely water.

To target this riffle, I positioned myself 20 to 25 feet across and slightly downstream of the target zone. I made casts with an upstream reach to change the angle of the tippet on the water. This allowed me to show my fly to the fish before they saw the tippet.

Three casts in, I watched a brown trout turn downstream and slowly inhale my CDC Flying Ant with all of the poise and confidence of a brown trout from a New Zealand fly-fishing video. It was stunning. Unfortunately, the trout, which was nearly identical in size to the prior two big trout, came unbuttoned as I reached to net it. Nonetheless, trout were definitely inhabiting riffles on that day, and I'm still enjoying the memories of stopping to fish them.

Riffle Case Study #2

In January 2018 my Fly Fishing Team USA mate Pat Weiss joined me for a couple of days of fishing. This case study and several of the case studies in future chapters came from this trip.

January is not usually a great time to fish riffles. However, the tailwater we were fishing has a high density of rainbow trout, which feed in faster water than what is often typical during cold conditions. Knowing this tendency, I suggested to Pat that we stop at a heavy riffle on our way downriver. He looked at its depth and speed and was surprised I wanted to fish it, given that the water was 41 degrees F, but he kindly stopped to fish at my request. We were both glad we did.

The upper part of the riffle started wide and shallow below the tailout to a run that held a lot of fish upstream. As it narrowed, there was a shelf that traversed at a slight diagonal across the river. Above the shelf the water was 10 to 12 inches deep. Below the shelf it dropped to 1.5 to 2 feet in depth. The surface of the water remained fast throughout. However, upon closer inspection, we found there were lanes of faster and slower water on the surface to help identify more likely holding lies with slight current breaks for the trout. If you look close enough, this is usually the case, even in riffles that seem uniform. Knowing that the depth change would also slow the current near the

Pat Weiss making the transition from downstream hookup to upstream leverage on his first fish in the riffle. Notice the diagonal line of rougher waves that crosses the river just to the right of his feet. These waves corresponded to the shelf that dropped off into deeper water below.

The location where Pat hooked his first fish. Notice the lane of flatter current surrounded by larger waves on both sides. This flatter water was created by a submerged boulder, and it held a fish on its downstream side. The seams on both sides of the white waves above the log produced the rest of his fish.

Pat working upstream-side leverage to move the fish into a position upstream where it could be landed.

The fish makes one last jump as Pat slides it into the net. Notice that the upstream-side pressure from the previous photo moved the fish upstream of Pat. This allowed him to use the current to help slide the fish into the net. When fish are downstream of your position, you have to fight the current to put them into the net, which results in a lot of lost fish.

Pat with his first fish from the riffle. Bigger rainbows were to come.

Pat Weiss with another hookup. That's my kind of splash pad.

bed of the river, Pat targeted his presentations to water downstream of the shelf.

Pat's first target was a lane of current, just over 2 feet wide, where the current was slightly slower and the surface displayed less waveforms than the surrounding water. This lane was formed by a shallower portion of the shelf above, which slowed and deflected the current somewhat to lanes of heavier water on both sides. In addition, Pat found a submerged boulder on the downstream end of this lane that provided a small hydraulic cushion with its upstream face.

Pat began working this area from just shy of 20 feet across the river. Instead of directly across from his target, he took a position several feet upstream to keep his shadow off of the water he planned to target.

Pat started with two flies featuring 2.8 mm beads. His first cast went through the lane uneaten and without touching the bottom. To adjust, he made his next casts farther upstream, at the lip of the shelf, to provide more time for the flies to sink. He also stopped his

rod high to form a hard tuck cast and drive his flies to depth. On his third cast a nice rainbow took his point fly. A long slug-it-out-style fight ensued before Pat was able to slowly work it over to his net.

We both anticipated another fish or two from this target, but Pat did not find any more willing takers. Pat took a couple of steps across the river and upstream to position himself to cover the far side of the riffle.

In this area the fastest vein of current cut downstream, with more-regular waveforms on the surface. The color of the water changed to a deeper blue-green here as the depth increased and the substrate underneath became less visible.

After the first location, Pat targeted the near-side seam of the fast water flowing on the far side of the river. He went through the same progression of making an initial cast and evaluating his presentation. He found his first drift did not slow down as he'd expected, nor did it tick the bottom. He cast farther upstream again in conjunction with a tuck cast. Two drifts later he

Before we left the riffle, I decided I needed to get in on the action as well. This fish grabbed my Blowtorch and went for a little ride downstream before I could land it.

A beautiful leopard-spotted rainbow that took Pat's dropper nymph. This fish had the kind of weight problem I can get behind.

set the hook and a nice rainbow danced on top of the riffle several times before saying uncle to Pat's lateral pressure on the rod.

Pat continued working the area over thoroughly. Despite making longer drifts with tuck casts, he still felt his rig was not reaching and staying near the bottom through enough of his drift. In response he switched his bottom nymph to a Frenchie with a 3.3 mm bead. With the weight change, his rig slowed down noticeably early in the drift, ticking bottom in the latter half every few drifts as well. This proved to be the right change. He caught five more rainbows from the riffle, including a couple of large ones. One came from a drift right down the middle of the fastest vein of current. The rest took on drifts along both the near- and far-side seams of this vein, where the velocity slacked just enough to allow trout to hold there easily.

There are three takeaways from Pat fishing this riffle:

1) Even during winter, trout can be caught in riffles despite their velocity. The likelihood of finding trout is higher if the riffle is deeper, and if it features large substrate to break up the velocity on the bottom of the river.

2) It is also more likely to find trout in riffles if the water is warming above 40 degrees F, and if there are lots of midges or *Baetis* in the drift.

3) Lastly, rainbow trout are more likely to hold in this type of water in the winter than brown trout.

Even though riffles are not deep habitats, they require you to make adjustments in order to fish them correctly. Pat did not keep making the same drifts with the same rig. Based on his initial drifts to a given target lie, he changed his drift length, casting entry angle, and eventually his fly weight to achieve the depth through the drift he needed. With these adjustments, he was able to catch seven trout from the riffle in quick succession. He would not have been as successful without tailoring his presentation to the situation.

Especially during winter, trout are not likely to move far to eat your nymph, so your nymphs must be accurately placed within narrow seams of current. Pat made quite a few drifts to both sides of the fastest vein of current. Most of the trout he caught took on drifts within bands of current only inches wide on the edges surrounding the heaviest flow. Before you move on from fishing a riffle, ensure that you have thoroughly and accurately covered the most likely lies. You may be leaving a lot of fish behind if you don't.

CHAPTER 7

This run was near the top of my beat on Slovakia's Bela River in the 2017 World Fly Fishing Championship. I caught quite a few grayling on dry flies from the soft edge on the right side of this photo. To fish here, I kneeled quartering downstream on the bank and made upstream casts with a downstream reach.

Runs

Depending on the stream classification manual you consult, runs can be described a bit differently. In general, they are considered fast-water habitats with low turbulence and surface agitation. What it boils down to is that runs are basically deeper riffles with substrate that is small enough or far enough from the surface that there are not many waveforms on the water, at least compared to riffles. Depending on the stream flow at the time, riffles can become runs, and vice versa, as the depth and speed of the water changes.

For fly anglers, squabbles over whether a water type is a riffle or a run obviously don't mean much. What matters is figuring out how to fish the water in the best manner possible.

Most runs are characterized by slow water on the inside edge if the run is on a bend in the river. If there is structure on the far bank, then there can be a slow seam or even an eddy. Somewhere in the center of the run, the fastest and deepest currents (the thalweg) flow. Unlike pools, runs usually don't display a distinct hammock or bowl shape to the bottom contour from upstream to downstream; depth changes up- and downstream are usually more gradual. However, they do exhibit a bowl shape from one bank to the other.

As with any location, when you work a run, it's important to observe first. I like to look for trout rising on the inside and outside seams in the slower water. Hatching insects are often pushed to the sides of the river by the main flow, so water near the banks is a good place to find rising fish.

When fishing dries in a run, upstream presentations are required for the inside edge. Typically, you will be casting over slow water to faster water near the edge of the main flow. In order to attain a dead drift in this situation, a downstream reach cast will place your fly line downstream of your dry fly and allow it to drift for a longer distance before starting to drag.

If you are approaching the outside edge of the run by wading from the inside edge, the opposite situation is created. Here your fly line will land in the faster center flow while your dry fly lands in the slower current beyond. Without an aerial mend, your fly line will rip downstream quickly and drag your dry fly with it. Therefore, an upstream reach cast is needed to place

If a run is wide enough that I cannot make drifts to the far bank effectively, I like to cover the run in parallel wading paths. For instance, in this run I started at position one and worked to the top of the run along the line extending from it. Then I dropped back down, waded out to position two, and fished to the top of the run again. The same tactic applied to line number three. Fishing this way lets me thoroughly cover runs with minimal changes in weight and less chance of spooking fish than repeatedly wading out into the river as I wade upstream.

In this photo I am setting the hook on a fish that just ate my dry fly. There was faster water in between my position and where the fish was rising. To achieve a dead drift, I made an upstream reach cast to mend my fly line in the air into the position of the arc drawn on the photo.

To make a reach cast, start with a normal forward-cast stop at your intended target. As the cast is turning over, extend your arm and rod tip across your body or out to the side. The fly will turn over in the original casting direction, but the rod-tip movement during turnover will mend your line.

the fly line upstream of your dry fly, to allow a longer distance to drift without drag.

When it comes to nymph presentations, I like to target runs in parallel linear bands from downstream to upstream. For example, I will fish the inside edge with a dry-and-dropper or Euro-nymphing rig from the bottom to the top. Then I will return to the bottom of the run, wade a few steps out, and cover from the

bottom to the top again. I repeat this process until I have covered the width of the run from bank to bank and from the tail to the head. If you traced my steps on the river, parallel lines the length of the run would be separated by a few feet.

The main reason for approaching runs this way is increased efficiency by minimizing rig changes. The amount of weight needed to drift a nymphing rig near the bottom consistently is determined by a combination of the depth and speed of the water. As the water gets deeper or faster, more weight will be necessary, and vice versa. As I mentioned above, from bank to bank in a run, there are usually significant changes in depth and the speed of current. But from the bottom to the top of a run, the depth changes gradually. As the depth shallows near the head of the run, the speed increases, which offsets the need to change the amount of weight to maintain proper depth.

Because of these characteristics, I find I can usually fish from the bottom to the top of a run without changing the weight of my flies. However, if I wade a few steps across, the depth or speed may change enough to warrant a change in weight; and if I back up near the bank again and take a couple of steps upstream, the amount of weight needed may change yet again. By fishing repeated parallel passes up a run, it may only be necessary to make one or two fly/weight changes to maintain proper depth and weight.

There are lots of fine details to contemplate when it comes to fishing runs effectively. Let's investigate two case studies to provide some concrete examples.

Run Case Study #1: Comparing Drift Mechanics and Rigs

This run provided a lot of great fishing for Pat Weiss and me; it also demonstrated the habitat preferences of larger fish, and provided some interesting comparisons of different drift mechanics, rig alterations, and their performance. At the winter flows we experienced during the trip, the surface of the run was fairly smooth. The water on the river left bank was shallow and slow, and gradually sloped into the deeper and faster water in the thalweg, which flowed closer to the river right bank, which was covered in trees.

In my mind, the run could be divided into two portions, and that is how we fished it. The upper portion had extensive tree branches extending out from the bank. An especially long set of branches reaching out over the river in the center of the run bisected it into separate fishable halves at the top and bottom. There were several gaps in the trees to put casts into, but certainly plenty of opportunity for hanging rigs up in the trees as well. There were a few larger rocks spread throughout the upper portion of the run, which

This photo shows the upper half of the run. The water became gradually deeper from the near bank to under the trees. There were a few rocks upstream beyond the right edge of the photo, which provided some structure. One of the biggest challenges of fishing this run was making repeated drifts back under the trees without snagging them.

provided some subtle but noticeable seams to which we could focus our drifts in and around. The surface was still relatively smooth, but the current was deceptively faster than it appeared.

The bottom portion of the run was a bit slower and shallower, and featured less structure. There was a cable at a stream-gauging station here, and brush had been removed from the far bank around the cable's tower. There were no large rocks in this portion of the run—only a gradual transition from slower water near both banks to the faster and deeper water in the thalweg. The bottom of the run featured an extended tailout, which gradually shallowed and slowed before narrowing into a fast riffle below.

We happened to be walking downstream from the parking access, so we stopped at the upper portion of the run first. The branches at the bottom of this portion broke up our silhouette and prevented the fish in the lower section of the run from spooking, allowing us to fish the run in two halves.

In the past I have had some good dry-fly fishing in this run. On this occasion there were not enough insects hatching to bring fish to the top, so we readied our nymph rigs as a result. The water here is smooth enough that I've been able to fish greased sighters or dry-and-dropper rigs on previous trips. This time the water was slightly tinged and the cloud cover was consistent, leading to conditions that I thought would make the full run approachable with up-and-across Euro-nymphing methods.

I started fishing first, working my way from the bottom near the longest branches toward the shallow head of the run, near the top. I was using a micro-thin Euro-nymphing leader with about 3.5 feet to my first fly and 20 inches to my second. I fished a 2.3 mm tungsten bead on my dropper tag and a 2.8 mm fly on my point to begin with. I made a parallel pass from bottom to top along the slower and shallower water nearest to me. This water was only 18 to 24 inches deep, with a smooth surface, so I fished at least 15 to 20 feet away. I used an across-the-river position to avoid spooking fish and to provide a long dead drift, with an up-and-across presentation.

I made initial casts quartering upstream and incrementally added length to them until I caught fish or ticked bottom every few drifts, during the last

This photo shows the lower half of the run, where there was less structure. The water was slightly shallower and slower in velocity. The brush had been removed from the far bank for the cable tower, leaving no overhead cover for the trout in this portion of the run.

Stepping into the run. Good things are about to happen.

There were plenty of colored-up, cookie-cutter-size rainbows like this one on the near side of the run. As we started fishing under the trees, the bigger fish showed up.

one-third of my drift. I expected most of my takes to come once the flies had reached maximum depth, directly across to slightly below me. I planned to work up the slower water near me, just outside from the tree branches, and then make a second pass to target the deeper water under the trees. My first fish ate on my third cast. It was a cookie-cutter rainbow about 12 inches long. As I worked up the shallow water

nearest to me, several more fish in the same category came quickly.

After my first pass I circled back down to the mid-point of the run where I had started, but stepped two steps farther into the river. From this position, I could cast into the gaps between branches and drift the deeper and faster water underneath them. The windows were tight, so I used a combination of helicopter

The weight change at the beginning of my second pass brought immediate results. Fly fishing is a game of inches in so many ways. A few inches closer to the bottom makes all the difference sometimes.

My first fish under the trees. Once we started fishing where there was overhead cover, fish this size were the norm.

casts (see chapter 10) and sidearm water-load casts to place my flies where I wanted.

My first few drifts after moving suggested I needed more weight. My rig drifted through the area faster than I expected, and did not display the typical abrupt slow-down that usually occurs once my flies have reached the layer of current near the streambed. Because of the tree branches, I was not able to increase the length of my cast upstream to allow more distance and time for my flies to sink. To cope I switched my dropper fly from a 2.3 mm tungsten bead to a 2.8 mm tungsten bead.

After the switch, I made my first cast to a slowed seam of current below one of the rocks in the run. The weight change made the difference, and I hooked a

The fish under the trees weren't just large, they were colored in ways that do justice to the name *rainbow trout*.

Pat, with a nice fish from under the trees, and a standard Pat Weiss "smile."

nice rainbow just below the midpoint of the drift. It became obvious that larger fish preferred this portion of the run. The fish on the first pass were all in the 10- to 12-inch range. After moving, five of the next six fish I hooked were over 15 inches. Pat hopped in once I was done with the pass and caught several nicer fish as well.

With a little observation, it was easy to see why larger trout preferred this zone in the run: The water I fished during my second pass was deeper and in the main current, with greater access to food; there were boulders to break up currents and conserve swimming effort; and it was under the trees, where the trout could seek protection from predators, including most anglers.

The lower half of the run near the cable held all of the adolescent trout. As long as we made good drifts, the fish came consistently and easily there. It was the perfect place to compare flies and rigs.

While fishing the lower half of the run, Pat stopped his rod early in the drift to form an inverted downstream angle in his sighter.

Pat's downstream drift might not have been a "standard" approach, but apparently nobody told the fish.

This produced a trifecta of attractions for the larger and more dominant trout in the social hierarchy.

After I had reached the top of the run, Pat and I circled out and downstream to the bottom portion at the gauging station. I had hogged the top part of the run, so now it was Pat's turn. Sidearm water-load casts offered the best option to avoid hitting the cable running across the river, as plenty of other anglers had done. Keeping hook sets at a low parallel angle to the water also prevented cable collisions. It quickly became clear that this portion of the run was packed full of smaller fish. Pat caught fish on five out of his first six casts!

Pat focused on the downstream portion of his drift, using an inverted sighter angle (see chapter 3). The arcing tension underwater on his tippet created some obvious takes where his sighter shot down 4 to 6 inches toward the water's surface. We laughed that night at how there were more casts that produced fish in this location than casts that did not. He was fishing a pink butt Walt's Worm, and switched his second fly between a drab Pheasant Tail and a Frenchie. Both featured 2.8 mm tungsten beads.

Comparing Rigs

After Pat had caught around 15 fish from a small zone of the run at the cable, I told him I couldn't handle watching him have all the fun. I started fishing, and caught several fish during my first couple of casts. Given the consistent success we were having, I decided it was a chance to compare how a drop-shot rig with more-imitative flies would perform.

I removed the tungsten bead nymphs I was fishing and re-rigged. I tried to come close to matching the length of tippet from my sighter to the split shot on the point of my leader, and I added two tags for nymphs above, each about 12 to 15 inches apart. I had pumped one of the fish we'd caught previously, and picked a Paintbrush Midge Larva and a Brown Mercury Midge, sized to match the food items found in the sample. These flies certainly did a better job of "matching the hatch" than the Walt's Worms, Pheasant Tails, and Perdigons we had been fishing. They are typical flies for most anglers who target winter fish eating midges in a tailwater.

The photo on the left shows a stomach-pump sample from a fish caught in the run, along with a quill Perdigon I was fishing at the time. The photo on the right shows the Midge Larvae and Pupae I changed to on my drop-shot rig versus the Walt's Worm and Pheasant Tail that Pat was having so much success with. Clearly the flies I changed to were more imitative of the food in the pump sample. Keep reading to see how the fish liked them . . . or didn't.

During my first few casts with the new rig, I evaluated the drift and the weight I had chosen. I added a micro shot and then another until my drifts ticked bottom every few drifts, similar to my prior rig with the weighted flies. I was surprised when after several dozen casts I still had not caught a fish. I started covering water on the far side of the run to make sure I was showing the rig to fish that had not seen our prior drifts.

By this time, Pat was bored watching me. He went back to the upper portion of the run under the trees and commenced fish catching yet again. I continued fishing new micro seams, changing flies a few times to see if different patterns might work better. Finally, after about 15 minutes, I caught an 11-inch rainbow, which ate the midge pupa on my top dropper. Unfortunately, during the fight it highlighted one of the shortcomings of the drop-shot rig: When the fish jumped, the weight fired upward through the flies like a slingshot, and I was left with a bird's nest of tippet. It was the kind of tangle that gets chopped and re-rigged instead of being picked out.

I decided to switch back to my prior rig and see if for some reason we had worn out the fish in the area through all of the catching we had done prior. This time I opted for a pink Lite Brite Perdigon and a Frenchie on the dropper. On my first cast, I landed a rainbow. During the five casts after that, I landed three fish. The trout had not spooked. They were still there and ready to eat.

I don't know why the tungsten-bead nymphing rig outperformed the drop-shot rig by so much. I would

After finally catching a fish with the drop-shot rig, it became a mess when the rainbow jumped during the fight. I've found this to be a common problem with drop-shot rigs, as the weight at the end of the leader often fires up through the weightless flies above when fighting fish or making quick casts.

have given anything to have been an underwater fly on the wall watching the drifts of the two rigs, and the trout's reaction to them. To be honest, the old small-fly tailwater angler in me thought the midge patterns I had chosen were going to wipe up the fish in the run. Yet they showed a distinct preference for the much larger and less-imitative flies that Pat and I had been fishing. More likely, I think they showed a preference for how the rig with weighted flies was drifting, as they seemed willing to eat most of the flies we tried in the run previously.

This trout ate my first cast after switching back to a standard Euro-nymphing rig with tungsten bead flies. The fish had not gone anywhere. For some reason, they just did not want more-imitative flies on a drop-shot rig.

Don't get me wrong; I'm not claiming that tungsten nymphs will outperform unweighted flies with split shot all of the time. This was only one quasi experiment. I certainly encourage you to make your own comparisons to help you feel confident in the approach you choose. However, I have read and been told by plenty of anglers and experts that unweighted flies will drift more naturally in the current because they are closer to the mass of actual insects, and move around more freely. If they drift more naturally, then they will always catch more fish, right? This line of reasoning has not panned out in my experience. I've fished a myriad of rigs with and without weighted flies during the many years I've been fortunate enough to fish, both before and during my competitive career. There haven't been many times I've felt I was held back by fishing tungsten nymphs on competition legal rigs, even on heavily pressured rivers. My experience comparing rigs in this run is one reason why I'm so confident in Euro-nymphing rigs with tungsten bead flies.

CHAPTER 8

A beautiful plunge pool on a mountain stream in Oregon. There were plenty of rainbow trout waiting here when I put the camera away and picked up my rod.

Pools

ools need no introduction for most anglers. I would lay odds that when most fly anglers dream of fishing at night, they have visions of giant trout rising to their dry flies in a deep, placid pool. Pools are simply a water type with slower water and greater depth than the surrounding habitat. They are produced either by faster water scouring the substrate to increase depth or by a dam that impounds the water. It is the combination of slower currents and deeper water that makes them desirable locations for trout. Here they can conserve energy by swimming less, as well as seek refuge from predators that would have access to them in shallower water.

Early in my fly-fishing life, I assumed that the bulk of trout in a river lived in pools and nowhere else. After all, when I saw other anglers fishing, they were usually parked on a pool. It is true that pools almost always have fish. However, as I've mentioned previously, pools are not the greatest sources of trout food in rivers. Riffles and pocketwater produce more, and larger, macroinvertebrates per area of river bottom. Therefore, when hatches are strong or the water temperatures are ideal, trout will spread into faster water types that offer better feeding opportunities, thereby lowering the density of fish found in pools.

Conversely, during colder times of the year, pools can be packed with fish. During the winter, action in pools can sometimes seem more like fishing a hatchery than a natural river. In fact, the availability of pools for wintering habitat has a great effect on the density of trout a river can support, at least in mountain streams. One study by Charles Gowan and Kurt Fausch (1996) showed a large increase in trout numbers and biomass in stream reaches after log weirs were installed to create pools.

The challenge in pools, then, rarely comes from decoding whether or not there are fish inhabiting them,

I've definitely relived the scene I enjoyed at this pool many times in my dreams.

but rather where they are, and how best to target them. Pools tend to follow a pattern of depth that resembles a bowl or hammock, depending on their length. The river bottom descends at the head of the pool where faster currents scour the substrate. The currents then begin to slow in the expanding space. It is very common to have a shelf across the head of a pool with an abrupt change in depth. The deepest and slowest portion of the pool is usually near its center. Due to the slowed velocity in the center of the pool, the water loses its capacity to scour the stream bottom. Substrate particles that were entrained by the scour filter out of the column and are deposited at the tail of the pool. At the tail, the river bottom slopes upward, which causes the water velocity to increase as it is forced through a smaller space.

Trout can be found in any of the zones in a pool, from the head to the tail. The most overlooked area is definitely the tailout. The center of the pool is the most likely place for fish to hold in colder temperatures, and will usually hold fish at all times. As long as it isn't overly turbulent, the head of a pool is often the best place to find a large fish. Fish that hold in the head have first access to the food drifting into the pool from the faster water above. The surface of the water may still hold some chop in this location as well, which obscures the view of overhead predators.

Strategies for Targeting Pools

Whenever I encounter a new water type on the river, I ask myself the questions covered in chapter 1. When it comes to pools, the first variables I think about are water clarity and surface disturbance. If the water is clear and the surface is smooth, fish will be able to see you from a long distance. In these conditions, you can either fish the pool from downstream; fish from a long distance from the side of the pool; kneel beside the pool to stay below the trout's vision; or a combination of all of these strategies as you move from the tail to the head. If the water is somewhat turbid, then you can approach the pool based on which locations will provide you the best presentation angles with the rig(s) you choose to fish.

Regardless of the methods I choose, I always work pools from shallow to deep water, back to front, and near to far. Because of the extra depth in pools, it is

This photo shows a beautiful pool in a slot canyon on the Sava Bohinjka River in Slovenia. After I took this photo I caught the silhouetted trout, and several others, on a dry fly. I then turned to nymphing presentations to work to the fish deeper in the column.

A dry-and-dropper rig on a Euro-nymphing leader, worked thoroughly from bank to bank, produced several fish in the tailout before moving to the heart of this pool.

common for fish to suspend in the column when there is sufficient food in the drift. It is also common for less-aggressive fish to be hard on the bottom while more actively feeding fish are above them. Therefore, working shallow to deep means within the water column, as well as to locations of overall shallower and deeper water in the pool.

My typical progression to work from shallow to deep is as follows: If there are fish rising, I will target them first with dry flies, unless I have to cast across water, where I'm worried I will spook fish if my fly line lands on top of them. In this case, I will cover the water in between with a dry-and-dropper or Euro-nymphing rig, and approach any rising fish that lie beyond after I feel I've caught any willing fish in between.

The tailout

The tail of the pool is where the trout will be most prone to spooking. Therefore, I always approach the tail with caution. If I'm not worried about pressure waves moving upstream from wading that will spook fish, I approach in the river from downstream. If there are no rising fish, then I usually start either with a dry-and-dropper or with a two-fly Euro-nymphing rig on a floated sighter in the tailout. I will cast 15 to 30 feet above me and work from bank to bank as appropriate. I consider each good presentation to have covered the water 6 to 10 inches on either side of where my flies drift. If the river is wide, it may require taking steps laterally to keep a manageable presentation distance, without laying too much drag-inducing leader and line on the water.

Once I've covered the width of the appropriate water, I will take one or two steps upstream and repeat the process again, working to grid all of the likely holding water. However, if I spot a fish, I will slow down and work to that fish until I catch or spook it.

If the conditions allow, I will creep to the side and make across-the-river presentations. If it is less than 2 feet deep, then I will usually opt for a dry-and-dropper rig for an across-the-river presentation so I can suspend the nymph above the streambed with the dry fly. If it is deeper, and the clarity and surface current make it approachable, then a standard up-and-across Euro-nymphing presentation is appropriate. The basic grid pattern from bank to bank remains the same as an upstream presentation, but the casts work from near to far. If the pool and tailout is quite large, then it can be a good place to swing a streamer or nymphs.

The heart of a pool

Once the tailout has been covered, it's time to move to the center of the pool. Unless the pool is on a small stream, most presentations to the center and head of a pool need to be made across the river. If the pool is on a bend, I pick the shallower inside bank to fish from. The arcing path of the river on an inside bend mirrors the natural arc of a Euro-nymphing presentation, and is also easier to fish with an indicator or dry-and-dropper method.

The center of the pool is a location where fish are prone to suspending in the column. Therefore, I will usually start with a dry-and-dropper rig to work from shallow to deep. Sometimes there can be several layers of fish willing to eat in a pool, and more fish will materialize as presentations work progressively deeper.

For example, during the Casting for Hope Tournament in 2017, I drew two consecutive beats with pools and followed the same pattern in both, with good success. The pattern was as follows: I spotted fish suspended in the column and would occasionally catch glimpses of fish near the bottom, below them. I covered the tailout with a dry-and-dropper rig (2.8 mm tungsten bead nymph) and kept the same rig to begin working the center of each pool. I worked from near me to the far bank and from downstream to upstream.

Once I had caught several fish and the takes dried up, I added about a foot of tippet and covered the center again. After that I switched to a two-fly Euro-nymphing rig and covered the area thoroughly, starting with lighter flies (2.3 mm and 2.8 mm beads), and caught several fish. I then switched to heavier beads, until contact with the bottom happened every few casts, and caught several more.

Finally, after working both rigs thoroughly through the center of the pools, I worked through again with two streamers on a Euro-nymphing leader. A dead drift with periodic jigging motions brought several more fish, which had ignored the previous presentations with nymphs. This progression from dry-and-dropper to nymphing to streamers brought several dozen fish from pools where other competitors had caught fewer

This was the pool at the bottom of my beat during the first session of the 2017 Casting for Hope Tournament in North Carolina. I worked the pool from the tail to the head and from shallow to deep with a dry-and-dropper to Euro-nymphing to streamers progression.

A dry-and-dropper or strike-indicator nymph rig can be a good choice for the heart of a pool, where this angler is fishing. However, look to the lower right of the photo, at the head of the pool. Here the currents are more complex and turbulent. A straight Euro-nymphing rig is a better choice for this type of water.

The perfect jump from a rainbow trout in the pool from the photo above. Look closely and you can see my dry fly on the dry-and-dropper rig I was fishing, to the right of the trout. (THANKS TO TUCKER HORNE FOR THIS AWESOME PHOTO.)

fish, likely because they only took a unilateral nymphing approach that went straight to the bottom, where they expected "all" the fish to be.

The head of a pool

The head of a pool can be an excellent place to find actively feeding trout. The head provides the first access to food drifting from the faster water above, so it's often a place for dominant large fish to be found. As you'll see in the case study below, it can also be a location where currents upwell violently, making it difficult to catch trout if they happen to hold there.

Dry-and-dropper rigs (and other suspension nymph methods) can still be a productive way to target the head of a pool. However, the currents are usually a bit more complex here, and the direction and speed can change in a matter of inches, from top to bottom in the column, or left to right. Therefore, my preferred method for the head of a pool is Euro-nymphing.

Due to their more-complex currents and depth changes, the challenge at the head of a pool is presenting your flies with a proper drift at the proper depth. Spooking fish is usually less of an issue if the head of the pool features waveforms on the surface. However, I will still approach the inside edge from quartering downstream, as currents are typically smoother there and the fish can be wary. Once I move to the middle or far side of a pool's head, I usually approach from an across position to increase the length of my drift and the depth it can attain.

It is important to carefully inspect the depth contours at the head of a pool. Often there will be a shallow upstream shelf followed by an abrupt increase in depth. It is usually necessary to fish below and above the shelf separately, due to the change in depth and speed. Be willing to switch to a lighter or heavier rig for each side of a shelf.

Accuracy is important around shelves. If you cast too far upstream, you will constantly hook bottom. If you cast too far downstream, your flies will sail over the head of the trout, which often hold where the depth break occurs. Even if you are accurate, it can still be difficult to get your flies to trace the increasing depth contour of the bottom. Tuck casts are useful in this situation to get your flies to depth as quickly as possible. If the water is turbid and you can't see the depth

transition, you may need to feel out the depth change with multiple casts of different distances. Work your way upstream until you tick bottom early in the drift. This signals that your cast is too far, and you'll need to shorten your cast until your flies can drift over the shelf and into the depths.

Lateral accuracy is also important. The heads of pools share many of the current seam complexities of faster water types. If you are fishing multiple nymphs, ensure that you watch their entry splashes. Land both flies in the same seam of current for the best drift.

Pool Case Study #1

This case study is another installment from the trip I took with my Fly Fishing Team USA mate, Pat Weiss.

Upstream of the riffle from the case study in chapter 6, there was a large, deep pool. The pool formed on a fairly hard right turn in the river. The water was 42 degrees F when I took the temperature before fishing the pool. With no hatch to bring fish up in the column or into faster currents, I anticipated the fish would be in the slower and deeper parts of the pool, with the

The head of the pool for this case study. The currents crashing into the far bank upstream forced an upwell of currents to rise to the surface in the lower half of the photo. It may not look violent, but the water was a bit of a churning mess here.

more-relaxed currents. No fish were rising, and the clarity and light conditions prevented us from seeing fish in the pool, but likely helped hide Pat's presence while he was fishing as well.

The far bank of the pool featured riprap that had been placed on the opposite bank to keep the river from eroding into the homes above. It was dodgy erosion control, and certainly not performed with fish habitat in mind. As the river collided with the riprap bank, faster surface currents were reflected down and laterally across the river, which scoured a deep trench along that bank. As the currents moved laterally back toward the near bank, they traced an upsloping deposition zone in the channel, which forced them back up toward the surface. This is a common situation at the heads of pools that collide with rocky outcrops or trees at a steep angle. It leads to excessive turbulence that can look like the water is at a rolling boil.

Generally, turbulent water like this is very difficult to catch fish from. Even when trout hold in these locations, the turbulence churns flies like a washing machine and spits them out with little control over depth and direction. It's not an easy place to convince fish that your flies are naturally in the drift when they are attached to tippet.

Pat and I both looked at the head of this pool and assumed it would be difficult to catch fish there. The pool was deep and wide enough that I wasn't worried about spooking fish downstream, so I asked him to fish the head on our way downstream. He added tippet to his Euro-nymphing rig and changed from a 2.8 mm to a 3.3 mm bead on his point fly to cope with the turbulence and depth. He worked the area thoroughly, making casts to the shelf and trying to get his nymphs to depth for the middle of his drift. Despite adjustments in tippet length and fly weight, the turbulence made it difficult to get flies near the bottom in a predictable drift lane. The only fish Pat was able to land near the head of the pool took at the extreme downstream end of his drift, below his position, where the turbulence decreased and the currents became more predictable.

After covering the head, Pat circled down to the bottom third of the pool. Without comparing notes, we both had identified this location as the best-looking water in the pool for the conditions. Here the main current coalesced into a band about 4 feet wide. There

Pat worked the head of the pool thoroughly with a variety of cast strategies to get his flies to depth. Despite his efforts, the churning currents at the head of the pool made good drifts and catching fish nearly impossible.

The only fish Pat caught at the head of the pool was on the extreme downstream end of his drift, where the current turbulence subsided. I took this photo immediately after he hooked the fish, and it's jumping at the location where he hooked it.

The lone trout that Pat caught while fishing the head of the pool.

Pat and I both expected the lower third of the pool to be the best area to catch fish. The water had good depth and speed for the cold temperatures. The slightly rippled lane of current was likely caused by converging currents. We both expected this to be the spot where a concentration of fish could be found.

Pat worked a grid pattern to thoroughly cover the bottom one-third of the pool. He caught multiple fish under the foam line in this photo.

Pat about to put one of the cookie-cutter-size rainbows from the pool in the net.

The fish from the pool were not big, but their iridescence was stunning.

was a slight ripple to the surface and a line of foam bubbles down the center. These characteristics are usually a sign that currents and food are converging in the area, along with fish.

Pat started near the upslope of the tailout. He switched back to a 2.8 mm tungsten bead on the point since he did not need as much weight for the less-chaotic currents. He made casts 15 to 20 feet, quartering upstream. His first few drifts covered the near side of the current. For the next few casts he would take a step forward, toward the opposite bank, and cover the center of the main flow; then he'd take another step, to cover near the opposite bank. After fishing from near to far, he backed up two steps and waded upstream two steps to form a grid pattern.

The rippled lane of current held the best concentration of fish. It did not take long before Pat hooked his first trout, and he soon followed with more. Though it was a decent holding spot, it did not offer the prime feeding lies of water in other locations up- and downstream, so most of the fish in this location were cookie-cutter 10- to 13-inch rainbows, except for one midsize trout. By the time Pat reached the water near the head, which he'd previously covered, he had caught a half-dozen trout, and we decided to move on to more-promising water downstream.

Pool Case Study #2

This case study was done with my friend and former Fly Fishing Team USA mate Charles Card. We fished a pool on a small spring creek with rainbow and brown

trout. Though it was early January, the springs on this stream retained a temperature in the 52- to 55-degree range. As such, we expected to find fish in all possible holding water, and our fishing prior to this pool that day had affirmed our expectations.

The main reason I wanted to include this quick case study is that it illustrates a couple of strategies from chapter 1 on making and executing a plan, as well as some benefits to longer, lighter Euro-nymphing rigs, as discussed in chapters 2 and 3. The water on this stream is very clear and the density of fish is high. As a result, before I fish any water there, I stop to look for fish and plan an approach before jumping in. Part of that approach is fishing from a kneeling position, or finding structure or water currents to hide my presence.

The piece of water we fished in this case study is hard to label as any one particular water type. I almost put it in chapter 7 (about runs), but I'm referring to it as a pool. It has the shape of a pool and soft water along the edges, but the current through the center was fast and fairly turbulent—not exactly a placid pool. The water's depth and turbulence made Euro-nymphing the obvious choice.

The tailout of the pool drops over a waterfall downstream, which made it hard to approach from downstream. However, the river left side of the pool abuts a large, car-size boulder. This boulder provides the ideal obstruction to hide behind while scanning for fish and making presentations.

Despite the low light and sleeting conditions, we were able to spot a rainbow and a brown trout to sight-fish to at the start. These fish were riding the hydraulic

The location for this pool case study, where most of the potential holding water is along the soft edges. The boulder on the right side of the pool provides a perfect hiding place.

Look closely just below the center of this photo and you'll see the brown trout and rainbow we spotted, to make our initial presentations to.

cushion of the upstream face of another boulder. The presentation to these fish was a bit difficult. It required hiding behind the large boulder. Sidearm casts had to be made upstream with enough sinking distance to reach their level. Predicting which location to cast upstream was difficult as well. If the flies landed a few inches to the right of the target, they were tossed to the bank and hooked the boulder. If they landed a few inches to the left, they were caught by the center currents and raced downstream.

We had sorted through quite a few flies earlier in the day and were able catch fish on most of the patterns

Charles Card scored a rainbow in his first few casts into the pool. Notice his location behind the rock. To land fish we had to play them into the side channel to avoid spooking other fish in the pool.

My reward for stopping to spot fish before jumping straight into the pool.

we tried. However, due to the somewhat recent brown trout spawn and the midwinter hatch doldrums, Tungsten Taco Eggs and Mops were high on the fish's list of favored patterns.

Charles was first up to bat. His second cast hit the right target and he caught a rainbow right away. The only problem is that it had made a sneak attack from the side of the largest boulder and wasn't one of the fish we had spotted. Charles had to play the fish past his original target trout to land it in the pocketwater below. During the process the brown trout slipped away out into the current, and we didn't spot it again.

The current in the center provided a nice veil to hide Charles's presence from the trout while fishing the far eddy.

The rainbow stayed around, though, which gave me a chance to target it.

It took me a few casts to dial in the specific location to cast to without hooking bottom or having my nymphs fly past through the fast current in the center. The bright-colored egg pattern made it possible to watch at least one of the flies on my rig and gauge which current seam my flies were drifting in, and what level in the column they had achieved. With this trick, I was able to place my flies exactly at the spotted rainbow's level. It took a few casts, but it finally ate my fly.

Charles and I continued to fish the seam near the rock from downstream to upstream. There were several more fish in the tailout riding the upstream faces of the other boulders. We also caught quite a few fish in the slow seam near the rock upstream of the fish we had originally targeted. We tried quite a few casts through the fast center of the pool but were not able to catch fish there, which we'd expected due to the velocity and turbulence.

To fish the rest of the pool, we used the surface agitation of the center flow to hide our presence. Charles drifted the near seam along the eddy on the opposite bank first. He missed several fish along the seam. He then placed casts along the far bank, where the current was recirculating upstream, and let them follow the path of the current until they entered the near seam again and continued downstream. (This is an example of the eddy Euro-nymph drifting technique covered in chapter 5.)

The uppermost holding water in the pool was the upstream end of the seam along the large boulder. This water was blocked from our original position by the curvature of the boulder. However, Charles was able to target this area by crossing at the tailout and positioning himself in the eddy where he had just been fishing. The center currents once again allowed him to fish within close proximity to his target lie without spooking the fish he was chasing. It didn't take long for a few more fish to come from along the base of the rock, and I was able to get in on the action as well.

The last thing I wanted to highlight about this case study was the performance of our two leaders. Due to the small size of the stream and the challenges of casting in tight spaces there, Charles had chosen a short, traditional Czech-style leader along with a shorter rod

The first rainbow trout, which Charles caught on a Mop.

An extremely colorful rainbow trout, which I caught from the head of the pool.

and line matched to it. I fished a 10-foot 2-weight Cortland MKII with a micro-thin Euro-nymphing leader.

Several times while fishing this pool, and throughout the rest of the day, Charles missed fish; he complained that he must be getting old, because his reaction time was slow. I assured Charles that his angling skills were as formidable as ever. In my opinion, Charles's strike-detection issue was not his ability but the makeup of his rig. His short leader forced him to fish fly line out the rod tip on his drifts. The fly line

To fish the head of the pool above the boulder, Charles crossed at the tailout and waded into the eddy. The fast center currents again hid his presence while making up-and-across presentations to the remaining holding water.

sagged back toward him, which forced him to approach from a shorter distance and fish heavier flies than I fished for the same water. The mass of the line also dulled his strike detection.

When making typical up-and-across Euro-nymphing drifts, the sighter/leader must stop or hesitate to show an indication of a take. This movement must overcome the inertia of the drifting leader and flies. Remember from Newton's first law of motion that an object will continue with a constant direction and velocity unless acted upon by an external force. In this case, the flies and leader will continue progressing downstream in the current where they reside unless the force of a trout taking and holding onto the fly halts their downstream progression.

Force is equal to mass multiplied by acceleration. With fly line and a thicker leader out the rod tip, the rig that Charles was fishing had much more mass out his rod tip than my micro-thin leader, as evidenced by the drastic difference in sag between the two rigs. Therefore, the force required by the fish to accelerate his leader upstream enough to signal a take was much greater than the force required to move my leader. A lot of times fish feel the pressure from this force early enough that they are able to spit the fly out before a strike is detected. That's why Charles had a few struggles with strike detection on this day. It certainly wasn't because he lacks capability, as he is one of the fishiest anglers you'll ever meet.

CHAPTER 9

An angler fishes a glide on Bosnia's Ribnik River. The fishing in this type of water could have been problematic here, but plenty of sight-fishing opportunities kept it exciting.

Glides

Low-gradient stretches of rivers typically feature glides. Stream habitat manuals often don't separate glides from other water types; they are generally described as low-velocity runs with very little surface disturbance. Glides feature the same gradual change in depth from upstream to downstream as runs. They rarely have woody or rocky structure to create currents with much complexity. This doesn't mean that all the currents are the same; it's just harder to identify the differences.

As a fly angler trying to read the water, there may not be a more intimidating water type to fish than a glide. Unless there are fish rising, it's difficult to isolate locations within glides that appear to have higher value as a holding lie for trout. However, that doesn't mean glides are void of fish. In reality, as long as the glide is deep enough, just about any place can hold trout. That's why the first thing I do when I come to a glide I plan to fish is to scan for rising trout and sub-surface fish that I can sight-nymph to. I also look for any changes in depth, small changes in current velocity from bank to bank, or changes in substrate type on the river bottom, as these can be higher-value targets. Underneath trees on the banks are also good locations.

Glides can be spooky locations to fish. It's best to target them in low-light conditions. If they are shallow, much of the time trout will abandon them in sunny weather for water types with greater depth. The most

Notice the smooth, nondescript water of the glide on the right side of this photo, upstream of my position. Just about any of this type of water can hold fish, and there is little to separate better from lesser holding water.

Floating the sighter upstream with a Euro-nymphing rig is a core presentation technique to target glides.

productive times to target glides are during hatches or drizzly weather.

Approaching fish in glides can be a challenge. There isn't enough surface agitation to hide your presence if you approach at close proximity from the side. The remaining options are fishing from a downstream position, across the current from a kneeling position, or with longer-distance presentations. Downstream presentations with swung flies or dry flies are also possible, but they must be made at distance, since trout can easily see an angler wading in upstream.

When wading glides, ensure that you make your movements slowly. Avoid making waves, which will travel to the nearest trout and alert them that a potential predator has entered the area. This is especially important for across or downstream presentations, since waves from downstream positions are dampened by the current before reaching trout upstream.

In shallow glides (12 to 18 inches deep), my first choice of method for covering the water is dry flies. I always hope for a hatch to bring fish to the surface to provide individual targets to cast to. If I'm not so lucky, I turn to a fan-cast approach and cover slightly different water from bank to bank and from the bottom to the top of the glide. Both strategies have worked well for me on difficult river beats during the World Fly Fishing Championships.

If dry flies are unsuccessful or the glide is deeper, dry-and-dropper rigs or Euro-nymphing rigs with a floated sighter are my next choice. These methods allow a longer-distance presentation to help avoid spooking fish. They also help to suspend nymphs so they travel as close to horizontally as possible. In more-turbulent currents,

a quick descent by your flies is beneficial. In the smooth currents of a glide, it is usually a red flag to the trout.

Kurt Finlayson and I studied the effects of sink rate in glides during another one of our river "lunch dates" when I was in college. One day we were fishing a very smooth and clear piece of water, behind my dentist's office, of all places. We could clearly see trout and whitefish in the glide ahead of us. In fact, the water was so clear that we could watch the glint on the bodies and beads of our nymphs and track them through the drift.

We were both fishing Euro-nymphing rigs with greased sighters that we could float upstream. Kurt was up first in the glide. He was fishing a Rainbow Warrior with a 2.8 mm tungsten bead. In the slow water, it quickly descended at a steep angle. Oftentimes, it touched bottom before reaching the fish he was targeting. I remember one specific fish he drifted to with about half a dozen drifts. It ignored his nymph even when Kurt was very accurate with his cast and drifted at its level.

Watching the nymph, I told Kurt I thought the descent was too quick and it looked unnatural. I switched to the same fly but with a bead one size smaller. To get the fly to the correct depth, I needed to cast farther upstream, because the descent of the fly was much more gradual, and followed a path closer to horizontal. My first two casts were a little off target, but the trout took my fly confidently on the third cast. There was nothing different about our flies; it was the weight that changed the rate of descent on the presentation. It was another lesson to avoid the common pitfall of fishing too much weight.

Let's put the above methods into practice in the case studies below.

Glide Case Study #1

During this case study, Pat Weiss and I fished a shallow, spooky glide on an urban tailwater in January. The glide was bisected by a bridge. The water below the bridge was quite shallow (~6 to 15 inches deep), and very smooth. The water above the bridge was a bit narrower, slightly faster, and deeper (~10 to 24 inches deep). Due to the trickle being released below the dam, the water was very slow and clear, which made it difficult to avoid spooking fish with our presentations.

When we arrived around two p.m., there were fish rising throughout the glide. They were a bit more spread-out in the lower portion, with about half a dozen fish rising regularly. Above the bridge there was a denser pod of a dozen or so fish rising frequently.

From the bridge I could see several of the fish rising in the lower half of the glide. Look closely and see if you can spot the four brown trout in the photo.

In this photo, Pat Weiss has spotted a rising fish at the tailout of the glide. He spent a minute observing its rise rhythm and decoding the currents before making his first cast.

Most of the riseforms were rings with no snouts breaking the surface (see chapter 1). This suggested that the trout were mostly taking midge pupae instead of the few adults we could see flying around.

I wanted to see how Pat would work the lower portion, so I settled in on the bridge. From my vantage point, it was easy to see a few of the fish that were rising.

Pat entered at the bottom of the glide and observed the currents and locations of fish before making any casts. He tackled up with a single dry fly on a leader similar to a modular Euro-nymphing leader. Pat has mastered the use of this leader to allow him to fish as many methods as possible with it. However, most anglers would have an easier time with a purpose-built dry-fly leader and fly line.

Pat started with a small Shuttlecock Emerger. This pattern fishes with the abdomen protruding below the surface and does a nice job of imitating midge pupae and emerging mayflies. His first target was a fish rising in inches of water at the tailout of the glide. The currents were deceptive here, with slow water between Pat and the fish, which held his leader and dragged the fly away from the fish. It took him a few casts to find a specific curve for his reach cast to achieve a good drift, and also to show the fly to the fish before the tippet. Once he did, the fish sipped the Shuttlecock and came to the net.

The rest of the glide below the bridge was a bit more challenging. The hatch was waning, and the rising became more sporadic. He changed flies several times to catch two more trout below the bridge, but

After a few casts and adjustments, Pat Weiss catches his first fish in the glide on a dry fly.

The first brown trout Pat caught in the glide, with the Shuttlecock Emerger in the corner of its mouth.

Pat used the bridge to help break up his silhouette as he approached the fish rising in the upper half of the glide. Sidearm casts were a necessity here, to avoid hitting the bridge with the fly or rod.

When Pat hooked fish in this location, he stayed downstream to avoid spooking other fish in the glide. The bridge provided some challenges to rod leverage angles, which he had to work around.

the commotion of the fighting fish seemed to put the fish down, and they stopped rising altogether. He also had the challenge of dogs jumping in the water and passersby feeding ducks in the glide. The joys of fishing in the city!

Pat moved to target the remaining rising fish just above the bridge. He approached from downstream, but the bridge forced him to crouch slightly and make sidearm casts. His tactics worked quickly, though, and he caught two more fish on the Shuttlecock, which he tied back on before fishing above the bridge. Despite the obstacle, he was careful when landing the fish to stay as far downstream as possible, to avoid spooking the fish higher in the glide.

After these first couple of fish on the dry, the rising slowed dramatically. Pat removed his dry fly, attached a Walt's Worm with a 2.0 mm tungsten bead, and greased his sighter. Though he had about 4 feet of tippet below his sighter and the water was less than 2 feet deep, the lightly weighted fly sank slowly enough to drift through the glide for 8 to 10 feet before touching bottom.

He fished the rig upstream with the sighter floating on the surface. Most of the takes were fairly obvious, indicated by a quick sinking of the front portion of this sighter. As soon as the tip sank or the sighter hesitated, Pat set the hook. Sometimes the "takes" were actually the nymph touching the bottom, but as often as not he connected to a trout.

A floated sighter and a Walt's Worm with a 2.0 mm tungsten bead ended up being the most successful technique in the glide.

One of the brown trout that fell victim to a floated sighter and lightly weighted Walt's Worm.

The success was immediate with this rig, and he quickly landed about half a dozen small browns and rainbows. I got jealous, so I hopped in. I had rigged a rod with Eduardo's dry-fly leader (see chapter 2). I turned it into a dry-and-dropper leader by adding about 18 inches of tippet with a tag to attach the dry fly. I chose a Griffith's Gnat–style midge dry to provide a little extra buoyancy, and added a midge pupa with a 2.0 mm tungsten bead on the point.

I made quite a few casts upstream into the same water where Pat had been catching fish. It took about 15 presentations before I finally caught a fish. I had misjudged the depth of the water and tied the dropper without enough tippet to get the midge pupa to depth. I asked Pat for his rod, and immediately caught several fish.

Take a look at all those midge pupae. Yet the fish this pump sample came from took the Walt's Worm, top in the photo. It certainly was not imitating the food that this fish was eating, but because it drifted at the right depth in a natural manner, the trout ate it anyway.

Stomach Pump

During my work as a fisheries biologist, I sometimes performed gastric lavage to assess diet in studies. Gastric lavage is simply a slightly more involved method of pumping a fish's stomach. Not everyone likes the idea of stomach-pumping trout, and that's okay. But if you do choose to pump a stomach, it's important to do it in a manner that does no harm to the fish. Follow the steps in the photos below to use the stomach pump properly.

Depress the bulb of the stomach pump and allow it to expand while holding the tube of the pump underwater. (PHOTOS BY CHARLES CARD)

Gently cradle the trout upside down. This position will usually calm the fish. Depress the bulb to empty the water before sliding it into the trout. If you expel the water when inside the trout, it will expand the stomach cavity, which can damage surrounding organs.

Gently slide the pump tube down the trout's throat. Stop as soon as you feel any change in resistance.

Slide the tube back out of the trout and let it go. The bulb will automatically inflate and provide suction as you remove the pump.

We pumped a fish to see if I had guessed wrong by fishing the midge pupa. I definitely had not, as the fish had been chowing on them. Why had the Walt's Worm been more successful when it looked like nothing the fish were eating? Simple; it drifted at the level of the trout in a convincing manner, while the midge pupa stayed too high in the column because of the way I had rigged my dry-and-dropper. This sequence provided evidence that dialing in the variables of your presentation is the most important strategy to successful angling. Before you blame your fly for lack of success on the water, always take stock of your drifts, depth, and approach, as these are often to blame before the fly pattern.

Glide Case Study #2

This case study is another illustrative sequence from the January trip I shared with Pat Weiss. It highlighted the importance of the proper choice of rig, along with the radius each rig can successfully fish, and how that can be limiting in certain water. We fished this sequence on a piece of water that transitioned from a medium-speed riffle to a long and progressively slower glide. The riffle formed on a right turn, but it straightened into the long glide, which most people would have labeled "frog water" in its lower half.

In the past, this has been a good location for rising trout during hatches. Unfortunately, there weren't

The upper end of the glide in this case study. The riffle coming into the glide can be seen on the far-left side of the photo.

The lower portion of the glide. Much of the water here becomes very slow and would be difficult to fish without rising fish to target.

A close-up of the middle portion of the glide. Notice the line of foam near the opposite bank. Foam signals a coalescing of currents and food; where there is foam, there are often fish.

Pat Weiss fishing the glide in this case study. Here he is focusing on the downstream portion of his drift.

enough bugs around to get the fish looking up on this day. The lower half of the glide moved slowly enough that we deemed it not worth fishing without rising fish, so we focused on the upper half.

The depth did not change much from upstream to downstream within the glide. From the inside bank to the outside bank the water gradually deepened from around a foot deep to 2.5 to 3 feet on the far side, along the willows. This deeper portion along the left bank was the obvious thalweg with the fastest velocity, in addition to the greatest depth. It also featured a sporadic foam line, which is usually a good sign that fish are underneath. The water for 3 to 4 feet on both sides of the foam line had similar depth, along with seams that signaled a change in current speed.

Pat stepped in first. He was fishing his Euro-nymphing rig with a couple of nymphs—one with a 2.3 mm bead and the other with a 2.8 mm bead. He had about

4.5 to 5 feet of tippet from the sighter to his first fly, and another 2 feet to his point fly.

He entered the glide at the top of the "frog water," where the current still had enough velocity to make nymph presentations easier. He made quite a few up-and-across presentations with the sighter floating during the first third of the drift, to keep the leader from sagging back toward him, which would reduce the radius of proper presentation. After some tweaking to his rig for depth, he caught his first fish, a nice rainbow, after 15 or 20 casts. He did not catch another fish afterward for at least five minutes, so I asked if I could take a turn.

I started in the same location, but I was fishing a dry-and-double-dropper rig on a modular Euro-nymphing leader (chapter 2). I had about 3 feet of tippet from the tippet ring to my dropper nymph and another 2 feet of tippet to my second nymph. I started with a Lite Brite Perdigon on the dropper and a Frenchie on the point. Both flies had 2.5 mm inverting tungsten beads. I chose a size 12 Front End Loader Caddis to add to the dropper tag on my tippet ring. I didn't anticipate catching any fish with the dry fly. I picked it specifically because it had just enough buoyancy to hold up my nymphs but not enough that it would resist sinking when a fish took. This buoyancy balance promotes more-sensitive strike detection.

I began by making quartering-upstream casts 3 to 5 feet shy of the foam line. I was fishing far enough away from me (~25 feet) that I could not lift the sighter off

Pat's first fish in the glide—a rainbow trout on a nymph he tied while we were in Slovakia for the 2017 World Fly Fishing Championship.

I began fishing the glide with a dry and two droppers. I made quartering-upstream casts and let the sighter float on the water to prevent the rig from sagging back toward me. Look closely in this photo and you will see my sighter floating on the water with my dry fly floating just beyond.

Sliding one of my first fish from the glide into the net.

One of the nicer rainbows I caught from the glide.

the water without the rig sagging toward me. I greased the sighter and let it float through most of the drift, with occasional small mends when required. On the lower end of the drift, I dropped the rod and shook line out to extend the drift a little bit. I planned to work the shallow water nearer to me first and then work the deeper and faster water around the foam line. When I made a second pass to cover this area, I ended up switching to a 2.8 mm tungsten bead nymph on the point position, as I was not ticking bottom or catching fish in the deeper water with the lighter nymphs.

Takes came quickly and often in this area. In fact, for a while I had more casts that ended with fish on the line than those that didn't. This was especially the

There's nothing quite like a leaping rainbow trout.

An early splash while Pat Weiss fights another rainbow from the top of the glide where it transitioned to a riffle.

One of the nicer rainbows Pat caught closer to the willows.

case after I took a couple of steps upstream into slightly faster water, which the rainbows seemed to favor. Most of the fish were cookie-cutter 10- to 13-inch rainbows, but there were larger fish near to the willows under the foam line.

Once I reached the transition between the riffle and the glide, my takes slowed a bit. I was still catching the occasional fish, but I expected more given the water I was fishing.

Pat jumped back in at this point with his Euro-nymphing rig. He worked from directly upstream to up and across through the water, where the glide started to have some small riffle waveforms. His action picked up right where mine left off. We actually started laughing a couple of times at the hard takes he was receiving early in the drift, before his flies had sunk very far. The fish in the open riffle were mostly small, but as

he reached the foam line near the willows, he caught several larger fish.

This case study provides a nice illustration of where different rigs do their best work. In the slower and deeper water, on the lower end of the glide, the Euro-nymphing rig did not perform as well as the dry-and-double-dropper rig, even in Pat's capable hands. As he neared the top of the glide, the situation flipped and the Euro-nymphing rig outperformed the dry-and-double-dropper rig I was using. This glide also revealed another instance of typical social dominance hierarchy. In the shallower and slower water in the middle of the glide, there were lots of smaller fish. As we reached the deeper water nearer to the foam line, and the security of the willows on the opposite bank, larger fish that had carved out their territory there made up more of our catch.

CHAPTER 10

Pat Weiss caught this beautiful leopard-spotted rainbow trout from a lie on the opposite bank. Fish don't get big if they are eaten, and large fish learn that the bank provides them refuge from predators in addition to energy savings.

Bankside Lies

One of my goals in writing this book is to try and help fellow anglers break out of their mold. One of the most important ways I've tried to do this is by recognizing the variety of water types in rivers that hold fish, and then devising and implementing casts and techniques that will provide the best presentation. I've already written about water types like pocketwater and riffles, which are either neglected or fished inadequately by most anglers. There's another area of the river that is often sorely neglected, and that's the bank. It's funny how most anglers who fish from a boat naturally look toward the bank for holding lies, yet those same anglers often look to the middle of the river for fish as soon as they step out of the boat and start wading. There is something about the wading perspective that naturally directs our attention toward the deeper water in the center of the flow. If we can't wade there, we naturally assume that's where the fish will be, right? It's important to remember that the bank provides a trifecta of attractions for trout:

1) On banks, the river's flow contacts the substrate, not just on the bottom, but on the side as well. With two zones of contact, the current is slowed even more, and trout can expend less swimming energy holding there.

Look closely in this photo and you will see a foam line and seam just off the bank, created by a protruding rock upstream. This seam may not appear all that inviting, but it provides a slight refuge from the faster flow in the center of this channelized river. Seven brown trout from this bankside lie fell to an upstream Euro-nymphing presentation.

2) The center flow eventually pushes aside most sand, pebbles, and other drifting objects. This means that food is forced from the faster water in the center of the river toward the bank.

3) Perhaps most importantly, the stream bank provides cover. When there are overhanging trees, undercuts, boulders, and log jams, there will be fish that hide under them.

So why don't anglers focus more on fishing the bank? The most obvious reason is that trees and other bankside hazards tend to eat flies. Most anglers do not possess enough skill to manipulate their casts around obstructions in an accurate manner. In the end, if you're worried that you will lose your fly, you're not likely to cast toward the bank.

The other reason I think most anglers avoid the banks is similar to one of the reasons anglers often pass by pocketwater. Bankside lies exhibit quick transitions between current speeds and directions. Eddies and hard-lined seams between fast and slow water are common. These are difficult locations to achieve a good drift. This is especially the case with a strike-indicator nymphing rig. The distance between the indicator and split shot/flies is usually long enough that it can be difficult to fit the entire rig in the same current seam. If the indicator lands in the faster flow off the bank, it is sure to pull the flies downstream and away from the slower target water on the bank.

How can you fix these issues and make banks a regular location for your success? The first strategy is to choose the right rig and approach, and the second is learning and practicing casts that are useful around bankside brush.

If you plan to fish dry flies, a standard quartering-upstream approach can be a challenge. Typically, the fly line will catch faster current near the center of the river and drag the dry fly downstream and away from the bank. Therefore, I find the best dry-fly approach to banks is to make a downstream cast with an upstream reach (see chapter 7).

If nymphs or streamers are on the menu, I usually fish both on a Euro-nymphing leader. Fishing a Euro-nymphing leader on the banks shares all of the drift benefits of fishing the same system in pocketwater (see chapter 5). In addition, a weighted fly (or flies) can be swung around obstructions with excellent accuracy when attached to the end of a long leader.

To cast to the bank, I use a trio of specialized casts:

1) The first cast I turn to is what I refer to as the **parallel kick cast.** In order for standard fly casts to be laterally accurate, the backcast needs to be close to 180 degrees from the target. If you are standing in the middle of the river casting toward the bank, this means that your backcast will be made toward the bank behind you, and your forward cast will take a diagonal trajectory toward your target on the opposite bank. The first problem with this strategy is that it may be easy to hook brush behind you if you're on a small river. The second problem is dialing in your length for the forward cast. If your cast is too far, you will hook a fly on the bankside brush. If your cast is too short, your fly (or flies) will land out in the river and not in the slower currents you are trying to target.

The parallel kick cast makes this situation much easier. Before you make the cast, you need to wade within about 12 to 20 feet of the bank you are trying to cast to, so that your rod can reach most of the way toward the bank when extended. Once you are in position, the parallel kick cast steps are demonstrated by Lance Egan in the photo sequence on the following pages.

There are a few atypical movements to this cast, and it can be a challenge to master at first, but it's worth it. By aligning the trajectory of the backcast with the bank, instead of diagonally away from it, your forward cast is also parallel to the bank, and the length of the cast becomes less of a concern. If your length is off by a few inches, your fly will no longer land in the brush on the side of the river, or out in the faster current, away from your target.

The parallel kick cast also sets up your rig for a proper drift. By lifting the rod tip and moving it downstream, the forward cast lands with tension already built into the rig. Tension can allow you to make micro movements with the rod tip while the flies are turning over, which can alter where they land by a few inches, for increased accuracy. If you are Euro-nymphing, this tension will provide the connection between your nymph and sighter, so takes that happen early in the drift will be detected.

The kick at the end of the cast has one last benefit. It aligns your fly line or your sighter in the same current seam where your flies land. If the

Helicopter Cast

Point your arm and the rod toward the bank you are trying to cast to.

Make a sidearm backcast low and parallel to the water. Ensure that the rod tip travels close to parallel to the bank so that the cast will stop close to 180 degrees from the target.

Raise the rod while the backcast is turning over with a pivot at the wrist.

Make the forward cast above the height of the backcast to create an oval path. Close the oval when you stop the rod.

While the forward and final cast is turning over, simultaneously lift the rod slightly, drift the rod tip downstream about one-quarter of the oval stroke, and kick the rod toward the bank by extending your arm and pointing the rod tip.

sighter or fly line lands out in the faster current, it will quickly drag your fly downstream and out into the river. Because the kick places all of your leader and rig into the same lane of current, your fly will stay near the bank and a natural drift will be much easier to make.

While I have placed the parallel kick cast in a chapter on fishing banks, I use it constantly wherever I need to make accurate casts into complex currents that require me to align my flies and leader/line within a narrow lane to avoid drag. Nymphing pocketwater is a prime example.

2) Another cast I use to fish banks is the **helicopter cast.** This cast is great for casting under tree branches that extend diagonally out over the river.

The cast is essentially an exaggerated oval cast with the plane of the cast tilted. I find it works best with weighted flies that will continue to curve under the branches when the rod is stopped on the forward cast. This cast can be done over either shoulder to slice the forward cast into any gaps you might have. The steps to the cast for a right-handed caster with the backcast over the right shoulder are highlighted in the photo sequence on the next page.

3) The last cast I use for targeting banks is the **bow-and-arrow cast.** This cast is certainly well known, yet I hardly ever see other anglers using it. I use it constantly. There is no better cast to get a fly into the tightest possible space under brush.

Make a sweeping backcast starting with a low rod tip, but aiming the backcast at a target high in the air behind you.

As the line is turning over on the backcast, cross your casting hand in front of your face to your other shoulder.

Wait until you feel the line or flies turn over behind you. Then make a forward cast, aiming low toward the water and under the overhanging tree. Stop the rod hard to curve the line and fly under the tree if needed.

Bow and Arrow Cast

Pinch the point fly on the bend of the hook behind the hook point.

Lift and extend your fly hand behind you. Simultaneously extend your rod hand toward your target and point the butt section of the rod in line with and slightly below your target. Manipulate the elevation and position of the fly hand so that the rod tip will trace the line through any small casting window you have when it's released. Extend hands far enough apart to curl the rod tip back toward you just slightly. This will store enough energy to propel the fly to the target. Heavier flies will require more curl in the rod. The amount of line out the rod may need to be increased or decreased to ensure just the right casting length and turnover power.

Cleanly release the fly while leaving the rod butt in position. As the rig is turning over, you can elevate the rod to prepare for the drift if needed.

Normally fish that inhabit these lies are pretty easy to catch, because they don't see a lot of flies. There is always a unique satisfaction that comes from catching a fish where other anglers are unwilling to fish. The bow-and-arrow cast provides this satisfaction quite often.

Before you start the bow-and-arrow cast, wade to within about 1.5 to 1.75 rod lengths of your target. For maximum accuracy, use a one-fly rig. The steps to the bow-and-arrow cast are demonstrated again by Lance Egan in the photo sequence on the previous page.

It takes some practice to learn to bow-and-arrow-cast with consistent accuracy. It is usually best to try the cast a few times over open water in the center of the river to gauge your length and turnover first, if you aren't confident in the cast. Now that I've covered some casts to help you better fish the bank, let me share a quick case study on bankside lies from the spring creek I fished with Charles Card in chapter 8.

Bankside Lies Case Study

I'm going to combine three separate short case studies into one here. I hope you will see that it does not take much water for trout to hold in near the bank, and that a proper approach with some gutsy casting can bring worthwhile rewards.

In the first sequence, Charles and I were fishing a short stretch of pocketwater just above where we entered the stream. Though it was January, with the 54-degree water temperature, we anticipated that the trout would be spread into all available lies. This proved to be true, as Charles caught a nice rainbow on a stonefly in the first mid-river pocket he fished.

Before moving up to the run above, featured in the next sequence, there were two small bankside pockets we stopped for. They looked to be typical brown trout holding water, despite only being a few inches deep. I fished the first one while Charles switched to a lighter fly. On my second cast tight to some underwater brush, a thick brown trout took the small-beaded Walt's Worm I had tied on for the shallow water.

A nice way to start this case study: Charles Card with a rainbow caught on a stonefly nymph.

The first bankside spot we stopped for, I had to be careful not to snag the thorny branches to catch a brown trout behind them in the slower water.

My first bankside trout in the sequence is coming to the net. I leveraged the fish upstream so that the heavy water in the center flow would help to bring the fish into the net.

Nice fish don't need a lot of water to sit in. This fish came from behind the thorny branches in just inches of water.

The small pocket below the rock produced a brown trout on Charles's first cast.

Charles's bankside brown trout, which took a Frenchie.

Charles took the next turn and fished a pocket behind a small rock. Typical of these types of lies, his first cast resulted in a colorful brown trout.

There is one important thing to highlight with these bank lies. Both of them were less than 10 inches deep, and very small in diameter. Accurate casts were obviously required. To gain immediate strike detection, it was important to lift the rod as the nymph was turning over on the forward cast. This movement created tension from the beginning of the drift. Most takes come early in these types of lies, and they will be missed if there is slack in the leader and tippet.

The upstream boulder on the left side of the photo created a long soft edge. This was a much more obvious bankside lie than the prior two small pockets, where we had caught brown trout.

When fishing in tight quarters, it is wise to look around your position for any trees that might steal your fly. In this photo, I'm scanning for a window to fit my helicopter cast through to fish the opposite bank.

The next bankside lie was just upstream about 30 feet. Charles was nice enough to watch and shoot photos from a high bank above while I got to do the fishing. Here there was a defined seam created by a boulder sitting near the bank upstream. The center of the river was fast, but the water on the bank featured some nice slower holding water.

Working up the seam from back to front I was able to land four rainbows. One of them was actually a few inches out into the main flow, a clear sign the water was warm. However, at the top of the seam there was a larger rainbow that I'd spotted before I started fishing the sequence. It was tucked tight behind a dead tree trunk that extended into the water. To ensure

Lining up a bow-and-arrow cast at the rainbow I've spotted on the bank just below the dead tree stump.

The rainbow trout is almost in the net . . .

Open up and say "Tungsten Taco Egg." It took a few casts and a fly change, but it was exciting to watch this rainbow take my fly.

In this photo I am fishing to several fish I can see in the shallow water on the near side of the run, before targeting the lies on the far bank.

A nicely colored rainbow trout that I sight-fished to in shallow water, on the near side of the run.

that I didn't spook this fish while landing the previous trout, I'd forced the other fish downstream during their fights before sliding them across to where I could net them.

To target the rainbow I had spotted, I made a few bow-and-arrow casts, almost touching the stump. The fish didn't seem to have any interest in the flies I was fishing. It's also possible that they were not able to get

to depth quickly enough, since I could only cast a few inches in front of the fish without snagging the tree. I switched to a Tungsten Taco Egg. It took a couple of casts to get the placement right, but I was able to watch the fish pursue and eat the Egg. It was an exciting end to fishing this bankside lie.

The last sequence in this case study highlights the different preference for holding water that rainbow and

The soft seam on the bank under the twigs held a nice brown trout I was able to sight-fish to.

After a few misses, I made an accurate cast 4 inches closer to the bank and hooked the brown trout. After this splash, I forced the fish downstream to avoid spooking the bigger fish I could see farther up the bank.

The reward of spotting fish on the bank and making casts into tight quarters.

The tricky spot where I spotted the larger brown trout holding on the upstream side of the rocks, on the left side of this photo. I made bow-and-arrow casts between the twigs on the water to land my nymphs upstream with enough time to sink before reaching the trout.

brown trout often show. This sequence took place on a run created by the cement slabs of an old gauging station downstream of where we had caught the previous fish. The near side was fairly slow and about 10 inches deep. Here I used a single 2.3 mm bead nymph to avoid constant hang-ups in the shallow water. The run transitioned into much faster water around 18 to 24 inches deep in the center. As I fished closer toward the center, I added a second 2.3 mm tungsten bead nymph to achieve greater depth. The far side of the run displayed a typical slow bankside seam under trees and overhanging bankside brush.

There were about a half-dozen fish visible on the near side in the open water. I was able to catch five of them before the last one spooked and slid into the current. Four of the five fish were rainbows.

When I stood up to fish the far bank, I spotted two large browns. The lower one was on a soft edge with some overhanging twigs from the trees above. I used a

helicopter cast to slide my nymphs under the brush. My first few casts didn't swing close enough to the bank and drifted to the right of the fish. Once I got the correct placement, only 4 inches closer to the bank, the fish took my Egg. I forced him downstream to avoid spooking the even larger brown upstream.

The brown trout upstream was in a more-difficult spot behind some branches that were touching the water. There was one small gap from a quartering-downstream position, which I could fit a bow-and-arrow cast into. I had to be able to get both of my nymphs to shoot past the fish to the top of the small pocket so they would have enough distance to sink to the brown trout's level.

Most of the time, fish in tight bankside spots will react to your fly within the first or second cast. This brown was a cagier old fish, though, and my first four casts went untouched. Thankfully I had been able to thread the needle with my bow-and-arrow casts to

This brown trout took some persistence with bow-and-arrow casts, but who would say a fish like this wasn't worth the effort and risk?

avoid hooking the overhanging twigs. On the fifth cast I was able to shoot my flies high enough in the pocket to increase their depth, and the brown trout took the Tungsten Taco Egg. The trout ended up being my biggest of the day—a great reward for taking the risk to target him in tight quarters.

Hopefully this chapter has convinced you to make bankside holding lies a focus of your fishing efforts if you typically tend to pass them by. These lies can appear too inconsequential to be worth stopping to fish. They can also be intimidating if you're not confident in your tight-quarters casting ability. However, they often hold fish ready and willing to eat your fly, especially if you're fishing a river with brown trout. The next time you see a bankside seam or pocket with just enough break from the current to hold a fish, stop and figure out a way to fish it. If you don't, you might just pass by the biggest fish the river is going to offer you that day.

CHAPTER 11

Proven Fly Patterns

n this chapter, I share some of my favorite fly patterns. These are all patterns that are featured heavily in my fly boxes. Their fish appeal has been proven in competitions around the world. Most of them are fairly simple, because the night before a competition is not a good time to tie complicated, time-intensive patterns. As you'll see, many of them are impressionistic or outright attractor patterns instead of specific imitations. Over time, I've become far more confident in these types of patterns, as they cover a wide range of insects, or simply capitalize on a trout's curiosity. I hope you'll try them out on your local water and find them to be good additions to your own confidence fly selection.

Dry Flies

Front End Loader Caddis

- **Hook:** #10-16 Hanak 130, Dohiku 301, or Orientsun 7214
- **Thread:** UNI 8/0 rusty dun
- **Optional tag:** 3 strands of Glo Brite Floss in chartreuse, fl. fire orange, or fl. red
- **Dubbing:** Hareline Superfine tan, callibaetis, or amber
- **Ribbing:** Micro to flashabou
- **Counter ribbing:** 5X tippet
- **Wing:** Natural cow elk hair
- **Over wing:** Hareline Para Post fl. pink
- **Hackle:** Grizzly dry-fly hackle wound in hackle-stacker fashion around 5X tippet

(Note: This fly is currently available from Umpqua Feather Merchants.)

Pliva Shuttlecock Emerger

- **Hook:** #14-20 Hanak 130, Dohiku 301, or Orientsun 7214
- **Thread:** Veevus 16/0 olive or olive dun
- **Tag:** A couple wraps of pearl micro to flashabou
- **Rib:** Veevus Power Thread 140D spun tight
- **Dubbing:** Hareline Superfine Adams Gray
- **Wing:** 1 to 3 CDC feather tips

CDC Flying Ant

- **Hook:** #12-18 Hanak 130, Dohiku 301, or Orientsun 7214
- **Thread:** Veevus 16/0 black
- **Dubbing:** Hareline Superfine black
- **Wing:** 2 to 4 CDC feather tips
- **Hackle:** Grizzly or furnace trimmed flush on the bottom

Parachute Mayfly

- **Hook:** #10-18 Hanak 130, Dohiku 301, or Orientsun 7214
- **Thread:** UNI 8/0 rusty dun
- **Tail:** Coq de Leon
- **Rib:** 5-pound Maxima Chameleon
- **Dubbing:** Hareline Superfine Adams Gray
- **Parachute:** Hareline Para Post white
- **Hackle:** Grizzly; can add more hackle or parachute post for buoyancy

Chubby Chernobyl

- **Hook:** #6-12 Hanak 130, Dohiku 301, or Orientsun 7214
- **Thread:** UNI 8/0 camel
- **Foam:** ⅛-inch closed cell tan
- **Legs:** Hareline Life Flex brown
- **Dubbing:** Hareline Ice Dub tan
- **Wing:** Hareline Para Post light gray or medium dun; can add fl. pink for visibility

(Note: For the purple variation, substitute black foam and legs, purple Hareline Ice Dub, and black thread.)

Nymphs

(Note: I have listed standard barbless nymph hooks for most recipes, but jig hooks could easily be substituted.)

Walt's Worm

- **Hook:** #10-20 Hanak 230, Dohiku 302, or Orientsun 7224
- **Bead:** Copper inverting or slotted tungsten bead
- **Thread:** Veevus 16/0 dun
- **Ribbing:** 5X tippet
- **Dubbing:** Hare's ear
- **Optional hot spot dubbing:** Hareline Ice Dub uv pink
- **Optional ribbing:** Pearl micro to flashabou
- **Optional thread collar hot spot:** Veevus Power Thread 140D fl. pink

Lite Brite Perdigon

- **Hook:** #12-20 Hanak 230, Dohiku 302, or Orientsun 7224
- **Bead:** Copper or silver inverting or slotted tungsten bead
- **Thread:** Veevus 16/0 (vary the color to change underbody tone as desired)

- **Optional hot spot thread:** Veevus 16/0 fl. orange
- **Tail:** Coq de Leon
- **Body:** Hareline Krystal Flash (lots of color options to suit your preference)
- **Wing case:** Black nail polish
- **UV Resin:** Solarez Bone Dry

(Note: This fly is currently available from Umpqua Feather Merchants.)

Quilldigon

- **Hook:** #12-20 Hanak 230, Dohiku 302, or Orientsun 7224
- **Bead:** Copper or silver inverting or slotted tungsten bead
- **Thread:** Veevus 16/0 dun
- **Tail:** Coq de Leon
- **Body:** Polish Quills stripped peacock quills (color to suit)
- **Wing case:** Black nail polish
- **UV Resin:** Solarez Bone Dry

(Note: This fly is currently available from Umpqua Feather Merchants.)

Egan's Frenchie

- **Hook:** #10-18 Hanak 230, Dohiku 302, or Orientsun 7224
- **Bead:** Gold, copper, or silver inverting or slotted tungsten bead
- **Thread:** Veevus 16/0 brown (red thread for the original recipe)
- **Tail:** Coq de Leon
- **Rib:** Small copper wire
- **Body:** 3 to 4 fibers of pheasant tail
- **Dubbing:** Hareline Ice Dub uv shrimp pink or uv pink

Soft Hackle Carrot

- **Hook:** #12-16 Hanak 230, Dohiku 302, or Orientsun 7224
- **Bead:** Gold or copper inverting or slotted tungsten bead
- **Thread:** Veevus 16/0 dun or brown
- **Tail:** Coq de Leon
- **Rib:** Veevus Power Thread 140D fl. orange spun in a dubbing loop
- **Dubbing:** Hare's ear
- **Hackle:** Wrapped CDC feather (pluck fibers to desired length)
- **Collar:** Hareline Ice Dub olive brown

Blowtorch

- **Hook:** #10-16 Hanak 230, Dohiku 302, or Orientsun 7224
- **Bead:** Gold or copper inverting or slotted tungsten bead
- **Thread:** Veevus 16/0 red or black
- **Tag:** Glo Brite Floss #5 fl. fire orange, three strands clipped short
- **Rib:** UTC brassie red wire
- **Dubbing:** Hareline Ice Dub peacock black
- **Optional flashback:** Medium pearl tinsel
- **Hackle:** CDC feather wrapped and plucked to desired length
- **Collar:** Hareline Ice Dub uv pink

(Note: this fly is currently available from Umpqua Feather Merchants.)

Straggle Stone

(*Golden Stone variation recipe*)

- **Hook:** #6-12 Orientsun 7246 or Hanak 900
- **Bead:** Copper or gold inverting or slotted tungsten bead
- **Thread:** UNI 8/0 camel
- **Legs:** Hareline Life Flex brown
- **Rib:** UTC brassie copper wire
- **Shellback:** Fino Skin brown
- **Abdomen and thorax:** Hareline Micro UV Polar Chenille brown

(Magneto variation recipe)
- **Hook:** #6-12 Orientsun 7246 or Hanak 900
- **Bead:** Fl. pink inverting or slotted tungsten bead
- **Thread:** UNI 8/0 black
- **Legs:** Hareline Life Flex black
- **Rib:** UTC brassie silver wire
- **Shellback:** Fino Skin black
- **Abdomen:** Hareline Micro UV Polar Chenille purple
- **Thorax:** Hareline Micro UV Polar Chenille black

(Note: this fly is currently available from Umpqua Feather Merchants.)

Mop Fly

- **Hook:** #10-12 Hanak 230, Dohiku 302, or Orientsun 7224
- **Bead:** Black nickel or copper inverting or slotted tungsten bead
- **Thread:** UNI 8/0 rusty dun
- **Body:** Mop body from BC Fishing Supplies (color to suit)
- **Dubbing:** Hare's ear or Hareline Ice Dub (color to suit)

Squirmy Wormy

- **Hook:** #10-12 Hanak 230, Dohiku 302, or Orientsun 7224
- **Bead:** Inverting or slotted tungsten bead (color to suit)
- **Thread:** Veevus Power Thread 140D red or fl. pink
- **Body:** Hareline Caster's Squirmito or Spirit River Squirmy Worm bodies

Tungsten Taco Egg

- **Hook:** #14-16 Hanak 450, Dohiku HDJ, or Orientsun 5240
- **Bead:** Slotted tungsten bead (color to suit)
- **Thread:** Veevus 16/0 red
- **Body:** Flybox UK Eggstacy chenille wrapped in front of the bead

Streamers

Slumpbuster

- **Hook:** #6-12 Orientsun 7246 or Hanak 900
- **Bead:** Copper, gold, or silver inverting or slotted tungsten bead
- **Thread:** UNI 8/0 rusty dun
- **Hook fouling guard:** Loop of 12-pound Maxima over rear of hook
- **Body and collar:** Micro rabbit or pine squirrel strip natural
- **Flash:** Red or pearl flashabou under the collar
- **Dubbing:** Hareline Ice Dub (color to suit)

(Note: I tie this fly in black and olive as well.)

The Humongous

- **Hook:** #6-12 Orientsun 7246 or Hanak 900
- **Bead:** Copper or gold inverting or slotted tungsten bead
- **Thread:** UNI 8/0 rusty dun
- **Flash:** Gold flashabou
- **Tail:** Ginger marabou
- **Rib:** UTC brassie gold wire
- **Body:** Gold tinsel chenille

- **Hackle:** Ginger badger or grizzly saddle

(Note: I tie this fly in black/silver and olive/copper variations as well.)

Sexton's Blanksaver

- **Hook:** #6-12 Orientsun 7246 or Hanak 900
- **Bead:** Fl. chartreuse or orange inverting or slotted tungsten bead
- **Thread:** UNI 8/0 black
- **Tail:** Black marabou
- **Body:** Black simi-seal dubbing

Rubber-Legged Bugger

- **Hook:** #6-12 Orientsun 7246 or Hanak 900
- **Bead:** Copper or gold inverting or slotted tungsten bead
- **Thread:** UNI 8/0 camel
- **Flash:** Pearl Krystal Flash
- **Tail:** Brown marabou
- **Rib:** UTC brassie copper wire
- **Body:** Brown chenille
- **Legs:** Hareline Life Flex brown and orange
- **Hackle:** Brown rooster saddle feather

BIBLIOGRAPHY

Barnes, Jacqueline B., et al. "Reappraising the Effects of Habitat Structure on River Macroinvertebrates." *Freshwater Biology*, vol. 58, no. 10 (2013), pp. 2154–67, doi:10.1111/fwb.12198.

Borger, Gary A., and Jason Borger. *Fishing the Film*. Wausau, WI: Tomorrow River Press, 2010.

Daniel, George. *Dynamic Nymphing: Tactics, Techniques, and Flies from around the World (Czech, Polish, French, UK, US, and More)*. Mechanicsburg, PA: Stackpole Books, 2012.

Elliott, J. M. "The Growth Rate of Brown Trout (*Salmo trutta L.*) Fed on Maximum Rations." *Journal of Animal Ecology*, vol. 44, no. 3 (1975), p. 805, doi:10.2307/3720.

Gatz, A. J., et al. "Habitat Shifts in Rainbow Trout: Competitive Influences of Brown Trout." *Oecologia*, vol. 74, no. 1, 1987, pp. 7–19, doi:10.1007/bf00377339.

Gowan, Charles, and Kurt D. Fausch. "Long-Term Demographic Responses of Trout Populations to Habitat Manipulation in Six Colorado Streams." *Ecological Applications*, vol. 6, no. 3 (1996), pp. 931–46., doi:10.2307/2269496.

Hughes, Dave. *Dry Fly Fishing*. Portland, OR: Frank Amato, 1994.

Krivanec, Karel, et al. *Czech Nymph and Other Related Fly Fishing Methods*. České Budějovice, Czech Republic: Grayling & Trout Publishing, 2008.

Lancaster, J., and J. D. Allan. "Stream Ecology: Structure and Function of Running Waters." *Journal of Ecology*, vol. 83, no. 4 (1995), p. 735, doi:10.2307/2261644.

Marinaro, Vincent C. *In the Ring of the Rise*. Guilford, CT: Lyons Press, 2001.

Nakano, Shigeru, et al. "Flexible Niche Partitioning via a Foraging Mode Shift: A Proposed Mechanism for Coexistence in Stream-Dwelling Charrs." *Journal of Animal Ecology*, vol. 68, no. 6 (1999), pp. 1079–92, doi:10.1046/j.1365-2656.1999.00355.x.

———. "Terrestrial Aquatic Linkages: Riparian Arthropod Inputs Alter Trophic Cascades in a Stream Food Web." *Ecology*, vol. 80, no. 7 (1999), pp. 2435–41, doi:10.1890/0012-9658.

Naman, Sean M., et al. "Habitat-Specific Production of Aquatic and Terrestrial Invertebrate Drift in Small Forest Streams: Implications for Drift-Feeding Fish." *Canadian Journal of Fisheries and Aquatic Sciences*, vol. 74, no. 8 (2017), 1208–17, doi:10.1139/cjfas-2016-0406.

Randall, Jason. *Moving Water: A Fly Fisher's Guide to Currents*. Mechanicsburg, PA: Stackpole/Headwater Books, 2012.

———. *Trout Sense: A Fly Fisher's Guide to What Trout See, Hear, and Smell*. Mechanicsburg, PA: Stackpole/Headwater Books, 2014.

Swisher, Doug, et al. *Selective Trout: A Revised and Expanded Edition of the Best-Selling Classic that Revolutionized Fly Fishing for Trout*. Norwalk, CT: Easton Press, 2002.

Todd, Andrew S., et al. "Development of New Water Temperature Criteria to Protect Colorado's Fisheries." *Fisheries*, vol. 33, no. 9 (2008), pp. 433–43, doi:10.1577/1548-8446-33.9.433.

INDEX

Italicized page numbers indicate illustrations.